SCATTERED SAND

SCATTERED SAND

THE STORY OF CHINA'S RURAL MIGRANTS

HSIAO-HUNG PAI

Preface by Gregor Benton

VERSO
London • New York

This paperback edition first published by Verso 2013
First published by Verso 2012
© Hsiao-Hung Pai 2012, 2013
Foreword © Gregor Benton 2012, 2013

The moral rights of the authors have been asserted

1 3 5 7 9 10 8 6 4 2

Verso
UK: 6 Meard Street, London W1F 0EG
US: 20 Jay Street, Suite 1010, Brooklyn, NY 11201
www.versobooks.com

Verso is the imprint of New Left Books

ISBN-13: 978-1-78168-090-2

British Library Cataloguing in Publication Data
A catalogue record for this book is available from the British Library

Library of Congress Cataloging-in-Publication Data
The library of Congress has catalogued the hardcover edition as follows:
Pai, Hsiao-Hung.
Scattered sand : the story of China's rural migrants / by Hsiao-Hung Pai ; preface by
Gregor Benton.
p. cm.
ISBN 978-1-84467-886-0 (hbk.) – ISBN 978-1-84467-920-1 (ebook)
1. Migrant labor–China. 2. Rural-urban migration–China. 3. China–Social
conditions–21st century. 4. China–Economic conditions–21st century. I. Title.
HD5856.C5P35 2012
331.5'440951–dc23
2012016668

Typeset in Fournier by MJ Gavan, Cornwall
Printed in the US by Maple Vail

This book is dedicated, with much love,
to my parents, Hsiu-Hsiung and Judeh

Contents

Foreword *by Gregor Benton*   ix
Preface *by Hsiao-Hung Pai*   xiv

Introduction   1
1. Exodus: Northeast Youth Head for the City   15
2. Earthquakes in Bohemia: Life and Death in Sichuan   41
3. Dust and Heat: Black Mines in the Yellow River Region   73
4. The Dark Kilns: Brickmaking in the North   104
5. 'Bad Elements': The Uprooted and the Permanently
   Impoverished in Shandong   129
6. The Factory of the World: Recession in Guangdong   164
7. In the Shadows of Olympians: Unorganized Workers
   in Beijing   207
8. Go West! The Migration Industry in Rural Fujian   223
   Epilogue: Trouble on the New Frontier – Ethnic
   Tensions in Xinjiang   282

Acknowledgements   293
Further Reading   295
Notes   298

Foreword

The present movement of Chinese peasants – around the countryside, from the villages to the towns and cities, from China to the world, and around the world – is the biggest mass migration in history. And it is among the world's biggest social upheavals ever, dwarfing centuries of European migration to the United States. The rural migrants who are braving abuse by employers, discrimination by urban natives, and repeated crackdowns and restrictions by the authorities have driven China's economy to new heights and changed the face of China's cities, while the earnings they send home have helped lift villages out of poverty. Much of the migration is seasonal, however, and during slowdowns and crises its direction is reversed, as many of those laid off move back to the villages to share their poverty and await the next rising tide. By disappearing not only when they lose their jobs but also when they grow old, fall ill, or get pregnant, peasant migrants subsidize urban employers, the state treasury, and the lifestyle of richer urbanites.

Chinese rural-to-urban migration has been the subject of dozens of books and hundreds of articles, written by experts and based on prodigious research; their work is an exemplar among international migration studies. Over the past few years, high-quality writing on this subject in Chinese, English, and other languages has exceeded in quantity the entire output of all previous such work, yet in it, the voice of the migrant is seldom heard. The merit of this book is that it lets Chinese rural migrants speak for themselves, so that we can experience their world from their point of view and in their own words. *Scattered Sand* displays the same empathy and sense of authenticity as *Chinese Whispers*, Hsiao-Hung Pai's acclaimed 2008 study of Britain's hidden army of 'illegal' Chinese labour. Both books maintain the rich tradition of socially progressive writing founded in China in the 1930s and revived in the 1980s, in which the narration is an act of collective identification and empowerment and a main aim is to give voice to the voiceless.

Hsiao-Hung Pai is a Taiwanese who was able to communicate uninhibitedly with her Chinese informants, which deepened her identification with them. As a person committed by nature to equity and justice, she is outraged by the self-interest of those in business and government who control migrant employment. Documenting abuses carried out on behalf of the rich and strong takes courage in a country where those forces monopolize power and are not used to being watched. Through her investigation, Ms Pai threatened the interests of the new composite class of officials, business people, and organized criminals who dominate the corrupt world of Chinese state capitalism. On several occasions, things could have turned nasty had her luck failed. As a British passport holder, she could count on some immunity, and she has a native ability to talk her way out of trouble. Even so, her work required greater nerve and determination than most people have.

What did her informants tell her? Having gained their confidence by showing sympathy and interest, she elicited a rich flow of ideas, views, and stories from them. Her journey starts and finishes at Moscow's Yaroslavl Station, where she joins homeward-bound migrants on the Trans-Siberian Railway. They paint her a sobering picture of the often romanticized reality of international migration. The pillaging by predatory police and other authorities starts at the Russian border, intensifies at the destination, and is rounded off with a final shakedown on re-entry into China. Migrant traders suffer endless official rip-offs in Russia and occasional attacks by xenophobic skinheads. Migrant labourers, driven out of China by poverty and despair, are paid pittances by their Russian employers and milked dry by the Chinese agents who recruit and run them. Those who publicly resist the abuse risk fines and deportation.

This picture bears little resemblance to that of the footloose globe-trotter moving around the world in a cocoon of global Chinese capitalism and culture, a representation that can be found in some writings of the currently influential school of transnational studies. Hsiao-Hung Pai's important contribution to the debate on transnationalism and 'Chineseness' is her unrelenting focus on the different fates that await rich and poor. Where other authors celebrate the migrants' mobility in a frictionless, deterritorialized age of 'transilience' and 'flexible citizenship' and play down the poverty, racism, and sexism of their world, she focuses on the 'permanent journey of the mobile proletariat' and the role of the hostile state – at home and overseas – in controlling and exploiting the petty trader and the migrant worker.

The bulk of the book records Hsiao-Hung Pai's encounters with rural migrants in Chinese towns and cities. They can suffer poor health, accidents, and even death through their work, and they are too poor to buy insurance. They accumulate debts they can't pay off. Local residents are more likely to show them contempt than fellow feeling. Their relations with agents and employers are rarely governed by rules, regulations, or contracts. The state-run labour unions make no effort to recruit or represent them, and they can't afford legal arbitration. When their bosses fail to pay them for months on end, or bully and deceive them, or subject them to other arbitrary abuses, they have no remedy. They are 'ghosts', people with no officially sanctioned existence, subject to routine harassment and random cruelty and violence. They live in ghettoes, aliens in their own country. Because conditions for them in China are so dire, many will do practically anything to get themselves or even their unaccompanied children to the rich West, where again they face oppression and discrimination.

An even worse life is that of the ethnic migrants, the non-Han segments in the Han cities, who form minorities within the minority and live in ghettoes within the ghetto. They are even more likely than the general migrant population to suffer random police searches on the streets and maltreatment by authorities and members of the Han majority. This is especially true in the current political climate, where the establishment is playing the dangerous game of stoking Han chauvinism disguised as Chinese patriotism. Hsiao-Hung Pai describes two of these internal colonies, Yi and Uighur.

There is little in this book to relieve the general sense of repression without redress. The author occasionally reports some small instance of verbal defiance, usually from older workers with a memory of the rebel days. Another act of self-assertion she describes is the Museum of Migrant Culture and Art, a samizdat project set up by volunteers in a poor neighbourhood in Picun in Beijing that proudly displays the history of migration with exhibits donated by migrant workers. The museum staff has raised a banner, 'To work is glorious,' an ironic play on Deng Xiaoping's 'To get rich is glorious.' Pai also cites the rise in labour militancy in 2010 to confirm that many migrant workers do not accept their fate, but although conditions for the emergence of an independent labour movement are better today than at any time since the 1920s, most observers agree that one is not yet imminent.

Pai's title, *Scattered Sand*, comes from Sun Yat-sen, father of Chinese nationalism and leader of its democratic revolution (which was not very democratic and not very revolutionary), who called the Chinese people a sand rope, without fibre, but had high hopes of the Chinese overseas, who he thought could be 'mothers of the Revolution' because migration would change them. Yet it is hard to see how he was right, for migration abroad has dissipated the energy of the enterprising, and migration at home has greatly widened the chasm between winners and losers, which bodes ill for progressive change there. China, once one of the world's most egalitarian societies, is now almost as inegalitarian as South Africa and Brazil.

Yet Hsiao-Hung Pai concludes her report on a note of optimism, describing the migrants' role in the recent unofficial strikes, which she hopes are a first step to greater equity. But although a movement of criticism and dissent does exist in China, it is less focused and more disjointed than in the past, and even if its members do manage to cohere, they will achieve little unless they can quickly identify a way to heal the division between insiders and incomers in the cities.

Gregor Benton
Cardiff University, May 2012

Preface

Like the 'American dream', the term 'Chinese dream' has become a political catchphrase. It is a phrase invented by China's political elite and is used to refer to aspirations for the future of the country. The national media discuss it endlessly, as do academics. Every five-year-old can probably recite a few lines from politicians about the meaning of these two words; China's new president Xi Jinping, for instance, describes it as 'the realization of the great revival of the Chinese nation'.

'This dream gathers Chinese aspirations and wishes for generations and manifests the interests of the whole Chinese nation,' Xi said following the Eighteenth Party Congress in November 2012, where a preordained group of new leaders took over positions from the old. 'As history has shown us, each individual's future and destiny is tied up with that of their nation.' He also predicted that this 'dream' would be realized by the hundredth anniversary of the founding of the People's Republic – in 2049.

China is far from achieving this universal dream. Millions lack access to basic public services due to their peasant origins (thanks to the household registration system), with 27 million migrant children unable to enroll in urban schools. Like their parents, they are part of the deprived, floating population existing on the edge of China's metropolis. During the two years I spent travelling across China researching *Scattered Sand*, I met rural migrant workers toiling under appalling conditions in urban sweatshops without any assurance of being paid at the end of their labours.

I collected stories from peasants who had to sell blood to support their families, only to die later on of AIDS. I witnessed the humiliating extremes endured by workers just in an effort to survive. The newspapers are filled with stories of migrants huddled under bridges freezing to death and of miners fighting to win compensation for industrial diseases. In one case, a miner opened up his chest to provide evidence of his lung disease as he struggled to receive compensation.

Despite all the talk of prosperity and economic improvement, it is hard to deny that China is divided by an apartheid-like system that separates the rural from the urban, the migrant peasant from the first-class citizen. Just contrast Premier Wen Jiabao's immense personal fortune (£1.68bn accumulated during his time as premier, according to an October 2012 report from the *New York Times*) with his reassurances to migrant workers that 'things have to change slowly'. (Readers who want a taste of Wen's bromides should refer to his hyped-up public relations tour from 2010, conducted amid growing discontent, during which a worker made the headlines by confronting the premier to ask why his son didn't have the right to an education.)

A first, necessary step toward achieving the Chinese dream is to abolish the distinction between the rural and urban hukou, which would mean removing restrictions on household registration in the cities and allowing rural migrants to register where they work, allowing them equal access to social services. In the past, the official position was that such reform would be 'too costly for the cities', but in fact, the Australian National University economist Xin Meng has shown that hukou restrictions have actually produced labour shortages in the cities by preventing peasants from migrating. Only 25 percent of the rural workforce moved to urban areas in 2010, while there were 10 million jobs to fill in China's coastal cities. Xin's theory is that removing restrictions on migrant access to social welfare and social services in the cities would prolong the duration of migration and abolish the labour shortage.

Since the hardback edition of *Scattered Sand* was published, the official position on hukou reform has begun to shift. Just a month after the leadership transition at the Eighteenth Party Congress in November 2012, China's top economic planning agency, the National Development and Reform Commission, announced that the authorities were committed to 'speeding up household registration reform' and to do so without delay—although the new leaders have avoided mention of the issue due to the projected costs of reform.[1]

This bold talk has proved to be little more than lip service. As the Party Congress was taking place, Miao Cuihua, a self-professed spokeswoman for migrant workers, posted a protest video online demanding payment of 3.4 million yuan in overdue wages to her and her migrant co-workers on a Hangu construction site in northeastern Tianjin. Though this case was only one among tens of thousands like it across the country, the video attracted over one million viewers within two days, while the national media busied themselves reporting on the official events and the 'model workers' sent to the Congress to praise the party.

Strikes involving more than a thousand people occur daily in the Pearl River Delta Region alone, with many more protests occurring on a smaller scale elsewhere. In 2010, the number of spontaneous industrial actions hit a ten-year high; there were more than 200,000 labour disputes. The widely reported Honda and Foxconn strikes were hardly the only ones – more than 4,000 workers went on strike in June 2011 at the Simone handbag factory in Guangzhou, fighting against low pay and harsh working conditions. Of course, the strike at Foxconn's Zhengzhou plant in October 2012 got the most media attention. There, 4,000 workers protested the company's insistence staff work through holidays and its pitiless demands for quality control from employees who lacked the proper training. More than 6,000 employees walked out to demand severance pay at Flextronics Technology's Shanghai plant in September 2012, and the month before that, 1,000 strikers called for higher wages at Youde, a Wuhan automotive components factory. And the list goes on. Following the Eighteenth Congress, President Xi Jinping made a symbolic visit to Shenzhen, one of Deng Xiaoping's pioneering cities, to embrace foreign capital and 'reinvigorate economic reforms'. He met a roadblock formed by 3,000 striking print factory workers – who were quickly suppressed by the police. Low-paid migrant workers have grown impatient for change, and this is particularly true of the youngest among them.

The Chinese ruling class is not short of supporters in the West. Certain Orientalist apologists in the Western media – for instance, British journalist Martin Jacques – have embraced the party rhetoric of China developing 'on its own terms, with its own rules'. According to them, China evolves according to its own unique system, with values and traditions not comparable with those of the West, and therefore must be treated in isolation. Chinese culture and values, they argue, do not support egalitarianism.

This is blatantly untrue. As Chinese society is as bitterly class-divided today as the rest of the world, millions of migrants from China's rural interior continue to travel into the cities (and, in many cases, abroad) in search of better opportunities and livelihoods for their families, despite the hardships that await. In fact, theirs is an almost universal aspiration. Like people all around the world, they simply dream of a better life.

Hsiao-Hung Pai
March 2013

Introduction

It was nine p.m. at Moscow's busiest railway station, Yaroslavsky. The platforms were dense with people, most of them of Russian or Central Asian descent. Kiosks and peddlers touted their wares — matryoshka dolls, hats, and T-shirts emblazoned with illegible English words — beneath high archways and portraits of Soviet soldiers and Arctic fishermen. It felt more like an open Sunday market than the terminus of the world's longest railway, the Trans-Siberian. And its peaked brown roofs seemed more suited to a Russian fairy-tale castle than to the point of transit in so many modern stories of personal migration, on trains heading to and from northern Russia, Siberia, Mongolia and China.

It was the beginning of my trip. I bought a loaf of black bread and a bottle of water. Large groups of Chinese men and women, carrying heavy plastic bags and suitcases, were arriving on the platform for the train to Beijing, obviously homeward bound. Immediately, a police officer approached, rattling off questions in Russian and singling out three of the men, apparently at random, lining them up against a wall, where they were searched. I could see the fear in their faces. They didn't dare move an inch. The other passengers, including the Central Asians, watched sympathetically. The sight was familiar to them — possibly the experience was, too — and I could see that they expected the worst for those men. Still the crowd did not linger, though some looked back as they walked steadily on.

How had all these Chinese migrants wound up here? What were they returning to?

As my train pulled away, the three Chinese men were still being questioned by the police. Their look of fear remained etched in my mind. I didn't know then that I would see that look again many times.

That day, I was bidding farewell to Europe, embarking on a journey through Siberia into China. I had spent 2004–2007 researching *Chinese Whispers*, my book on the life of undocumented Chinese workers in Britain, and often found myself wondering about the origins of these migrants. What forces drive migration? What compels migrants to journey to the West, despite the exploitation that awaits them? Why would the widow of a Chinese migrant who died working in Britain want to borrow another £20,000 to send her young daughter there?

Today, an estimated 200 million Chinese peasants have left their homes in search of work; 130 million of those have left their home provinces, according to the China Labour Bulletin (CLB). They represent half of the urban workforce and are responsible for half of China's GDP, as reported by the Organisation for Economic Cooperation and Development (OECD), with jobs largely in construction, services and manufacturing. This indispensable army of labour from the vast rural interior, moving from city to city and country to country in search of a livelihood, has been described, by academics as well as by migrant workers themselves, as 'scattered sand'. More often, and less accurately, they are called peasant workers – *nongmin-gong* – reflecting their society's deep-seated ideological reluctance to regard them as part of China's industrial working class. They are not organized as a workforce and experience institutional discrimination and social exclusion. They remain the most marginalized and impoverished group of workers in China.

Sixty years ago, the Chinese Communist Party (CCP) rose to power on the strength of the peasantry. The misery of rural life under the corrupt Kuomintang – the Chinese Nationalist Party –

and the KMT's unwillingness to oppose the imperialist powers ensured the revolution's success. The new Chinese state could begin to carry out its work: to develop and industrialize China with the aim of achieving full socialism.

In that process, the peasantry has been considered an unchangeable social class, one of Mao Zedong's 'four blocs of society' along with workers, the national bourgeoisie, and the intelligentsia. This theory of 'four blocs', known as New Democracy, bypasses the bourgeois-democratic revolution that classical Marxism holds to be necessary for establishing a working-class majority – the universal class through which a socialist revolution must be achieved. Instead, socialism is instituted directly through a coalition between the four blocs, led by the Party. Once the old ruling powers had been overthrown, the CCP claimed that this coalition had been forged. The bourgeoisie were not abolished, only expected to realign themselves in the interests of the country.

Thus, in revolutionary China, a citizen's class position was fixed and permanent, no matter what his occupation or relationship to the means of production. Those born as peasants were *nongmin* on their ID, a status they carried for life, determining their rights and entitlements in society. (For example, peasants are not entitled to pensions.) Movement into the cities was strictly controlled and in effect prohibited via the system of *hukou* (household registration) set up in 1958. It was impossible for peasants to move their *hukou* to the cities.

As in Stalinist Russia, national investment during China's industrialization was focused on building heavy industry and increasing industrial output. The rural population served as a massive backyard production team for the urban one, feeding the cities that were modernizing the 'Chinese nation' but agriculture as an industry in itself was neglected. There were no initiatives to develop rural infrastructure or improve life in the countryside, both widely studied and documented by Marxist academics. In the Great Leap Forward of 1958, the collective power of the peasantry was institutionalized as simply a vast resource to help develop industrial

China. About 53,000 communes were set up to direct the 700-million-strong rural labour force for national use (remaining in place until 1985, when they were replaced by townships), and local cadres inflated figures to meet unachievable grain production targets set by the state;[1] the tragic result was the death of tens of millions of peasants.

After the four years of fierce political power struggles that followed Mao Zedong's death in 1976, Deng Xiaoping emerged as leader and embarked on *gaige kaifang*, a process of economic reforms and 'opening up' that established 'special economic zones' for international investment without state restraints; that is, he opened China up to the forces of global capitalism. Yet the farm remained the backyard of production. Reforms directed at the countryside were still geared toward developing the cities and the country as a whole, under the banner of the 'four modernizations', in agriculture, industry, national defence, and science and technology, which were to transform China into a global economic powerhouse. Increased agricultural production required measures to 'release the productive forces', which amounted to decollectivization and commercialization of the rural economy, along with decentralization of national industries. Many communes were disbanded after the Household Responsibility System was established in 1981. Peasants were given limited rights to the use of land through fifteen-year contracts (later, thirty-year contracts), and with the increase in grain prices, production increased.

However, because of poor administration, the amount of land distributed to each household was very limited and fragmented. According to a survey conducted by the Chinese Ministry of Agriculture among 7,983 sample villages in 29 provinces in 1986, the arable land allocated per household was only seven *mu*,[2] or little more than an acre, hardly sufficient to feed the average household of more than four people.[3] Half of China's 400 million rural working people became unable to sustain themselves and therefore 'superfluous', the government term for off-work, 'extra' labour.

The growth in agricultural production lasted only a few years.

Long-term state investment in agriculture was lacking; there was no political will to develop the countryside. After 1985, as growth stagnated, rural income began to decline. Class divisions intensified, and inequalities deepened within the villages as peasants suffered from heavy taxation and the corruption of local party bureaucrats, who profited hugely from the increasingly commercialized rural economy. Under these conditions, the 200 million 'superfluous' peasants could no longer depend on the land for a living.[4] About 100 million of them became workers in newly developing village enterprises, including nonagricultural enterprises. Another 100 million were without work and had to find other ways to survive. They began to move cityward and opened up the restricted rural-to-urban movement, and the authorities allowed this as cheap labour was much sought after now the economic reforms were gathering pace. These people became the new mobile proletariat, going from one city to the next searching for work – from service industries and food to electronics manufacturing to construction. Meanwhile, the per capita income gap between the cities and countryside continued steadily to widen, from a ratio of 2.49 in 1980 to 3.3 in 2009. Rural unemployment also continued to rise.

The millions of unemployed rural migrants were referred to as 'blind flow' (*mangliu*). This derogatory term was coined in the early 1950s, when state media (especially the *People's Daily*) began to describe rural to urban migration as 'blindly leaving the countryside' and 'blind penetration'. *Mangliu* came into wider use in the 1980s and 1990s as migration grew, and has helped to shape urban prejudice against the rural population. But the term also reflects the desperation and directionless movement of the migrants in search of a livelihood. The government tried to control this growing rural migration by directing it abroad. Unemployed former peasants were sent out of the country in a variety of work and construction schemes through national government corporations (with foreign building contracts), local government corporations, and trading companies. Throughout the 1990s, up to 200,000 workers from China's countryside were recruited and sent abroad in this way, mostly to Asian countries, where they received payment below the local rates and were isolated in their own enclaves. According to the Ministry of Foreign Trade and Economic Cooperation, the remittances from Chinese migrant workers abroad generated $8 billion for China in 1994.[5] But despite the contributions of this diaspora, most of the superfluous rural workers were left in China, travelling internally in search of jobs. Some, from China's border regions, crossed over with short-term visas that did not permit them to work, in search of better opportunities, but the majority eventually returned to their families back home.

My train was packed with homebound Chinese migrants. Their suitcases and food parcels lined the floor. The mass exodus was largely due to the closure of Moscow's Cherkizovsky Market, a 400-acre outdoor space where about 100,000 migrants (half of them from China, the rest from Tajikistan, Azerbaijan, Vietnam and North Korea) sold counterfeit goods – purses, jeans and shoes – out of wooden shacks. My cabin mates, Ah Sheng and his wife, Xiao Ning, both in their late twenties, had run a handbag stall, and now they sat at the foot of another passenger's bunk, anxious to relate their story.

They'd been in Moscow less than a year, said Ah Sheng. Xiao Ning missed her seven-month-old daughter, who was being looked after by her parents back home. She often asked Ah Sheng when they might be able to return. 'Soon enough,' he always said. They had once worked on the land in Changchun, Jilin Province, but Ah Sheng had quit farming and gone to work in a joint-venture car assembly factory in Changchun, earning 1,000 yuan (£91, $145) a month, better than his farming wages but not enough to support his and Xiao Ning's parents, all retired farmers, who as peasants did not qualify for state pensions and were dependent on their children's income. Xiao Ning's relatives in Moscow had told the couple that despite the difficulty of living in a foreign country without speaking the language, money was fairly easy to make because there was a strong demand for their products. They also spoke of Moscow's well-established Chinese migrant community, which acted as a constant network of support. In 2008, Ah Sheng and Xiao Ning decided to join them there.

They were led to the Cherkizovsky Market, like many migrants before them. A vibrant multicultural community, like its ancient predecessors in the Silk Road era, the market had been established in the early 1990s as the Soviet Union collapsed and China began opening its doors to world markets. The 1997 border demarcation agreement between Russia and China, coupled with political and military rapprochement, reinvigorated Chinese migration to the Russian Far East.[6] As soon as the doors were opened along the 4,300-kilometre Russian-Chinese border, Chinese peasants began to cross in waves. Many had been trading in consumer goods for more than fifteen years near the border areas, in towns like Manzhouli, China's busiest entrypoint on land, with a population of 300,000.

Trade expanded further into Siberia, and small-scale bartering along the railway flourished in response to the disruption of economic links after the disbanding of the USSR. The Chinese migrant garment trade filled the gap left by Russia's lack of light industry and met the needs of lower-income Russians from villages outside of Moscow. And for fifteen years, the Cherkizovsky Market was part of normal Russian life, until one day at the end of June 2009, Prime Minister Vladimir V. Putin ordered it shut down. Reportedly, Putin was angry that the market's owner, Telman Ismailov, was using his wealth, earned in Russia, to open an opulent resort in Turkey. Ostensibly, the closure was mandated by safety regulations.

Xiao Ning recalled that day when their flatmate Dakuan stormed in with news of the crackdown. 'We are finished!' he shouted, 'The bastards have shut it down!' All Ah Sheng could think about were the unsold handbags left lying in their containers. It would be a huge loss of money for him and Xiao Ning. But Dakuan warned them not to go near the market. The police were making arrests.

Dakuan was right. The news that night reported that the police had seized a total of $5 billion worth of goods belonging to the migrants. The authorities claimed that the products had been illegally smuggled into Russia, without explaining why they had turned a blind eye to smuggled goods for more than a decade.

'We spent a lot on the containers for the products,' said Ah Sheng. 'On top of that we had to deduct the cash we spent paying penalties to the police. Every time we made money, we lost some. In fact, only three months out of the entire year were relatively good ones, when we made money instead of losing it. But now our $30,000 worth of containers – one million roubles' worth of products – have been taken by the authorities.'

The market had been the only place the migrants knew well in Moscow. It was ten minutes' walk from their flat. Each day, this short trip to and from work was fraught with fear: They feared the police, the frequent random arrests resulting in heavy penalties each time, the name-calling, and, worst of all, the skinheads and robbers lurking on street corners, awaiting the most vulnerable. For this reason, many migrants hadn't left the market's confines in years.

Xiao Ning and Ah Sheng recalled being regularly stopped and searched on the street. 'The officer would tell us that our tourist visas were too old,' Xiao Ning said. 'And then he would ask us where we lived, although it was obvious that he had been told already. It couldn't have been a coincidence for him to find us in the street right in front of our flat.'

Ah Sheng thought that the large number of Chinese migrants was seen as a threat by the Russian authorities. There are currently 200,000–400,000 Chinese working in Russia, and about 30,000–50,000 new Chinese migrants entering each year, mostly as traders and temporary workers. But with the Russian population decreasing, particularly in the Russian Far East, the Chinese presence became alarming. 'The real reason they've closed the market, I think, is to put a halt to migration into Russia, particularly Chinese migration,' he said.

Indeed, more than 100,000 migrant workers were immediately made jobless by the closure. Some Tajik migrants were camping out, as they had nowhere to go to outside their workplace. The atmosphere in Chinese-occupied flats was dense with anxiety. A group of long-term Chinese migrants decided to do something: a hundred of them, joined by a number of Vietnamese migrants, attempted to block traffic on a highway. The police acted quickly and deported them all.

'We can't do anything about it. They make the rules and they can change the rules,' said Xiao Ning. 'I thought we should leave and see what happens after a while – maybe things will quiet down and we can come back to Russia later.'

Unable to recover their confiscated goods, two thirds of the Chinese migrants were returning to China. Most of those who stayed couldn't afford to go home.

Ah Sheng mentioned that Dakuan was known among their community for the rap songs he wrote in his moments of depression during his time in Moscow. He recalled one his friend had written after their release from the police station:

> Trading in Russia is a lousy life!
> Our goods go cheap, there's too much strife.
> Twelve cents' worth we sell for four,
> Then come the cops to ask for more.
> Strip your ass, they'll search you all!
> Give em cash to keep your stall,
> Drag you down to the bloody station,
> Pay the slap to stay in their nation.
> Aren't we here to make good cash?
> No ticket home, not enough in the stash.
> Every single day feels like a year,
> Better go back, even China beats here.
> I'll never get rich from farming the land,
> But at least I will have peace of mind.

Yet another ordeal awaited the Chinese at the border. Those who had been working on Siberian farms, who had a different immigration status, had to leave our train at the Russian border town and follow a 'facilitator', who would negotiate with the border officers and lead them back to China by bus. Many would be fined for 'minor visa problems' and others detained – then charged by the facilitator for 'accommodations' while they were being held. Most had not even been paid by their farm employers, and here they were held at the mercy of the border authorities, terrified about being prevented from returning home.

As I entered China, just before arriving at Manzhouli, the border officers insisted on checking all my laptop files. It was all 'part of the anti-terrorist procedures', the other passengers later said, against the Uighur 'splittists' – a key word used by the state to silence ethnic minorities, including Tibetans, and to justify, for the sake of national identity and security, the repression of discontent.

From that moment on, I heard two distinct, conflicting voices. The first was that of the Chinese state, emphasizing the national progress of the 'Chinese nation', material bounties, and a bright, sustainable future for all. Sometimes paternal in tone – lecturing and condemning, as during the Olympics and anti-terrorist campaigns – it proclaimed: 'Unite against the separatists and splittists' and 'The twenty-first century is the Chinese century.' At other times maternal, it persuaded, cajoled and encouraged: 'Love your country'; 'The Chinese astronaut takes the nation's first step into space, with tears in his eyes – he has triumphed for the Motherland'; and 'The five-star flag is greater than my own life.' The voice lingers permanently in the air, permeating every inch of society.

But another voice could always be heard from below – all over the cities and the countryside, in the factories and down the coal mines, by the brick kilns, at the job centres and the labour markets in every city. This was the cry of China's mobile proletariat, always on the move, from the rural interior into the cities of their unevenly industrializing country and from those cities to the metropolises of north and southeast Asia and the US, and Europe. These workers were struggling to survive –and barely subsisting – through all the upheavals of the global market economy.

Their journey began three decades ago, and since then the global economic downturn has exacerbated the causes of their migration: rural poverty, the collapse of urban job security, mass unemployment and rapidly falling living standards.

Despite state proclamations of a 'rising China', the reality is that China has been struck hard by the global recession and is as bitterly divided as the rest of the world. The 'iron rice bowl' no longer exists. More than 600,000 small- and medium-size firms closed in China in 2008, throwing millions out of work. The deepening slump has encouraged a reverse migration, back to the countryside. The area most affected has been the export-led manufacturing heartland of southern China, where millions of migrants from rural Sichuan, Henan, Hunan, Guangxi, Yunnan and other provinces normally congregate for work.

China's agricultural adminstration revealed that 15.3 percent of the 130 million rural migrants in the cities – about one in seven – had returned to the countryside jobless following the mass layoffs between 2008 and early 2009.[7] By spring 2009, more than 25 million migrant workers had found themselves without a job. Though the National Bureau of Statistics (NBS) reports that 'the average (annual) urban wage rose 13 percent in the first half of 2009 to \$2,142', these figures exclude the private sector, which accounts for 40 percent of China's GDP, more than 120 million workers, most of them migrants.[8]

One can be easily fooled. The skyscrapers continue to shoot up in Beijing. Top-range department stores are doing well; 27.5 percent of the world's luxury goods are consumed in China, more than in the US and second only to Japan. Money is made and spent by the middle classes as if they were still living in a boom. A successful Beijing filmmaker, Li Yang, on his first visit to Britain sneered at the housing and the lack of super shopping malls in London's East End, where I live. 'You're missing out on a lot, living in this part of

London,' he said, referring to his own upmarket district in Beijing, Haidian, a world away.

During 2008–2009, I followed the footsteps of migrant workers from Russia and the border region to China's industrial northeast; from earthquake-affected Sichuan to the building sites and brick kilns of the northern cities and to the isolated factories of Shaoguan, Dongguan and Guangzhou of the manufacturing south; from the region west of the Yellow River to the east, where class divisions in the townships and villages are intensifying, decades after the Revolution; from the dazzling special economic zone cities to the impoverished coal-mining villages of Henan; and finally from central to northern Fujian, where communities are being rebuilt thanks to remittances from abroad.

I witnessed the living conditions of peasant families. Their annual income – barely a third of the average urban wage – continues to decline. I witnessed the impact of layoffs and the growth of local corruption as desperate workers waited for jobs. Meanwhile, working conditions and wages have deteriorated, and some workers, out of sheer hopelessness, have taken their own lives – a bitter testimony to the tragic impact of *gaige kaifang*. Yet local governments have been reluctant to penalize companies who laid off their workers without pay or to punish directors who simply hid or fled. Prime Minister Wen Jiabao, acknowledging the 'huge impact' of the recession, launched a $585 billion government stimulus package and $1.1 trillion in bank loans to encourage domestic consumption, but little of this money was allocated to public services, housing or health care.

Yet many of the workers dismissed as 'scattered sand' are not prepared to accept what is thrown at them. In May and June 2010, a series of spontaneous strikes, involving thousands of migrant labourers, broke out at large multinational plants such as Honda and Toyota in southern and northern China. The strikers demanded wage increases, improvement of working conditions, and the right to form their own independent trade unions. At the Nanhai Honda plant in Guangdong, migrant workers won a 500 yuan ($79) monthly pay increase, with a further increase of 611 yuan set for 2011. At Toyoda Gosei in Tianjin, workers won a 20 percent pay increase. In fact, such strikes or 'mass incidents' now break out every day throughout the country.

As 'socialism with Chinese characteristics' reveals itself to be little more than a variant of the brutal capitalist order that the Communists once denounced, the strikers have shown that they will not wait passively for their iron rice bowl.

'No matter if the cat is black or white, as long as it catches mice,' Deng Xiaoping used to say of China's urgent need to embrace market economics by any means necessary.

When I mentioned this to a migrant worker from Henan, he said, 'But no mice have been caught.'

1

Exodus: Northeast Youth Head for the City

Peng, a twenty-one-year-old man with large black eyes and a look of genuine innocence, approached me as I stood inside Shenyang's Lu Garden Labour Market. Hundreds of people gathered here each day to wait for work. Right outside the building, men were selling watermelons to thirsty job seekers, some of whom had queued overnight, just to be first to see the ads in the morning. Inside, large slogans of national economic progress were hung on the four walls and propped against the lifeless old marble floor. Workers crowded around the job boards, some wearing placards to advertise their skills, such as catering and decorating. I was speaking to one of them when Peng walked up and introduced himself, then launched into his story, speaking freely, delighted to have someone to talk to about the years of hardship and solitude. He had been living in Shenyang for three years, in a room five metres square that he shared with four other men from nearby villages. The bed cost him ten yuan a day, which meant he couldn't afford to remain long without work. He lived on four meat buns (*baozi*) a day, bought near the labour market for three yuan. He would waste no time on meals – he ate his buns while he searched the job market, which he visited daily. He hadn't much in his life apart from looking for work. Once, he'd been stopped in the street by a cosmetics company representative who tried to persuade him to become a salesman. He would have to sell hard and earn a commission. Although he was tempted, he turned the offer down; he'd heard too many stories from other villagers about getting trapped in sales work (*chuanxiao*), where you earn little and are constantly under huge pressure to sell products to your personal network. The companies subject recruits to a militaristic training and the work regime is harsh. Recruiters always target young rural migrants, who are more desperate than other job seekers.

Peng had lost his last job, as a security guard, a month before, and was still unemployed. 'What's the bloody point?' he exclaimed. 'Work at Lu Garden always comes through a middleman, who charges 50 yuan for a job worth 50 yuan.'

Peng was a farmer from Fuxing village in Liaoning province, three hours' bus ride from Shenyang. He called Fuxing a 'poor old place'. The main produce there is sweet corn and wheat, incomes are low, and many young farmers had left to work in cities – mostly Shenyang – in recent years. Peng's mother had died when he was young; his father was strict and temperamental. Peng was the only child and had grown up lonely. At thirteen, he'd had to go to work, helping his father on the farm. He was expected to work hard because he was a boy, which he resented very much.

Peng had not otherwise had a memorable childhood. He remembered only that he'd spent all his time in the fields with his dad. Home life was monotonous; the work was tough and never-ending – but then it was the same for everyone else. If you stayed in the village, that was the kind of life you led. In the evening, Peng cooked for his father. Occasionally he would read a book. He'd taught himself to read – he liked Chinese historical tales. He'd gone only to primary school and wasn't expected to further his studies – only to work on the land and bring in income for the family. Sometimes he was asked to help out on his uncle's farm too, particularly during harvests.

On two *mu* of land per person – a third of an acre – he and his dad farmed wheat and sweet corn, for sale and their own subsistence. In total, they brought in 6,000–7,000 yuan (£545–630, $952–1,111) a year —enough to feed and clothe themselves but not much else. His dad had tried to look for other work nearby in order to improve their income, but there wasn't much industry around

Fuxing. They saw that the sons of many families had left for work outside the village.

In 2004, his uncle developed heart disease and could no longer work on the land, and so could not afford the frequent checkups and treatment. He had no wife or children to support him. No medical insurance was available to peasants. Peng's father tried to shoulder his brother's medical costs – more than 1,000 yuan per month – taking a job transporting timber into town in his horse cart, but the extra income was hardly enough. He was too old to leave the village, and so after two years, Peng, then seventeen, volunteered to go work in the city, and became the main breadwinner in his family.

'The ruling clique doesn't care that most peasants aren't insured for basic medical care,' Peng concluded.

From 1952 to 1982, health care institutions in China were funded by the state, with communes providing free health care to all. The Cooperative Medical System established health centres in villages staffed by 'barefoot doctors', medical practitioners with basic training. These health services were poor in quality, but at least available, and during this period infant mortality fell from 200 to 34 per 1,000 live births, and life expectancy increased from about thirty-five to sixty-eight years. Infectious diseases were controlled.

When the communes were abolished in 1982, the system was dismantled, and peasants instantly became uninsured. Health care was privatized and decentralized, as the central government drastically reduced its funding for social services. Between 1978 and 1999, the government's share of funding for national health care fell from 32 percent to 15 percent. Now doctors are paid according to a performance-oriented system, in which bonuses are granted according to the amount of money doctors generate for their hospitals from drugs and tests. Sales of expensive drugs – the chief source of income for China's hospitals – have boomed. In 2007, the total revenue of public hospitals in China was 375.4 billion yuan; 200 billion were from drug sales, compared with 28.5 billion yuan in government funds – just 7.6 percent of total hospital revenues.

The result is that health care is no longer accessible to most Chinese. Local authorities in the interior provinces and rural regions in particular have been unable to properly fund health care. In 1999, only 7 percent of rural residents and 3 percent of residents in the interior had health insurance, compared with 49 percent of urban residents.[1] In 2006, according to the Ministry of Health, fewer than 10 percent of rural residents were insured, compared with 50 percent of urban residents. It was also reported that 87 percent of rural residents paid for *all* of their health care. Experimental initiatives, like the New Rural Health Cooperatives (NRHC), launched in 2003 in 300 counties, have largely failed. NRHC offered limited health insurance to peasants: 30 yuan per person per year – 10 yuan each contributed by the participant and central and local governments – proved insufficient to cover participants' medical costs. Even in 2006, when the central and local authorities both increased their contributions to 20 yuan per year, the 50 yuan total per peasant covered only 25 to 35 percent of yearly health care costs in rural areas. Many peasants, too, suspect that the usual rampant corruption plays a part – that local authorities are skimming the funds.

Recent health reforms have brought new problems. In 2010, as part of the national plan to promote domestic consumption, the government put forward guidelines for health care reform, along with an investment of $124 billion, 40 percent of which would come from the central government and the rest from local ones. The thinking was that if health care were improved, people would not have to save so much for medical costs and would spend more on consumer goods. However, the government never announced how the money would be allocated. The reform itself consisted of two parts: increasing funding for medications and medical equipment, and improving medical insurance coverage. The government planned to raise funds for the rural cooperatives to $18 per person in 2011, although at the time of writing there had been no release of information on how and where that would be done. Moreover, this was not a universal reform: Only sixteen cities (six each in central, western, and eastern China) were chosen to pilot it, with 5,000 township hospitals targeted for upgrading. InMedica, a medical research company, predicted that in China's largely privatized health care system, the biggest winners in this reform would be medical equipment suppliers like Mindray, Beijing Wandong and Yuyue Medical. Private hospitals, too, including private foreign hospitals, would be favoured by the scheme. The rationale was that opening the door to foreign investment in health care would ease the burden of public health care, since middle-class patients would be more inclined to use foreign hospitals.

Peng's first security job in Shenyang paid 1,300 yuan (£118, $206) per month. He sent two thirds of this money home, and kept the rest for his living expenses. He was able to pay rent, and spent very little on food – a few yuan a day. The best meal he made himself was two eggs fried with tomatoes, and he cooked this only occasionally. He had no other expenses – no transport costs, because he walked to work. He was guarding a local three-star hotel. There were three other guards working with him, who also came from nearby villages. Many of the hotel's guests came from the southern provinces; others came from abroad. He had wondered about them and why they came to a place like Shenyang, a city he found dull and depressing. His job was not easy; hardest to bear was his supervisor's daily bullying – shouting and name-calling – and one day he talked back. Two weeks later, he was dismissed without notice. Since then, he'd been back at the labour market, looking for work, but had found only a temporary job as a labourer on a building site not far from the market. The pay rate was two-thirds that of the security job, and the work only lasted two days.

The month before I met him at Lu Gardens, he'd found another security job, at a local brewery. The ad, like many listed at the labour market, had given no information about fixed wages. Such ads say only 'good starting wage' or 'guaranteed good wage for the experienced.' Peng took the job because he had no other option. When the first paycheck came, 1,000 yuan (£90, $158) for the same work he had performed at the hotel for 1,300, he asked for a raise and was immediately fired. His bosses said they couldn't pay more, because of the global economic crisis – and they knew that they could find a replacement immediately.

'Bosses can do anything they like,' Peng said. 'Heaven is high above and the emperor is far away. They don't care about breaking the rules, precisely because the rules are not enforced.

'In Shenyang, no one is on your side in these kinds of situations,' he continued. 'Arbitration is unfair and slow and always in the interest of the businesses. If worse things happen and you get injured, you can't afford the costs to take the company to People's Court. A Shenyang builder fell on a building site and lost his leg. He didn't sue the company because he couldn't afford to. Who cared about him? He's one of us – from the countryside.'

Now Peng came to Lu Garden every day. He got up at around 6 a.m. along with his roommates. They usually cooked porridge for breakfast and ate it with pickled vegetables. Peng never had much appetite that early in the morning, so he'd leave the flat and walk alone to Lu Garden, through the quiet alleyways and streets. He enjoyed it; it was the most tranquil part of his day. When he arrived, a crowd of job seekers was already there, well ahead of him, all eagerly waiting to see that day's new opportunities. He would push himself to the front and scan the ads on the walls, taking notes, and then call up each number and ask for an interview. If he saw no suitable ads, he would walk around the market and chat with fellow job seekers. Sometimes he would sit on the floor in a corner and rest, before getting up again to look for more incoming ads. He would also walk around seeking potential employers – sometimes they would come down to look for individual workers to do a casual job, just for the day.

At noon, Peng would leave the market and buy his lunchtime buns from a vendor he'd known since his first day at Lu Garden. The bun seller had been a job seeker himself, but had given up looking for work and taken on this little street trade instead. The watermelon seller was in the same situation: unemployed labourer turned trader. Peng would take a fifteen-minute break, chewing his buns and chatting with them about news of the day. After lunch, he would get back inside Lu Garden and start searching again – new ads did come in throughout the day, so everyone carried on, hoping for a job. The latest Peng ever stayed was till 8 p.m., when his flatmates also packed up and went home.

As I was leaving Lu Garden myself that day, another man walked up to me and said, 'Wait! I have something to show you. Would you like to see my poems and essays?' His eyes sparkled with enthusiasm. 'I wrote them in my years working away from my home village.' He was Ren Jianguo, from Hugou village, Shanzuizi county, Liaoning province.

I followed him to his flat, like Peng's just ten minutes' walk from the labour market. We entered a tiny alleyway and turned a corner into a dingy-looking block of flats. He said these were mostly occupied by retired urban poor. I saw some men and women in their seventies doing calisthenics in the tiny public area in between the flats. They were in their pajamas, leaning on a metal pole and stretching their legs. I followed him up the stairs, which smelled bad. The railing had rusted. No doubt, this was among the most modest housing in Shenyang, as he told me – and migrants cannot afford anything better. All of his flatmates were still at Lu Gardens, waiting for work. By the look of the place, there must have been at least a dozen people living there besides him. But Ren Jianguo didn't seem to care about the mess and the lack of space. He seemed interested only in what he'd written in black ink. He searched anxiously in a pile of documents on a desk next to an old washbasin. Finally, he found it: some fifty pages of handwritten poems and essays. 'There! Please read it. It's my sweat and tears,' he said, pushing the papers into my hands.

The first page was titled 'To My Parents.' It told of his regrets over the years when he had not brought sufficient income from his job in Shenyang to support his aging mother and father, who had been farming the land in Hugou village:

One of the most pointless things in life is to exhaust yourself in rearing children. I say this for you, Mother and Father... I left home in tears, to make a living in the world outside. You had fed and clothed me for twenty years, and I had to leave to know what it's like to be so giving. You had toiled in the fields, suffering and bearing the heat and the cold, just to pay for my schooling. You had cared for me and provided me with everything that there was. All you were hoping was that I would make a good life for myself one day. But how I broke your hearts – earning such a poor wage on a building site in a heartless city ... getting drunk in my depressed moments ... I do not deserve you. I would like to go down on my knees, to beg for your forgiveness ...

Ren Jianguo began writing down his thoughts from the day he left home for the city. Peng, instead, found consolation in sharing his experiences with other migrants. He told me that for him, solitude was one of the most distressing things about living and working in a city as an outsider. The day I left Shenyang, Peng accompanied me through the dusty lanes of the city to the train station, confessing that he was trying to look after his mental health by not being alone.

Shenyang's past glories and tragedies are no longer very visible in the city today. Still the capital of Liaoning Province in northeastern China, and historically known as Mukden, it had been the legendary Manchu general Nurachi's first capital after Nurachi overthrew the Ming Dynasty in 1625. It remained so until 1644, when the Manchus invaded Beijing and established the last dynasty there, the Qing.

Toward the end of the Qing dynasty, when the imperialist powers were dividing the country into their spheres of influence, Shenyang was an object of competition between Russia and Japan. The former built a railway connecting the city with the South Manchurian Railway, in an attempt to tap into the region's natural resources; the Japanese used a train-car explosion north of Shenyang in 1931 as a pretext for invading the city, seizing all of northeastern China, and establishing a puppet state called Manchukuo. The anti-imperialist sentiment among the people of this region has lasted and evolved over the years into a strong nationalism.'[2]

Shenyang has developed into an important industrial centre since the 1920s, and in the 1970s it became one of China's top three industrial cities, alongside Shanghai and Tianjin. Shenyang today is the largest city in the northeast of China, with a population of 8.1 million. Its historic heavy industry (it has been known as the rust belt since the industrial decline of the 1980s) is still manifest: you cannot ignore the polluted air when you enter Shenyang. You also see the city's new look: the inflow of foreign investment and the fast growth of the city's service industries apparent in the ubiquitous high-rises housing foreign banks and insurance companies.

As a fast-growing city, Shenyang boasted a total GDP of 383 billion yuan in 2009, and has been recognized as one of the top twenty emerging cities in China. Its income level is known to be the highest in the region. In 2010, the average income in Shenyang was reported to be 1,708 yuan per month,[3] an enviable one compared with other northeastern cities and towns. For that reason it has pulled in many rural people from the northeast as well as from the south. Currently, there are around two million migrant workers in Liaoning province, most of them seeking opportunities in the private sector, particularly in Shenyang's manufacturing and service industries. Thousands of labourers, a massive reserve army, crowd the streets and labour markets each day, waiting for jobs.

The Lu Garden Labour Market in central Shenyang is the city's largest. Two or three hundred jobless migrants gather there each day. Near Lu Garden is a well-known antiques market much liked by the city's middle class. In fact, it is much better known to them than the labour market. 'Just cross the bridge and it's on the left-hand side,' is what everyone tells you when you walk in that direction. The labour market itself is an unimpressive, grey-looking concrete building that can be seen from the other side of the bridge.

Street sellers with three-wheeled carts crowd around Lu Garden. Job seekers can be seen waiting and talking to one another even hundreds of metres before you reach the bridge. When you push yourself into the building, you feel the heat coming from the mass of people inside. In midsummer, it was just as the migrant workers described it, 'like being inside a steamer'. The heat of competition is just as fierce: people try to grab the first job around; they cannot afford compassion for other aspirants. The place is particularly overcrowded at the beginning of the year when migrants return to the city from their winter break, with the number of job seekers rising to more than two thousand each day. Then it's like a movie scene of a wartime train station. It is all about survival.

Lu Garden's labour market was originally formed spontaneously by migrant job seekers who gathered here looking for work, and it has been regulated by the local authorities since 2003 as a casual-labour exchange. Official estimates say that 2,000 to 5,000 job seekers visit Lu Garden every day – up to a million people per year. Big companies advertise their vacancies on the walls, but some construction employers and small- to medium-size catering businesses come here in their cars and look for workers themselves. Employers often go through middlemen, because it is the easiest way for them to find migrant workers. And employers prefer migrants because their labour costs much less than urban workers'. This is particularly the case in the private sector. The middlemen receive fees from both the employers and the workers. Some middlemen are labour contractors themselves, which means they will take a regular cut from the migrants' wages.

In 2011, the number of Lu Garden's migrant job seekers has apparently increased while in similar markets in other provinces employers have complained about a labour shortage. At Lu Garden, employers now complain instead about workers' reluctance to accept low wages.[4] One caterer was reported to have said: 'These workers nowadays … they want their wages on the day. And those workers you want to employ are just unaffordable!'[5] An employer from a cosmetics company who had visited Lu Garden five times said, 'I'm now offering 1,500 yuan per month and still can't find workers!'[6] It seems that in Lu Garden, migrant workers' self-confidence has grown.

Even so, Shenyang is now known not only for its fast growth but also for its mass unemployment, which affects workers in both the state sector and private sector. The mass layoffs here are largely a result of the conversion of state-owned enterprises (SOEs) since the era of reform and opening up.

Previously, all enterprises in China had been publicly owned and managed, and the state was the largest employer, providing work for more than 75 million people. But since the late 1970s, the government under Deng sought to increase the competitiveness of the economy by dismantling or privatizing them, a process that took more than two decades. In the first stage, 1978 to 1984, greater autonomy was given to the management, and enterprises were allowed to keep a portion of their profits instead of submitting them to the state. In the second stage, 1984 to 1992, this autonomy was increased, as enterprises were given freedom to hire and fire staff and to establish direct links with suppliers. Increasingly, traditional administrative relations between the state and entrepreneurs were replaced by contractual relations. In the third stage, 1992 to the present day, the central government has limited its ownership to 500 to 1000 large-scale SOEs, allowing all smaller SOEs to be leased or sold; by 1998, a quarter of China's 87,000 industrial SOEs had been restructured. By the end of 2001, this number had grown to 86 percent, 70 percent of those having been partially or fully privatized.[7]

The result was mass unemployment. From 1998 to 2004, six in ten workers in SOEs were laid off, or 21 million workers from 1994 to 2005, according to the Ministry of Labour and Social Security (MOLSS). In the northeast, as the centre of heavy industries, which were all state-owned, layoffs were nearly twice the national average.[8] Although workers are entitled by law to compensation when laid off from an SOE, there is no national standard for the amount of compensation: It is completely up to the individual enterprises. In

certain enterprises, particularly in those SOE-concentrated provinces such as the northeast, workers often receive no compensation
at all from a corrupt management. In March 2002, 10,000 workers
at the state-owned Liaoyang Ferro-Alloy Factory in Shenyang
embarked on a series of protests against the corruption of factory
managers during the forced closures of the local state-owned enterprises.[9] While company assets disappeared, the company failed to
pay workers their pension contributions and full wages. Following
a closure, workers were promised only the minimal compensation
of 600 yuan for each year of their service. After receiving this compensation for two years, workers would not be eligible for further
unemployment benefits. As the workers' petitions had brought no
solution to their misery, they took to the streets. Adding insult to
their injuries, the worker activists Yao Fuxin and Xiao Yunliang
were arrested and convicted of 'subversion of state power'. Yao
was sentenced to seven years in prison, Xiao to four.

A report titled 'No Way Out' put it this way: 'The government's
failure to implement clear policy guidelines for the process [of the
enterprise closures], combined with a lack of transparency, flawed
auditing of company assets, and widespread corruption, left millions of workers out in the cold, with no job and barely enough
income to support their families ...' In 2006 alone, according to the
report, a total of 2.05 billion yuan was owed in unpaid wages and
a total of 700 million yuan in unpaid compensation by SOEs that
were undergoing closures in eleven provinces.[10]

There is a basic living subsidy that the laid-off SOE workers
are entitled to receive for up to three years, but this is lower than
the minimum wage. The monthly minimum wage in Shenyang
is 700 yuan. For workers with families to support, the subsidy
isn't enough to live on even in the short term. As a result, some
have started to seek work in the private sector or tried to set up
their own small businesses if they've managed to accumulate any
capital. Others, in their thousands, have opted for a more ambitious project: migrating abroad, seeking work in South Korea and
Europe, including the UK.

Among the unemployed I met in Shenyang there were also migrant workers who had lost their land in their home villages. Some of these migrants had left the countryside as a result of local government land seizures. Nationally, these official seizures of land for commercial or industrial use have driven an estimated 70 million peasants from their farms and have been a major cause of peasant pauperization.[11] In Liaoning province alone, millions of peasants are estimated to have been affected. Land grabs in Liaoning are related to government debt. Eighty-five percent of local government borrowers in Liaoning could not afford their interest payments.[12] Banks were willing to loan to them in the first place because there is a huge amount of land that the local authorities can grab. It is modestly estimated that 23 percent of the total loans to local governments in China depend on sales of appropriated land for repayment.[13]

Although farmland was decollectivized through the 1980 Household Registration Act, and peasants given rights to till and manage allocated parcels of land under contract with the village production team, all of that land remains state-owned, and can be transferred only through expropriation by the state. Since the early 1990s, local governments have been seizing peasants' allocated land and converting it to industrial and commercial use to fuel economic growth. This has increased steadily as a direct result of the uncontrolled growth of property development and the anarchy of the market since the reform and opening up. And although local authorities are required by the Land Administration Law to compensate peasants for expropriated cultivated land, in practice peasants' petitions against the loss of their homes and farmland are almost always ignored.

When peasants protest, they are often attacked by armed thugs sent in by the local authorities. In March 2011, police officers and hired thugs attacked a group of 300 peasant protesters in Fuzhou. Ten of them were beaten up and injured; in 2004, peasants were protesting against land seizure in Sanchawan village in Shanxi province and many were seriously injured by rubber bullets; in

June 2005, six villagers of Shengyou in Hebei province were killed
by hired thugs; in May 2009, Yingde villagers near Guangdong
province were attacked by armed police; one villager suffered
brain damage and was left paralyzed.

Hence the migration into cities like Shenyang, where they scramble for the few jobs they can find. Many migrants to Shenyang
arrived during the worst of the recession in 2009, when manufacturing and service industries in the city were seeing large layoffs
of migrant workers – an estimated 0.4 million lost their livelihood
then. Even so, Shenyang tempts migrants with a manual labour
wage that averages 1,200–1,500 yuan per month, higher than other
cities in the region.

Li Long, twenty-nine but older looking, weathered from years
of farm work, stood out among the job seekers I saw for his energetic manner, his keenness as he talked to other migrants, while
he walked up and down the streets of Lu Garden with his shirt
rolled half up to relieve the heat. He'd come from Yuelai, a village
in Heilongjiang province with 600 households – a fair size. But
most of the villagers had nothing but small, fragmented plots of
land to work on, and in recent years many had left for surrounding towns in search of work, though many of those soon returned
after being laid off. He himself had been a farmer, with less than
an acre of arable land, and what he could earn in a year – 1,500–
2,000 yuan – was such a pittance that he'd moved to Shenyang,
where he'd worked as a loader and general labourer for two to
three years. But now he had been jobless for several months. He
lived with two other job seekers from Heilongjiang, and they often
came to the labour market together. He would wait around Lu
Garden for the whole day, if no work came up. When he got tired,
he would walk to the bridge and sit on it, watching the crowd. 'I'm
always ready to put up with hardship,' he said. 'Poor Mom and
Dad, they are still tilling the land, at their age ... I feel so incompetent. It's so hard to survive in Shenyang.' Even when he was
employed and sent his income home, it had not been enough to
support them.

Two months after I left Peng in Shenyang, I was staying in a guesthouse in Beijing. I'd just come back from a short trip to visit Ying, a Chinese who had returned to his hometown, Handan, from London. The train journey had exhausted me. At five minutes to midnight, the phone rang. It was Peng.

'Did I wake you up, sister?' he asked.

'Not at all!' I replied. I'd been kept awake by the calls from the local saunas anyway – the reception kept putting them through to the rooms. The female callers, mostly rural migrants, would offer 'special services' – a massage and sex – if a man answered, but would hang up without a word if they heard a female voice.

'How have you been?' I asked.

'I'm not good. Not good at all. Couldn't find any work at all in Shenyang,' he said. 'I've tried really hard in the past month. Since you left, things have got considerably worse and most people have given up their job search in Shenyang – sixty out of a hundred migrants have returned home to their villages. I've hung around here long enough. But no sign of a job.'

'I'm so sorry, Peng!' I said, not knowing how to reassure him. 'What are you planning to do now?'

'I'm going home, back to Fuxing. I'll help out on the farm for a while ... and see what happens. I can't stay in Shenyang anymore – I'm going mad! And everyone's leaving. I am dead scared, sister. I don't want to end up like Ah Shan.'

There was a pause.

'You know Ah Shan?' he asked.

I struggled to remember.

'You met him in the Lu Garden labour market,' Peng said. 'Ah Shan couldn't live with the pain and shame of staying jobless for more than six months. He took his own life – just a week after you left. One day, he just jumped into the river right by the labour market and drowned himself.'

I was speechless. I really didn't remember Ah Shan. He must have been one of the many job seekers who had gathered when I talked to Peng. Peng described him as an honest man, 'although you probably wouldn't notice him in a crowd.' Peng was obviously upset about the death. He'd spent days searching for work alongside Ah Shan and they must have built up a friendship. For Peng, friendship meant a lot. He was trying to hold back his tears as he spoke. I advised him to return home for a break and told him to call me whenever he needed to talk. Then we hung up.

The next day, he returned to Fuxing on a three-hour bus trip. Going home didn't turn out to be much of a break. His father, who had never left to work in the city, did not sympathize with him. 'Other villagers' sons can make money in the city. Why can't you?' he nagged. The accusation was hurtful, but Peng ignored it because he didn't want to talk back to his dad. He tried to justify staying in the village for a while. But it wasn't yet harvest time and there was little farm work. So he spent some time cleaning the front yard and sorting the farmhouse storage for his dad, and cooked dinner for him every evening. 'Have you learned a few dishes in Shenyang?' his father asked, not knowing that Peng had never had time to cook during his time in the city.

Two weeks later, his father got on his case again, and this time he was much harsher: 'If you don't move your ass and go work in the city, we won't be able to survive.'

Peng packed his bag and left home the next morning. Shenyang was the only large city nearby. He had to return to the Lu Garden labour market, which held nothing but memories of failure and Ah Shan's suicide. How could his father understand? 'I am just like his working buffalo,' Peng told me.

One day, waiting around Lu Garden in the early morning, Peng met a recruiter from Hebei province who was looking for candidates to go and work as security guards in Beijing. Peng was thrilled with the opportunity. He had worked as a security guard before. And wouldn't it be great to leave Shenyang and work in the capital? He took the offer immediately, without negotiating.

The security company was called Tianhe Antai 'Heavenly Peace'. It was one of the largest security companies in Beijing – and infamous for its covert operations, which included running drug deals, regularly bribing the public security department, and deceiving and transporting rural migrants into unpaid jobs. But Peng was a stranger to Beijing. How could he know? All he knew was that he was to board a bus from Shenyang to Beijing, along with fifteen others – all older than Peng – to start a new life.

The whole busload would soon be joining the army of migrant workers who performed the dirty work for China's grand capital: building apartments for its new rich, cleaning its streets, planting trees along its avenues, guarding its properties. Each of them was as hardworking as the next, but the younger migrants, like Peng, were more equipped with information about life and employment in the cities and less willing to tolerate poor conditions and more prepared to stand up for their rights. Would his father ever understand?

The trip to the capital was a long one – ten hours. Peng had taken so many bus trips before, and each time he'd told himself that he would make a success of himself and send the much-needed money home. He would be proud of what he could do for his family. He nibbled at the steamed buns that he had brought with him for the trip. He had only two.

It was well past midnight when the bus finally arrived. As it turned in to the depot, Peng wondered where they were: the place didn't look remotely urban. A few other buses were parked, but no one was around. Under the dim streetlight, Peng could see two men selling steamed buns on the side of the empty street. Wasn't this Beijing? 'Gongzhufen,' said the conductor – a quiet part of the city.

Peng and the other fifteen villagers got off the bus and looked around in the semi-darkness. Another bus would take them from this east Beijing depot to Daxing district, in the south of Beijing, where the company was based. Though the depot was not well lit, their many pairs of eyes found the right bus stop soon enough. Daxing, it said. This second ride lasted another hour.

Daxing district, situated on the periphery of Beijing, is clogged with factories of all kinds – ugly even at night. The district comprises nine towns and eighteen townships, and has a total population of 650,000, more than 75 percent of them migrant families who have created their own communities. They come from Hubei, Henan, Shandong and Hebei provinces, as well as from the northeast.

Tianhe Antai has many security contracts with companies in Daxing, to whom they supply migrant workers recruited from Shenyang and elsewhere. The company is housed in a first-floor office in an ordinary-looking street. You can easily miss it. On arrival, Peng and the others were asked by the recruiter to hand in their IDs. 'It is just our normal procedure,' he said. 'It's for our records.' But after a few days, the workers realized that they weren't going to get their IDs back. Peng's repeated requests for his were refused. But none of them protested, for fear of offending the company.

They were then sent to guard a business nearby which they were told was an insurance firm. During the first two weeks, they were also told by the security company not to leave the premises under any circumstances. They were to station themselves right at the gate, but they were not to step outside the compound. They were to eat in the company canteen. Peng became very concerned, because this was the first job where his movements had been restricted – but without his ID, he couldn't simply get up and leave. As time passed, he began to feel trapped. He and the other workers talked about what to do. Should they approach the management collectively? Should they be more confrontational? The shared feeling, however, was that there was little recourse, so the subject was dropped. Meanwhile, the men were desperate to be paid.

Passive cooperation did not bring them peace. In fact, things got worse. When they asked for their weekly pay, they were told that there was no pay yet and they'd have to wait. At the end of the second week, their request was again rejected, without any reason given. The workers realized then that they would not be paid at all. Not one yuan. They didn't voice their concern because they didn't really understand what was going on. Peng, however, did: He and the others were simply being treated as rural peasants who were so desperate for work that they'd accept whatever deal was on offer.

Peng wanted to flee. But to do so, he'd have to fight a large security company. How many bodyguards and thugs did the company have at its disposal? Peng had no idea, though he had heard that workers had been beaten for demanding owed wages and that one of them had been stabbed. There was enough talk like this to keep him frightened.

By the third week, Peng felt like a prisoner. He wanted to get out – there was no way he could go on like this without pay. One day, he noticed that his team leader, a simple-minded man, was easily placated by the offer of a bottle of spirits. Peng came up with an escape plan. He shared it with only two coworkers, because the others seemed too frightened to do anything.

The next week, as their shift ended for the day, Peng invited the team leader for a drink in their dining area. The man had no suspicion about Peng's motives, as so many workers had offered him alcohol to sweeten him up in the past. As cup after cup of liquor was poured, the leader became less and less aware of what was happening. 'Have more, my elder brother! It is my fortune to have met you!' Peng cheered and toasted him.

Finally the team leader downed the last drop in his cup and, voice slurred, said he had to go to bed. Less than a minute later, he was asleep. Then Peng and his two companions snuck out of the building, into the dark night of Yellow village, in central Daxing. They ran as far as they could, although no one was chasing them, slowing down only to catch a bus headed away from Daxing. They had nothing to show for their three weeks' work, but they knew they had done the right thing.

The bus took them to the east side of Beijing, where they stayed with another job seeker from Liaoning, who let them sleep on his floor and fed them for two days. Peng and his two coworkers then tried to recover their IDs, calling the recruiter and threatening to call the police. Of course, this was an empty threat, since reprisals from the security company for carrying it out might be anything from an ordinary beating to a disabling one by company thugs – but it worked: the recruiter sent the IDs via another migrant from the northeast. The company still refused to pay them; Peng had to give that up. He didn't know what became of the workers who had remained on the job.

Eventually, he and his two friends learned the security company's real reputation – much too late. Tianhe Antai is well known for its criminality. Their labour recruitment is used to make illegal profits. Many of the rural job seekers they hire are underage and made to work for nothing. The migrants even have a saying: 'You can get work from Tianhe Antai, but you can't get money!'

It is as if the Labour Contract Law never existed. The law was passed on 1 January 2008, thanks to momentum generated by a child labour scandal in May 2007 that caused a great deal of public anger: Thousands of children, some as young as eight years old, had been kidnapped and sold for 500 yuan a head to 7,500 illegal brick kilns in Shanxi and Henan. Of these, 576 children were rescued. The kidnapped children were found to have been beaten, burnt, and disabled, and some were killed. Those who survived were forced to work in the kilns under the most subhuman conditions. It was found that these illegal brick kilns employed 53,036 migrant workers.[14] At the time, many feared that this scandal was only the tip of the iceberg. Its aftermath was also shocking: A few foremen and middlemen (one of them a Labour Bureau official) were prosecuted, and one of the kiln owners, the son of a Party official, was sentenced to nine years in prison for what amounted to a crime against humanity. Other than that, little was done. But the public outcry had worried the government. It was in this context that a call for the enactment of new labour legislation was heard. A law to protect workers' basic rights was recognized as necessary. Eventually, the Standing Committee of the National People's Congress, that is, China's top legislature, decided to adopt the Labour Contract Law, which had been under consideration since 2005 but never became reality until after the brick kiln scandal.

The law contained ninety-eight articles setting out rules requiring employers to provide workers with signed contracts of employment, which must be based on 'equality and free will' and designed according to the principle of 'negotiated consensus and good faith'. The government claimed that the Labour Contract Law aimed at providing greater job security than the old contract law enacted in 1994, for example stipulating that employees of more than ten years' standing are entitled to non-fixed-term contracts, requiring employers to contribute to workers' social security, and setting wage standards for workers on probation and those working overtime.[15] At the time, Wu Bangguo, chairman of the Standing Committee of the National People's Congress, promised that the new law would 'regulate employers' use of labour and protect workers' rights'.

In practice, however, the law has made no difference for workers like Peng and his colleagues. 'Even when you are given a contract by these companies, you'll find that the contracts are always written in the interest of the company!' Peng told me. '[The law] doesn't take into account the workers' position at all. Some of us simply don't dare to sign the contracts because they are written in such ambiguous ways. We are afraid of being cheated.'

Utterly demoralized by their experience in Beijing, Peng and the other two workers returned to their villages. This was the second time in a month that Peng had returned home to Liaoning without any pay.

And the relentless cycle continued. Two months later, I received another call from Peng. Back at home, his father wouldn't stop hassling him, and he'd returned to Shenyang and the Lu Garden labour market. 'But I've been unlucky,' he said. He'd found absolutely nothing. Now, his plan was to head back to Beijing. Word was that Daxing's labour market was flush with jobs. 'I am determined to find something.'

I was in Beijing at the time and met Peng at the Gongzhufen bus station when he arrived. Dozens of villagers, mostly young men and women in their twenties and thirties, some with children back home, all from Liaoning, filed off the bus. They'd come to Beijing looking for work, some in the building industry, others in domestic service and cleaning. They were all carrying bags of belongings, looking as if they intended on settling for a while.

Then we all boarded another bus, as Peng and his fellows had done just a few months back, and proceeded on to Daxing district. 'I'm gonna make it this time, sister,' Peng said to me. 'I've got to find a job that lasts.' We got off at Yinghai township on the east side of Daxing, where Peng said he knew of cheap lodgings for new arrivals, where you could sleep five to a room. He led me up the stairs of this place and we had some green tea. There was obviously no room for me to stay, and so I wished him good luck and left.

The next day, Peng went to the Daxing labour market at around 9 a.m., a mistake, because most jobs are taken early in the morning. He told me the Daxing market is smaller than Shenyang's and full of people from everywhere – from the northeast, Shandong, Henan, Zhejiang, Jiangsu. Competition seemed even harsher than Lu Garden. He met four other migrants from Liaoning, and they told him that there were many jobs advertised around Beijing's train stations, so together they took a bus into the city centre, some fifteen kilometres away, to have a look. At West Station, they found plenty of ads on shop windows, all for low-paid, temporary manual work. Peng spotted one that read: 'Grand four-star hotel near Beijing West Station. Looking for fit, young men to do security work. Call to discuss pay.'

The five of them, including Peng, felt encouraged and called the hotel recruiter immediately. The ad was clearly aimed at migrants from rural areas, and so Peng and his group did not expect an offer of a reasonable wage. However, they did not expect to be offered only 35 yuan (£3.1–£3.5, $5.5) per day. Beijing's legal daily minimum wage, meagre enough, is 54.40 yuan (£4.9, $8.5). On top of that, they were asked to pay for their own uniforms, and to do three days' work, called training, without wages, and they would have to work without a contract.

'You take it or leave it,' said Peng. 'Stay like a slave, or go back to the countryside – who gives a damn about you?' Without other options, they took the jobs and were housed in a garage by the hotel, where they were given hard bunk beds, no sheets or pillows provided. Peng slept on top of his jacket and jeans. The floor was concrete, and filthy, as if it were never cleaned. The work was straightforward enough, though – guarding the hotel entrance. The men worked eight-hour shifts and were sometimes asked to do overtime. They felt lucky that they all got paid.

But it is impossible to live in an expensive city like Beijing on 35 yuan per day, let alone send money home. After three weeks, Peng was forced to move on. His co-workers stayed. Work isn't easy to find, and they didn't feel confident enough to leave.

'Did I do the right thing, sister?' he later asked me, obviously looking for reassurance. I told him he had, and he returned to the Daxing labour market next day to try his luck again.

Peng resented the idea of security work, but it was the only work he had substantial experience in and a likely chance of getting. He continued his search. He had only 200 yuan left and couldn't remain unemployed for long. When I saw that he'd cut down to one tiny meal a day to save living costs, I offered to help. But he refused – he was far too proud.

'I'm OK. I just need to take up the next job available and make no fuss,' he said.

As I left Peng at Yinghai township, I wondered how I could possibly help him. The fact is that there is no national minimum wage in China. The minimum wage law that came into effect in January 2004 makes local authorities responsible for setting their own minimum wage standard. The law stipulates that this should be 40 to 60 percent of the average wage in the particular area, making the so-called minimum wage very difficult to live on. In Beijing, what was the monthly minimum wage of 640 yuan (£58, $101) could provide little more than a substandard lifestyle, but what other options do workers like Peng have?

I could have helped Peng only if I'd had connections. *Guanxi!* A word heard so often in China. You need connections to open doors for you in every aspect of your life. This is particularly true in post-Mao China, ruled by monetary values and the social relations they establish. Sadly, I had no *guanxi* good enough to help Peng. I was a foreigner.

Fortunately, times, like tides, do change. A week later, Peng called with good news. 'I've got a new job!' he said excitedly.

'What is it? And where?' I asked.

It was another security job, he explained, but this time in the biggest hotel in Yinghai township, Daxing district, the Golden Sail Holiday Hotel. 'And this time, I am here to stay!' he said.

I had never heard Peng sounding so positive. I was thrilled for him. He invited me to visit his new workplace for a hot pot (*huoguo*) dinner when he would be off duty in the evening. We would celebrate his new job and a new beginning.

Peng had just finished his shift when I arrived. He greeted me with a warm hug, wearing a dark blue uniform, and introduced me to his colleagues – Qiang, the thirtysomething team leader from Jiangxi province, and Mr Li, a security guard in his fifties from Henan province.

'We have ten security guards here, all from rural areas in other provinces,' Peng explained. It wasn't a marvellous job, but it paid more than his last, 1,100 yuan (£100–110, $174) per month. 'I don't mind working ten hours a day for the whole week,' he said. 'I'm gonna work hard.'

I knew that Peng was determined to send money home to his father. He felt that he must do that, no matter what.

Qiang joined us inside the hotel café. 'Please sit,' he said. He poured *baijiu*, or sorghum wine, into our cups, sat himself down and raised his cup: 'Let's toast to Peng's new life here! Success! Let's toast to sister Hung's health and safe journey!'

I had to drink up. It's easy to get drunk on *baijiu* – its alcohol content is 40 percent – so I followed with a gulp of hot pot soup to dilute the effect. It was delicious, a mixture of all types of mushrooms, spinach, bean curd, and beef slices.

Qiang had another cup of *baijiu*, and conversation turned to the security industry in Beijing and how it is one of the shadiest industries here, with only 25 law-abiding security firms, compared with over 500 unregistered ones. (Other migrant workers also quote a similar figure.) The companies work with recruiters to pull in migrants from the countryside who are desperate enough to take anything, Qiang explained, and the recruiters also charge the workers a 'tax per head', on top of the money they're taking from the security companies. Both recruiters and companies are crooked.

No wonder then, Peng said, that around 7,000 labour disputes have been reported in Beijing each month. His figure is not far from the statistics given by the Beijing trade union's law department, which said the number of workers filing grievances with the Beijing municipal authorities reached 80,000 for the year 2009.[16] According to the trade union, Beijing's Labour Dispute Arbitration Committees (LDACs) were understaffed and had a backlog of cases. Each dispute now took around ten months to resolve, very often in favour of the employers. The Beijing courts have also reported seeing an increase in labour disputes for the same year – a total of 4,506 labour cases were heard. Nationwide, courts heard a growing number of labour cases from 2008 to 2010. Resolving them became one of the most difficult tasks for the Chinese courts during the peak of the economic crisis. Wang Shengjun, head of the Supreme People's Court, said that courts across the nation handled 295,500 labour dispute cases in 2008, 317,000 in 2009, and then 207,400 in 2010.[17] He noted that a large proportion of these disputes involved back wages, nonpayment of overtime and insurance contributions.[18]

And lawsuits do not always end justly. A high level of incompetence in the courts has been reported in Shenyang. In July 2007, Wu Guangjun, a worker at Liaoning Cotton and Hemp Company, filed a lawsuit against the company seeking reinstatement of his employment contract. After a 'talk' with the company, the Huanggu district court in Shenyang told Wu that the court could not accept his case. Wu revisited the court and was told the same thing by the judge himself, and offered no justification. Wu couldn't get a written copy of the rejection ruling, and was unable to appeal to a higher court. By April 2008, Wu had sold his house to meet the costs of his numerous petitions, which had received no response. Eventually, he became homeless and was seen camping out on the streets of Shenyang. This was a direct result of the failure of institutions and legislation to protect the basic rights of workers.

'With so many labour disputes, it's obvious what is happening,' said Peng. 'Why doesn't the government do something to stop the unregulated security middlemen?'

'These underground security firms are run by criminals,' Qiang replied. 'Criminals are the reason the police receive their pay and keep their jobs. Without criminals, the police can't justify their good salary. They work with each other – they need each other to survive. I am sure you know that these underground firms feed the police with never-ending bribes.' Tianhe Antai, Peng's first employer in Beijing, was notorious for that, in fact.

'As if they gave a damn!' said Qiang, downing another cup of *baijiu*. 'Without migrant workers, Beijingers would starve.'

Eventually, their colleague Mr Li joined in as well. 'We definitely need to be given more respect and more rights,' he said quietly.

As we drank more and more *baijiu*, Peng began asking me about London and whether security guards have a good life over there, in a 'world-class city', as he called it. I told him about a place in east London I knew quite well called Canary Wharf, guarded by hundreds of non-British security guards employed by dodgy agencies, to which he listened with wide-open eyes. 'Really, sister? Are most of them also migrants? From where? Surely they're not earning peanuts like us ...'

Peng toasted me near the end of the evening. 'Sister, I hope that when you return to Beijing one day, you will see that I've got myself a more senior position at work and have done something better with my life,' he said. 'I truly hope that conditions will improve for us all.'

2

Earthquakes in Bohemia:
Life and Death in Sichuan

The footsteps of Sichuanese migrant workers can be found everywhere in China – in the factories, down the coal mines and brick kilns, on building sites in every metropolis. Rural poverty in Sichuan, the country's fourth-largest province and western China's largest source of migrant workers, has driven 20 million peasants to the cities. Among them, more than 11 million have left the province entirely.

Numerous government programmes have attempted to deal with Sichuan's poverty. The '8–7 Plan', launched in 1994, sought to eliminate absolute poverty within seven years. Whether that goal was reached depends on the definition of 'absolute poverty'. China's criteria for rural poverty reflected one of the lowest thresholds among developing countries. In 1986, the 'absolute poverty' line in China was 206 yuan per year. In 1988 it was raised to 1,067 yuan, then to 1,196 yuan in 2009, 1,274 yuan in 2010 and 2,300 yuan in 2011. The raising of the poverty threshold has put three times as many people below the line: since 2011, 128 million among the rural population.

Back in 2005, a five-year plan was launched to reduce the income gap between town and country, which had increased dramatically as a result of the reform and opening up. Yet the gap has continued to widen. Rural per capita income remains below subsistence level: by official measures it was 4,140 yuan (£350) in 2008, less than a third of urban per capita income, and all of the Sichuanese migrants I met were earning *below* this level. Meanwhile, what the state considers the problem of 'superfluous labour' has worsened in rural areas over the years: Lacking state social security provisions for their elderly, peasant families create their own by having more children, in defiance of China's one-child policy. The government has lost count of the scale of the problem. In the 1990s, when it roughly estimated 200 million unemployed in rural China, 50 percent of rural Sichuan's workforce was described as 'superfluous'.

I set out for Sichuan's capital, Chengdu, just a few months after the 8.0 degree earthquake of 12 May 2008. The Information Office of the State Council placed the province's death toll at 69,197, with 374,176 injured and 18,379 missing. Wenchuan and Beichuan, at the epicentre, had suffered the most. At least 60,000 Wenchuan residents were missing and there was little hope for their survival; nearly half of Beichuan's 20,000 residents were dead. Even today, the government has not released a final death toll for Wenchuan, and meanwhile other natural disasters resulting from the quake, such as landslides following rainstorms, have killed more people, and fifty sources of hazardous radioactivity have been discovered in Beichuan's affected areas. When I arrived in August 2008, four months after the quake, residents were still waiting for the local government to clean up the rubble. Between May and June more than 600,000 Sichuanese migrant workers left their badly needed jobs nationwide to visit their families. Life, they knew, was not short of natural disasters – which would always be accompanied by man-made catastrophes. But it was only acceptable to speak of the first.

I had been to Chengdu before, in 1997, and I remembered it as a haven. Known as a city of poets – a bohemian city – its relaxed atmosphere was a welcome change from the constant social struggle that many visitors feel elsewhere in China.

Chengdu sits in a sheltered basin surrounded by mountains, far from the Yellow River Delta where the dominant Han Chinese culture has historically been centred. Through the centuries these conditions attracted poets and writers, most of them travelling hermits, the most famous being Li Bai, whose family migrated from Central Asia and settled in Sichuan. Famed for his wild life-style and his unrestrained, individualistic literary style, a style unknown in the court-influenced writing of ancient China, Li Bai came down in legends as a Chinese Robin Hood (*xiake*). He helped the poor as he travelled with the money he begged from the rich; he caroused and played his lute (*dombura*) to accompany his poems.

> We drink face to face in the midst
> of these mountain blossoms,
> one glass after another, and another;
> Let me go home, I'm no longer sober;
> In the morning I shall return with my dombura.

Sichuan was never far from his mind – many of his poems describe his delight in the beautiful landscape and his joy in the music of others, including his famous 'Listening to the Sichuanese monks', in which he describes feeling overwhelmed by the monks' perfor-mance of music in the misty Emei Mountains:

> For me, he waved his hand,
> strumming and sounding
> like millions of pine forests;
> Mind as clear as water;
> the echo remains
> when the bells toll the dawn;
> Forgetting even when dusk comes
> In many layers of autumn clouds ...

The romantic image of Chengdu – what the Chinese call a *shi wai taoyuan*, 'a peach garden not of this world' – has lasted for centuries; the city was a sanctuary even during the final years of the Qing dynasty as the country was being carved up into con-cessions by the Western powers. I can imagine the Sichuanese strolling in parks, playing *majiong* on the street, and chatting away

in teahouses in their provincial capital while the imperial dynasty
fell apart 1200 kilometres away. Since that time, the number of teahouses in Chengdu has continued to grow: from 454 in 1900 to
598 just before the Chinese Communist Party's rise to power in
1949, and up to the present day, when there is one on every street.
Every day, one in five Chengdu residents visits a teahouse. And
Chengdu's literary scene also continues to flourish, with poets
and poetry lovers alike gathering in clubs throughout the city to
recite the poems of ancient masters and exchange notes about their
own creative work. Even in the open space in Renmin Park, such a
scene can be witnessed. I saw a group of poetry lovers of all ages,
men and women, gathered inside the little pagoda, displaying their
work on the marble table, some reading their poems aloud as others
applauded.

After the earthquake, Chengdu's authors produced an outpour-
ing of work. The forty-five-year-old writer and poet He Xiaozhu
was writing a novel on the second floor of a teahouse in Chengdu
when the earthquake struck. He was terrified and tried to find a
place to hide. He escaped injury, but when he heard of the deaths,
he was heartbroken and wrote the poem 'Elegy', which was circulated all over the country:

> Thousands upon thousands of anguished cries;
> Return to silence and tranquillity;
> Heavenly acts cannot be predicted;
> The moon over Wenchuan;
> Still, a question mark;
> Aftershocks extend to Chengdu;
> Sorrow engulfs half the world;
> Tears turn to ice;
> Let candlelight melt them away;
> Children, climb on a dandelion
> and line up for heaven.

I thought of the words of the ancient poets as I travelled by train
to Chengdu – a twenty-five hour trip, across Hebei, Shanxi, and

Shaanxi provinces. Though the ancient poets loved the region's liberalism, they, too, had dreaded the long journey:

> The path to Sichuan is filled with hardships,
> harder than going up to the blue sky.
>
> — Li Bai

I had boarded the train with my then boyfriend, John Davies, early in the morning. I was fascinated by an array of golden shades outside my cabin window. I climbed down from my bunk bed and saw the dusty land of the Shanxi province unfolding in front of my eyes. The barrenness looked strangely beautiful. I was struck by the magnificence of the country's landscape as well as by the breadth and depth of its rural poverty. Shanxi, a large mountain plateau some 1,000 metres above sea level, is bound on the north by the Great Wall and on the south by the Yellow River. It was China's strategic bastion against the 'barbarians' from the West for many centuries. The land is clearly poor here along the northern border, eroded by rainfall and by lumbering and ruthlessly scoured by sand and dust moved in constant wind and water, giving the bare earth a distinct yellow polish. The Gobi Desert seemed to spill over into this place. There were no traces of livestock. Many of the houses here are extremely basic – caves built up with mud walls.

When we entered the dining car the next day, we were greeted by restaurant staff in stewardess-like uniforms. Two public security officers sat at the back of the car, chain-smoking and keeping an eye on what went on. We ordered our favourite mapo tofu and minced pork with aubergines, as a first taste of Sichuan.

A young woman and an older man asked to sit with us. She was in her early twenties, a biology student at Chengdu University. The man was in his late 50s. 'We've just met,' he said. 'I have a daughter in Chengdu University, too. So we have a lot to talk about.' Like everyone else, they were curious as to why we were heading to Sichuan at this time, when the province had barely recovered from the earthquake. 'We visited Sichuan years ago and would like to see it again,' I said, sticking to our preplanned story. The student nodded.

Then dots of blue came into view outside the window: overcrowded tents, inhabited by villagers who had been made homeless by the earthquake. Not only had the Sichuanese had their homeland and their limited infrastructure destroyed in the eight mountainous counties, and now had to worry about aftershocks and heavy rain causing further disasters, they were also still waiting for their homes and communities to be rebuilt. Although the government had pledged to spend £100 billion ($15 billion at the time) on reconstruction, as reported by international media, no one I spoke to during my journey in China had a clue about this cash, let alone when it would arrive, how it would be spent and over what period of time. In fact, earthquake reconstruction was rarely in the news here, buried under the glory of the Olympics, even after the Olympics were over.

The Chengdu government had estimated that three years would be required for reconstruction to be completed – a frightening length of time for the victims, long enough for their plight to become dormant in the general collective memory, at least until the next tragedy. While the homeless waited in their tents, local officials experienced their share of stress: They'd been ordered by the central government to reduce their expense budgets, for example, by eliminating all 'unnecessary official banquets'.

I couldn't help asking the student, 'Do you think the government is doing enough, or putting enough resources into reconstruction?'

The student seemed offended by my question. 'Of course! No doubt about that!' she said. 'Our government has done all it could to help the victims.'

I said nothing, noticing her rising anger.

Altogether, 4.45 million households had been damaged by the earthquake, including 3.47 million in rural areas. Ten million people were living in temporary housing (tents) three months later. When winter came, the majority of villagers were still waiting for their homes to be rebuilt. By November 2008, 195,000 homes, less than one eighteenth of the total needed, had been completed. Even in May 2009, a year after the disaster, millions were still in temporary housing, and many will continue to live in those tents for years to come. State compensation in money – for those who actually received it – ranged from 16,000 yuan (£1,609, $2,540) and 23,000 yuan (£2,313, $3,651) per family, which most found insufficient to build a home themselves.

'Maybe you've read negative reports about our government,' said the student, provocatively. Her tone reminded me of students I had known in 1970s Taiwan, who had been deeply indoctrinated by the nationalist ruling party there, the Kuomintang. 'So, do you support Tibet's rioters? A lot of the reports in the West are anti-China. They picked on our government about everything.'

This would be my first direct experience of nationalist ideology on the trip, an ideology that wasn't purely relative, expressed in terms of East vs. West, with the East a victim of Western encroachment, but instead increasingly positive, expressed as Chinese nationhood. It was the year of the Beijing Olympics, and the Chinese press was busy bombarding its viewers and readers with self-congratulating propaganda, including street ads exhorting them to 'Fight for your Motherland.' There can be no understanding of the history of modern China without facing up to its nationalism; since the reform era, no other ideology has been as powerful.

My nostalgia for Chengdu proved to be overly romantic. A decade of new development had changed the city. Most of the tranquil avenues dotted with teahouses were gone, along with the little surprises hidden in alleyways, like street snack stalls and sellers of pirate CDs who happily engaged in conversation. The town's past simplicity and richness had been replaced by a crude and impersonal display of private affluence. Chengdu had become another grim and depressing Chinese city with chaotic traffic, suffocating pollution, oppressive high-rise shopping blocks and Starbucks everywhere, along with other multinational companies.

As always on this journey, the first place I visited was the city's largest employment centre, the City East Labour Market, which advertises all types of jobs. It's situated in the extreme east end of the city, that is, in the middle of nowhere. A row of cargo tricycles was parked near the market, and the riders were trying to get customers. Like the job seekers in the labour market, these riders come from the surrounding villages. Outside the gate, hundreds of rural workers were gathered, from Pengzhou area, An county, the Dujiangyan area and as far as Wenchuan, the earthquake's epicentre, about five hours away by bus.

When I began to talk to one of them, others surrounded me and curiously asked me where I was from.

'Taiwan? The treasure island!' a man said.

'I wouldn't mind going to Taiwan to work!' another man added.

The crowd grew bigger still, and I suddenly found myself in the centre of a large circle of job-seekers, all eager to talk. I asked if any had worked outside of Sichuan before.

'We worked in Beijing!' a man pointed at himself and his friend.

'Taiyuan! For two years!' shouted another.

'Shanghai!'

A white-haired man in his fifties said he was from Huangtu village, five hours from Chengdu, and had been a migrant worker for ten years, including a long stint as a builder in Shenzhen, some 2,000 kilometres away. 'I came home because I was worried about my family,' he said. 'Our house was damaged in the quake.'

He was interrupted by others around him, pushing and nudging, all impatiently waiting for their turn to speak.

A man from Wenchuan broke in, 'My family and I have become homeless and are now staying in temporary shelters. The local government promised permanent housing and job priority for people in Wenchuan. But we are all waiting, for months now.'

Then a man whose thick eyebrows over deep-seated eyes distinguished him from the Han Chinese workers approached. He was in his mid-thirties. He introduced himself as Shen Wei, from the Liangshan Yi autonomous prefecture in southwest Sichuan.

Liangshan contains the country's largest population of Yi, the seventh-largest of the fifty-five ethnic minority groups in China. 'I come here every day, to look for work. It's been so difficult,' he said, his accent flatter in intonation than the others'. 'They don't want us Yi. We don't know why. I told them that I'd take any kind of work.'

Shen Wei left Liangshan at the age of twenty. The poverty and the scarcity of opportunities in his rural home gave him no choice but to live a life of constant migration. Liangshan is a largely agricultural region, and one-third of Liangshan residents live below the poverty line. Agricultural income in most Yi households is well below subsistence level. Shen Wei went to work as a security guard in Chengdu in 1996, and then left the province to work, also as a security guard, in Shijiangzhuang, a city in Hebei province, in the late 1990s. After that, he travelled to Beijing when offered a job in the same trade. Soon enough, he had spent his youth toiling in various industries in eight provinces all over China, and now his parents, who lacked a pension in their old age, depend on his earnings.

Shen Wei described working as a security guard in Beijing in 2001. The job paid 800–900 yuan (now £72–81, $127–142) per month – low, considering the high cost of living in the capital, but considerably better than what he could have made at home. He'd lived with other migrants in shabby, overcrowded shacks in Daxing, and his commute to the city centre took two hours each way, but it was the fact that he couldn't save enough to send money home that eventually made the job not worthwhile.

He returned to Chengdu's labour market. There, in 2005, a Sichuanese recruiter – there were many of them around – offered him a job making toys and mobile phones in a factory in Dongguan city, in Guangdong province in the south. Jobs down south were seen as a lot better, offering better terms and conditions, than those in the north. Recruiters often targeted Liangshan, seeing the Yi people as cheap and docile, eager to work and desperate to earn, and therefore much more vulnerable and easy to control as a workforce, more apt to accept poor working terms and then stick with the job. Liangshan's unemployment rate was as high as 4.12 percent in 2009, and it was a known fact that most Yi youth were unemployed.

A few of those workers from Liangshan were only fourteen to sixteen years old. They went south in order to support their parents back home. Once out of the province they would be expected to stay out and keep earning. This job was the beginning of a long journey. After being laid off from the Dongguan factory, Shen Wei said, some of the kids were sent to a new workplace, a brick kiln up north, back in Hebei. When leaving Guangdong, they spent some of their meagre wages on the bus tickets home. The trip took a day; they couldn't afford to buy food or water. The company – a Japanese and Korean joint venture, which employed hundreds of people – knew the workers were underage, of course. 'But they don't care,' said Shen Wei. The middlemen and supervisors were responsible for recruitment, and the company knew how to avoid blame for employing child labour.

So, Shen Wei made his own journey to Dongguan with a group of ten young men from Liangshan who had all been recruited at the same time in Chengdu's labour market. He didn't like the look of Dongguan and found it instantly depressing. Immediately, they were put to work assembling mobile phones, ten hours a day, seven days a week. For that, the monthly pay was about 850 yuan.

Shen Wei stayed in Dongguan for three years. Management withheld their wages for the entire year, calling it a deposit. The workers were paid just before they returned home to the villages for the Chinese New Year. (Migrant workers always return home for the Chinese New Year and go back to work in the spring.) Legally, employers are supposed to pay workers each month, but the Dongguan workers were told that annual pay was the common practice in Guangdong province. Shen Wei was never able to send money home during the working year. The policy was intended to keep the recruits from leaving the job, and it worked.

But that was not the worst of their situation. The Liangshan

Yi did not apply for a temporary residency permit in Dongguan, because they simply couldn't afford one on their scanty pay. So they lived and worked in Dongguan without the permit, that is, without *hukou*, and without status. That meant they had no access to local heath care – if they became ill, they would have to pay the doctor themselves, which they couldn't afford either. Any children they brought with them would not be able to go to local schools. And apart from being denied access to public services, they would face punishment if caught without papers by the police.

As Yi, they were not only looked down upon, but also faced open hostility on the streets. Shen Wei knew personally of co-workers who had been verbally abused, and one who'd been badly beaten and kicked in an unprovoked attack in an alley, late at night, by local men. He'd heard of many other similar attacks. Yi were easily singled out by their facial features and strong accent. In Guangdong province, ethnic minority migrant workers usually have a hard time and find it difficult to be accepted by local people. 'People of Yi origin get the worst pay and the worst treatment,' Shen Wei said. 'Not only in that factory, but in the cities generally. Everywhere we went in Guangdong, we faced hostile eyes.'

But in spite of the prejudice and violence, the workers from Liangshan stayed, because they had to. They worked even when they were sick – they were not allowed to take sick days. Even when Shen Wei had a high temperature, he'd gone to the factory, not the doctor. He'd heard about two young workers from Liangshan before his time who'd become ill in Dongguan and died. One of them, working sick and untreated, had developed pneumonia. When he died, not much fuss was made at the factory. His family was informed and that was the end of the matter. Somehow, the news never became public. 'But our lives are cheap,' said Shen Wei. 'There was no compensation. No one would make a noise.'

I asked if this was why he'd eventually left the job.

'No,' he said. 'Actually, I would have stayed if I could.' But the scandal of child labourers in the Shanxi brick kilns had been exposed not long before, and local media had become interested in the issue of child labour. On 28 April 2008, a report highlighting how Dongguan factory foremen used child labourers from Liangshan was printed in the *Southern Metropolitan Daily*, and the factory bosses got scared and fired all the Yi workers, regardless of whether they were adults or kids. The report read in part:

> [The trafficked children] came from faraway Liangshan in Sichuan, and most of them are not yet 16. The overseers sought and recruited them from families mired in poverty, promising them high wages; some were even abducted and sent off in batches to Dongguan and from there distributed by the truckload to factories across the Pearl River Delta. On unfamiliar soil, these children are often scolded and beaten and only have one proper meal every few days. Some little girls are even raped. Day after day, they undertake arduous labour. Some children think about escape, but the road is blocked. The overseers threaten them and warn them that if they try to run away, there will be a price to pay.

In fact, the foremen in these factories were regularly recruiting children. Thousands of Yi kids from Liangshan were working in Guangdong. At Shen Wei's factory, more than twenty kids were recruited every year. 'But even before the report came out, I heard that the factory was thinking of cutting down its workforce,' said Shen Wei. 'I guess it was easy for them to sack us because they didn't really need us anymore.'

Fei, a twenty-five-year-old Tibetan, spoke up. He had been deceived by a local job recruiter, who knew that he was desperate for work, into selling the drug ecstasy in Beijing. The recruiter had promised him a security job, but not one guarding a company. He took the offer without hesitation; the pay was 150 yuan (now £14.5) a day. 'Good money, isn't it?' he said, and everyone around us perked up: Indeed, it was a large sum compared to usual urban wage levels. Every day, Fei was instructed to stand at a particular location, to wait for buyers. Sometimes it was outside a building, sometimes on a certain street corner. He had no idea who the buyers were, only that they were regular. 'But I was so frightened of getting caught all the time. You wouldn't want to spend a minute in prison – as a Tibetan, you would have a hellish time there. I was so scared of that,' he said. 'When I wanted to quit the job eventually, they wouldn't let me.'

The crowd listened quietly. 'I fled in the end,' he said. One day, he simply didn't show up. He went to buy a ticket home and stayed waiting in the train station for hours, always looking around him, scared that someone might be after him. 'When I returned to Chengdu that summer, looking desperately for work again, a middle-aged Sichuanese recruiter approached me and told me he had a job transporting goods,' Fei went on. The man had been there, recruiting young people, for weeks by then, Fei believed. He made a bad impression on Fei; he didn't seem honest. He wouldn't give specifics about the job, just said, 'You'll find out when you get started.'

'What was the job?' asked a voice in the crowd.

'He sent me to Yunnan province. The job covered food and accommodation,' Fei said. 'But it wasn't any ordinary transporting job.'

Fei took a bus to Kunming, Yunnan's capital, and another bus to a border town, Yingjiang, where he was picked up by the recruiter's contact. The contact drove him to a house miles away from the town centre. At the house, another two men came to meet him. They explained the job to him: transporting heroin. By then, Fei knew that he couldn't get out. He was reluctant to give us details, and didn't want to identify the people he met there. 'I had to swallow the heroin and transport it across Yunnan, all the way to Chengdu. I swallowed eighteen condoms filled with heroin, five kilograms total, every time they sent me. I felt really sick, and I kept vomiting. I had to leave the job after just a few days.'

Two other men had worked with him, both Tibetans, recruited in a labour market in Yunnan itself. All the people transporting drugs were males. Fei hadn't talked much to them, just knew that they were carrying the same amount of heroin. He'd felt too unwell to think about the others.

Fei ran away, taking the first train back to Chengdu one morning. Again, he believed that the recruiters would be after him, but nothing happened. Perhaps young Tibetan boys running away from this job was a usual occurrence. He didn't know. But he'd been worried enough to start wearing dark glasses to disguise his appearance. He wore them for months.

Opium poppy cultivation is a huge enterprise in Burma, and Burmese smugglers account for 80 to 90 percent of the heroin that enters Yunnan. The authorities currently seize two to three tons of opiates per year, and the majority of heroin in China is trafficked through Yunnan or Guangxi to Guangdong or Fujian, and then on to the international market.

Now yet another worker in this crowd of more than 100 stepped in and told his story. He was tall, tanned, handsome and well-built, with hair to his shoulders, quite unusual for a Chinese man. He had been working as a security guard in a bar in Shanghai, he said, and was determined to stay in that job, until one day, he met a woman.

He hesitated. I urged him to continue.

'She was in her mid forties. Wealthy. I mean, stinking rich,' he said. 'Her husband was never at home, doing business abroad, heaven knows what business. She met me outside the bar where I worked. She stared at me as she passed, then turned back and approached me. She liked my looks. She asked if I'd be interested in meeting. So we met the next day and she took me to an expensive café for coffee and lunch.'

'There was Western food on the menu. I'd never tried American steak, I said to her. She encouraged me to order it. During lunch, she told me she was interested in me and set up the next meeting, in a posh hotel in central Shanghai, which she paid for. She needed a young man, and offered to pay me for sex.'

The crowd exploded in laughter. It wasn't the most usual kind of work around.

'I was only nineteen!' he said. 'I was confused. But it was a large amount of cash she was offering. So I said yes.'

'The word "prostitution" didn't come into my head, until later, when the offer was repeated, again and again,' he said. He managed to earn 10,000 yuan (now £909) a month working as her lover.

Someone shouted at him from the back: 'Worker, you're the tool!' The crowd laughed again.

But the story wasn't so funny for the man recalling it.

'We began to meet regularly, once a week, after that,' he said. He knew for certain that the meeting was purely for sex – she didn't seem interested in anything else. She never asked a question about his background and what he'd done in his life. 'I thought that I could continue working like that and earning good money in Shanghai. I was young and in good condition. Having sex with a woman more than twice my age was no big deal for me. I could carry on like that for years, and bring in good income for my parents. I was really naïve then.'

'Time went by, and soon she became tired of me. One day, three months later, at the end of our session, she told me that she wouldn't be seeing me again. She said my job was over. And she never called again. From other security guards at the bar, I heard that she's picked another boy, from the countryside, to replace me. She's got a new lover.'

His story was unusual; the majority of China's three million sex workers are still migrant women, most of them peasants between fifteen and forty years old. I had received those calls from female sex workers in the hotel saunas in Beijing, but in fact these women were in every city, selling their services in karaoke bars and shopping malls and on street corners as well. Shenzhen, with the highest number of migrant sex workers, has more than a thousand of these 'karaoke bars,' where more than 300,000 women are estimated to work. The majority of them are from Sichuan.

Then the subject of the earthquake came up again. Yuan Gang, a middle-aged man who'd been a railway worker in Shaanxi province when the earthquake hit – spoke about how his house had collapsed, how his wife and three children were put into temporary housing, and how the compensation he had been entitled to was withheld, for no reason. 'Knowing the past record of our local authorities, we believe our compensation is being permanently withheld!' he cried. He was shivering with anger, and people in the crowd began to nod.

Encouraged by Yuan Gang's open denouncement of the local government, others began to speak up about their own experiences with it, and their frustration. A white-haired, frail-looking man in his sixties, named Xue, who had accompanied his job seeking son to the labour market, had been listening at the edge of the crowd, nodding repeatedly at the things people were saying. Now he spoke, too.

'Rulers in China know about the power of those from the countryside,' he said. 'China's history is all about how the peasantry has been burdened and oppressed, and how each time they rose up to overthrow those in power. But then those new rulers would oppress the peasant masses again, until our anger could not be contained any longer and boiled over, once more, into a revolution.'

The crowd was silent as they listened to him speak.

'We peasants brought the Party into power. Without the power of the peasantry, China wouldn't have defeated the imperialists and the corrupt Kuomintang.'

Now the crowd around him cheered.

'But once they came into power, we became burdened and exploited again! Because, they said, our Motherland needs to grow fast and catch up. Industrializing China and increasing output was the only thing they wanted from us in those years,' he said. 'And do you know what we peasants had as our reward in the decades that followed the Revolution?' He paused, and I waited for him to continue. The crowd was rapt.

'Poverty! Did they ask the peasants if they wanted to be collectivized in the early 1950s? Peasants just took the orders from the top. They had no right to say no. Around 130 million peasant households at that time were turned into around 7 million mutual-help groups, and then into 700,000 agricultural cooperatives. This was for the peasants to produce on a mass scale, and then produce more! And more! All for the nation! But not for our livelihood!

And then those at the top used the Hundred Flowers movement in the end, to put down half a million peasants who opposed the collectivization.[1]

'But they didn't stop there. I'm sure you know of the Great Leap Forward in 1958? That mad policy played with peasants' lives and turned cooperatives into over 50,000 people's communes in a short time. They used the communes to take whatever they wanted from us! We must produce and produce, and devote whatever we had to the nation! Peasants had truly become propertyless! But what could they say? It was the state, the Motherland, that needed our input, down to the last piece of steel in our house and the last metal coin in our pocket! Millions of peasants died of starvation as a result of inflated production targets imposed by the so-called people-loving local cadres in the Great Leap Forward. And they carried on with their power games – all the way through the Cultural Revolution! And what a revolution!'

The crowd laughed, clapping and cheering, encouraging him to go on. The gateway of the City East Labour Market was becoming a soapbox, and a true orator had emerged. Xue went on, 'My parents weren't even allowed to grow their own bloody melons in those wild days of the Cultural Revolution. That would be a very bourgeois thing to do – to grow your own food and eat it. You had to remain propertyless, as propertyless as everyone else. We must rejoice in our equality of poverty! That's the principle upheld by our great leaders!

'But some were much more equal than the rest of us. Those were our local officials. They did what they pleased, imposing extra taxes on top of our existing agricultural taxes. People started to wonder: Has there really been a revolution?'

The crowd was murmuring now, and the noise grew.

'Now we don't have the agricultural taxes anymore, but we are still heavily burdened. We still have many charges and fees to pay. And who are we to ask them why? Also, our little plots of land can be seized by the authorities for other uses, and as cities are booming and expanding, that's a growing trend. Will we be left waiting for some compensation for that, too? And we are now talking about not being paid compensation for the earthquake? This is just part of what local officials do.'

Yuan Gang chimed in, 'The laws in this country aren't for us.'

As I was scribbling furiously, trying to take down Xue's speech, a small stone hit me on the side of my head. A man shouted at the crowd from a distance, 'Do not talk to her! Stop talking to her! She is a spy! A spy!' Rubbing my head in shock, I looked around.

The man was in his thirties, medium height, thin, wearing a white T-shirt. Was he a plainclothes police officer? Or simply a nationalist passer-by? I had no idea. But the crowd of workers was disturbed by his assault and his 'warning'. They began to whisper.

The man didn't give up. 'Spy! Spy! Go away!' he continued to shout.

I had to say something – all this was happening because I was there – so I defended the crowd's right to remain. 'This is a public space, and we are staying here to talk,' I said.

Everyone around me clapped and cheered. It was obvious that they wanted to continue telling their stories. The stone-thrower looked embarrassed and quickly left the scene.

Later that day, I went to the North Station, a smaller labour market where rural job seekers gather. When I got there, I noticed many Yi waiting just outside. Some of them could be distinguished by their traditional colourful costumes – the women wore embroidered dresses, the necklines stitched with silver flowers. Some were sitting on their luggage, waiting for the next train home. Others were hanging around for job offers from local recruiters, although there didn't seem to be much action. The only visible placards advertised an 'earwax remover' and a 'blind masseur' who performed their services in the alleyway next to the station.

I also noticed the presence of the police as soon as I entered the station. They seemed to be patrolling the area around it too. Their presence made the atmosphere different from other labour markets – the job seekers seemed uncomfortable and looked around constantly to observe the movement of the officers.

I wondered what had made North Station a public-security issue. It looked as insignificant as thousands of other small stations around the country. Then I saw that the officers' eyes were fixed on the Yi workers. Ten minutes later, I saw two cops, batons in hand, chase a woman in traditional costume and her child out of a street café. The woman had apparently been having lunch with her child when the officers stormed in, shouting 'Get out! Get out!'

The frightened woman spoke a few words in Yi language, a Tibeto-Burman variant, but did not dare resist the order. She took her child and fled the station area. The police had made no attempt to search or arrest her. It seemed they simply wanted to frighten her. I went up to the officers and asked what the chase was about. They ignored me and walked away. I was told by other onlookers that this happened all the time. But how did they justify it?

'They say Yi have a bad reputation for dealing drugs. Every Yi person is a suspect,' one man said.

I witnessed the same police surveillance and harassment at the South Station, also a labour market frequented by Yi residents from rural areas. When I visited, Yi job seekers had gathered to wait for the local recruiters. They looked restless and too worried to talk. A Yi woman told me, 'The police are always around, scrutinizing our movements. They can stop and search us whenever they like, without a reason. They have no respect for us at all.'

Nationalism has always been part and parcel of 'Chinese social-ism'. Chinese socialism originated not in Marxism but in an eclectic amalgamation of intellectual trends current at the beginning of the twentieth century, including republicanism, anarchism, volunta-rism, and populism. At the time, many Chinese intellectuals were being educated in Japan, where they were introduced to Western reformist and radical thinking, and the Western order came to be seen among the Chinese intelligentsia as the ideological model for nation building, which eventually gave the nationalist New Culture Movement its anti-traditionalist character. But that move-ment, which lasted from 1915 to 1919, was largely liberal, Social

Darwinist, and youth-oriented – not Marxist – and Chinese intellectuals did not openly support the Bolsheviks.

Not until China's betrayal by the Allies at Versailles in April 1919 would this change. China had entered the First World War on the Allied side, on the condition that all German spheres of influence in Shandong province would be returned to China following a victory, and Chinese intellectuals even began to see their participation in the war as the emergence of China as a nation-state. 'The time had come [to establish] the Chinese nation, which with its enduring civilization encompassed the culture and history of Asia, and for its glory to rise again in the near future,' wrote Li Dazhao, a leading intellectual at the time.[2] But at Versailles, instead of rewarding China as promised, the Allies granted all German rights and privileges in Shandong to Japan.

On May 4, students amassed in Beijing for a demonstration, launching the national anti-imperialist movement that would come to be known as the May Fourth Movement. Demonstrators criticized the incompetent warlord-run government for failing to resist China's humiliation at Versailles, and May Fourth also marked the beginning of the growth of a fervent Chinese nationalism. The Chinese working class – there were over three million industrial workers in the 1920s – was a new social entity, its members largely from the countryside, and their participation in strikes and anti-imperialist actions would be their entry into political life. In his essay 'Youth and Villages', published in 1919, Li Dazhao, one of the movement's leading theoreticians, wrote of a necessary union between the country's youth and its peasantry: Though the peasants embodied a movement's revolutionary energies, they needed to be awakened by the young, who in turn would learn from the peasants the means of liberation. From the May Fourth Movement, with its populism (taking the peasantry as the base for socialist revolution and society) and voluntarism (emphasizing the role of the young intelligentsia), emerged the Chinese Communist Party (CCP), established in 1921.

The growing nationalist movement, which cut across classes, would eventually turn against the workers. In 1920, the Comintern in Moscow conceded the possibility of an alliance with a nationalist bourgeoisie in colonial and semicolonial countries, and under the stewardship of Stalin and others, a United Front was formed between the CCP and the Kuomintang, the bourgeois nationalist organization founded by Sun Yat-sen. In 1923, a proposal was passed at the third conference of the CCP that allowed communists to become members of the Kuomintang, and for the Kuomintang to be considered part of the 'revolutionary alliance' of the four classes.

This would turn out to be a disastrous mistake on the part of the CCP. As the labour movement grew in strength, with many trade unionists being CCP members, the Kuomintang grew nervous and in 1927 massacred tens of thousands of workers and trade unionists, destroying China's labour movement and sending the nascent CCP into retreat in the countryside. There, they found their base among the peasantry and sharpened their vision of Chinese socialism. In the ensuing battles with the Kuomintang in the 1930s and 1940s, 'Chinese socialism' developed to become what it largely is today: collective, though party-led, and ultimately aimed at ending foreign invasions, maintaining national sovereignty and establishing an independent republic.

Marxism was largely absent from the beginning. Anti-imperialism and nationalist resistance – backed by a coalition of social classes – drove the 1949 Revolution, and the ruling class used patriotism to mobilize this bloc of the four classes for nation building after 1949. Since then, Chinese socialism has become a reactionary ideology of the state, markedly in its suppression of dissent. In 1980, Deng Xiaoping stated that 'the only goal of socialism is to make our country strong and wealthy' – essentially collapsing the difference between Chinese socialism and nationalism.

Throughout my time in China, I could see this everywhere I looked. Not only is there blatant public prejudice against minority migrant workers, there is also little institutional protection for them. No existing legislation ensures punishment of discrimination against ethnic minorities. Racial crimes are not even recognized. There are no statistics on the number of racial attacks and incidents. Some companies offer better pay and working terms to Han Chinese than to migrants who are also ethnic minorities. Other firms have taken children from impoverished minority communities in rural areas and made them work for a pittance, as in Guangdong. But the most important minority issue for the authorities is crime control. In late 2007, the Guangdong public security bureau highlighted 'public safety' as the most important aspect of 'migrant worker management'. I saw how migrant workers in the cities are physically segregated from the rest of society. In public places, such as the train stations, they are put into a special queue for peasant workers (*nongmin-gong*), to be dealt with separately. I asked a station staffer in Guangzhou why. He replied, 'You never know what problems they will cause ... and there are too many of them.' Public security officers often walk up and down these queues armed with taser guns, in case of trouble. Despite all this 'public safety' management, in reality it is the migrant workers' personal safety that is in jeopardy.

The frustration of the villagers affected by the earthquake lingered in my mind. I wanted to see for myself just how slow the reconstruction process was. I decided to go to Wenchuan. But in inland China, thinking about visiting a place is one thing, and getting there is another. No trains went to Wenchuan, though it was only about four hours' journey northwest of Chengdu. I called the bus station.

'There are no buses going to Wenchuan. The road is closed,' I was told. 'Even the taxis can't go there. The roads are still under reconstruction.' This was four months after the earthquake, but after all, a lack of transport had been the main reason given for the delay of rescue immediately after the disaster.

I decided to travel to Dujiangyan, sixty kilometres northwest of

Chengdu. From there, I was told, it would be a three-hour trip to Wenchuan. Although the roads were in poor condition, I thought a taxi driver might well say yes if I paid a bit extra.

Dujiangyan, a tourist resort, was once chiefly known for its 2,200-year-old irrigation system, built in 256 BC, under the provincial governor Li Bing, to harness the wild Min River. It was an impressive engineering project using a central dam and artificial islands to split the Min into an inner stream for irrigation and an outer channel for flood control. The irrigation stream is still in use today. But Dujiangyan is now famous not only for its ancient history but also for the terrible damage it suffered during the 2008 earthquake. Five schools and a city hospital collapsed along with other buildings and all were still under reconstruction at the time of my visit.

When my then partner John and I arrived at Dujiangyan after a forty-five-minute bus ride, we were confronted by ruined buildings and piles of rubble. The streets were so much quieter –few signs of tourism after the quake, obviously. I asked around for taxis. No one wanted to go to Wenchuan. 'It's not permitted. All roads are closed,' the drivers all said. Eventually, I had to give up the idea of ever getting there.

On to Plan B: A visit to Juyuan Middle School in Juyuan village, on the outskirts of Dujiangyan, 110 kilometres from the quake's epicentre. Chinese media had reported 250 students and teachers killed; the international media put student deaths at 900. Sixty parents of children buried under Juyuan Middle School attempted to deliver a petition to the local authorities in June 2010, asking the government to launch and publish an investigation, and were instantly arrested by the police for crimes of 'subversion'. Meanwhile, local courts wouldn't take up the cases, and lawyers have been warned by the authorities to stay away. Huang Qi, an activist who demanded an official inquiry, was detained on June 2008, then sentenced on 23 November 2009 to three years in prison for 'illegal possession of state secrets'. In early February 2010, Tan Zuoren, another activist, who had investigated the deaths of children in a number of schools that had collapsed, was jailed for five years for subversion.

Juyuan looked like a postwar village. Not a sound along the street. I asked John to walk away in another direction, to avoid attracting attention, since he is white. He went off to see a river that runs alongside the village, while I walked slowly toward the ruins of the middle school. I saw a few villagers sitting on benches outside their residence.

'Is that the Juyuan Middle School?' I asked them, pointing to a huge pile of rubble circled by a metal wire fence.

They looked slightly worried. One of the two women replied. 'Yes, that's where the school was. It will be rebuilt on another site a mile away.'

'Is it being constructed at the moment?' I asked.

'No. The building work hasn't started yet,' the woman answered. 'It's been four months already.'

'Do you know why there's a delay?' I asked.

One of the men became cautious. He raised his eyebrows and said: 'You are supposed to report to the local authorities first before talking to any of us.'

'Have you been told not to talk to people from outside, then?' I asked.

'Yes. You report to them first. If they permit you, then you can come back to talk to us,' the man replied.

I walked on, toward the school. It was a horrifying sight. Its four-storey buildings had collapsed completely, like a spilled box of matches. There was only rubble, surrounded by metal wires around the site. Nothing had survived.

But this was not the work of a natural disaster; this was a man-made catastrophe. At the time of its original construction (the east side was built in 1988, the west side in 1995), the building had been certified as meeting the standards of China's 1978 Construction Earthquake-Prevention Guidelines. However, following the quake, construction ministry expert Chen Baosheng told the *Southern Weekend* that there had been many fundamental problems with the building of the school. The plank boards pulled from the wreckage 'were like something that someone just hurriedly put through a wire-drawing machine, without considering its load-bearing capacity, so that when the layers pressed against each other, the thing naturally just collapsed'.[3] The steel main beams had been considerably smaller than normal, and the school's prefabricated architectural structure was poorly equipped to deal with earthquakes.

'[In this type of structure,] the steam beams don't have connecting beams,' said Chen. 'So when an earthquake hits, the connectors between the walls and the beams, the area between the posts and the boards, and the connectors between the boards all get severely damaged. It'd be surprising if such a building *didn't* collapse under the force of a strong earthquake.'

Yi Ancheng, the former principal of Juyuan Middle School, revealed that the school's classrooms had been made from cement and gravel stone dating back to the 1950s. When construction began in 1986, she had applied to the village party secretary for funds to construct a new classroom building, but her school was granted only 10,000 yuan for the project. In the 1990s, when construction projects were put under the management of the education department of the municipal government, which became directly responsible for the projects' quality control, the department's engineer simply borrowed the blueprints from another school, Congyi, and changed the name to Juyuan Middle School, in order to save cash. After that, the Juyuan village authorities passed the building job to a local contractor. 'As the village government only had a budget of 10,000 yuan, the cost of the construction had to be minimized as much as possible, and the contractors still wanted to squeeze a profit out of it, so you can just imagine what the resulting quality was,' Yi said.

In 1998, another principal of the school, Lin Mingfu, filed a report on the dangerous condition of the building with the Dujiangyan education department, claiming that it had serious flaws. He was told to use steel wires to secure the part of the roof that was about to collapse. These few wires, as it turned out, were the only things that were holding the building together when the earthquake hit.

Lin Mingfu said that the four-storey classroom building had been constructed to satisfy the national aim of the 'nine-year compulsory education' initiatives. He noted, 'If the higher levels of government had a demand, our local leaders had to promise to carry it out.' The government's demand for another building at Juyuan Middle School had to be met, despite the village's lack of sufficient funds. In this situation, cost-cutting was inevitable. All of the elementary schools that collapsed in Dujiangyan had been built in 1993–94, the middle of the period of 'nine-year compulsory education' initiatives.[4]

I pointed my camera at the rubble and took a number of shots.

'What are you doing over there?' said an aggressive male voice behind me. I turned round and saw two police officers. Knowing what this could mean and certainly not wanting to lose my photographs, I pretended that I knew nothing about the site that I was photographing.

'What is this?' I asked innocently. They were fooled. Another mindless tourist.

'*It is just a collapsed building.* Please leave. There is nothing here for you to tour around,' one of them said, waving his hand to invite my immediate departure. They also found John with his camera, and asked him to leave the area, too.

We walked on past private houses and shops and realized that all the other buildings in the village had survived the earthquake. They stood strong and intact. The Juyuan Middle School had been the only building hit.

Out of sight of the police officers, I tried to chat with a fruit seller, Mr Zhu, at the edge of the village. Here is what he said:

The surviving students out of the 1,000 at Juyuan Middle School have been moved to study in a school at another village. My neighbour's niece is among the survivors. The contractor, Juxing Construction, that built the school also built the hospital in

Dujiangyan city centre, and as you probably know, that also collapsed. It was no coincidence. But where is the investigation? The authorities dared to ignore our wishes to find out the cause of the tragedy. We all know that the local government helped make this tragedy possible. But you can't trace the responsibility here, can you? Not if you are resourceless peasants. The company director of Juxing disappeared immediately after the quake. No one can find out where he is. The local government allows few to come into the village, because they don't want the truth to get out.

Throughout Sichuan, the local authorities have tried to stop international journalists from visiting the collapsed schools and the nearby areas.

In December 2008, the *Chongqing Daily News* wrote the following report:

> A group of migrant workers have travelled thousands of miles on improvised motor tricycles. They all worked in a plastic factory in Dongguan, Guangdong province. Recently, their boss suddenly disappeared, taking all the factory's money with him. The workers decided to go home without being paid. They found ten discarded motorcycles in the factory and refashioned them into three-wheeled mobile homes ... When the riders were stopped by Chongqing traffic police on an expressway yesterday, they had been on the road for ten days.

This happened just after the financial crisis hit the West. Guangdong, in the manufacturing south – the factory of the world – was seeing a significant decline in the number of orders from multinationals, and Chinese investments in US financial markets had shrivelled up. China's exports had declined by 15.2 percent since 2008; in March 2009 they were 17.1 percent lower, down to $90.45 billion. (During the same period, China's imports dropped by 43.1 percent. The country's foreign direct investment also began to decrease from 2008, falling by 5.73 percent in the last month of that year.) With a third of China's economy based in exports, many Hong Kong–run and local manufacturers were going bankrupt, and when I arrived in Chengdu, half of all toy factories and one third of all shoe factories in China were being shut down in the south. Employers were fleeing as their factories closed down, one after another, all over Guangdong.

But local governments sided with the companies. The Guangdong provincial procurator instructed its officers not to arrest factory employers suspected of 'white-collar crime' and in January 2009 Guangdong's justice department announced 'Six Nos', rules that established protections for businesses, in order to 'help enterprises through the economic crisis and promote enterprise development': no freezing company assets 'at random'; no monitoring or closing down company finances 'at random'; no blocking enterprise communications; no reportage or news coverage that damages enterprises' reputation; no 'casual' arrests of company chiefs; no measures that would have negative impact on enterprises' production activities. Currently, there is no law in China to punish employers who flee without paying wages. In most cases, migrant workers can do nothing but return home with empty pockets.

By January 2009, an increasing number of Guangdong's migrant workers were heading home, to Sichuan, Hunan, and Hubei. Despite the official statistics showing the national unemployment rate at 4 percent, the real figure was much higher. The majority of rural migrants are not registered in the cities. In Sichuan province, the unemployment rate was now said to be 4 percent, and 3 percent in Chengdu. These figures did not include migrant workers, either.

In the spring of 2009, I went to Jintang county, two hours south of Chengdu. By then 70,000–80,000 people had returned from Guangdong province, following the continuous layoffs and closure of factories since winter 2008, and the streets felt bleak: There were few residents around, and little trade in the shops. Even fewer rickshaws and unlicensed taxis were parked along the street. Many of the unlicensed cab drivers were migrants who had returned home from Guangdong. I spoke to one of them, Mr Zhong, as he scouted for potential customers on the main street.

Mr Zhong, in a strong Sichuanese accent, told me that he worked as a security guard in a company called Yin Yu Lights, the largest manufacturing firm in Heshan city, in the Gonghe township in Guangzhou. The company is part of the Hong Kong Zhen Ming Li Group, with a head office based in Hong Kong, and it employs over 10,000 people from all over China, including a large number from Jintang and Jianyang in Sichuan.

Zhong had moved to Guangzhou in 1997, the year of the hand-over of Hong Kong. At that time, people felt that things were looking better down south and many were heading that way, and more than a hundred visas were issued each day for travel to Hong Kong. (These visas were still required to control migration from the interior.) Zhong was young and willing to take low-paid work, but for the next ten years, he earned only 700–800 yuan (£64–73.5, $111–127) a month while working twelve to thirteen hours a day, seven days a week, with only two days off each month. His requests for a wage increase were turned down repeatedly until early 2009, when his pay was raised to 1,360 yuan (£124.9, $215). Workers also had the cost of food and accommodation deducted from their wages, though these were supposed to be covered. There were then no written rules to protect the workers, so the company could change terms as they liked, and often did.

In 1999, Zhong became depressed by these conditions, and many of his colleagues felt the same. They resented being treated like another race. They wanted a raise, and discussed among them-selves what they should do to get one. One of them broached the idea of a strike, and people became excited. They knew that it would be illegal, but they also knew that stopping work was the only way to put pressure on the management to implement changes. At the same time, they had no clear idea exactly how it should be done. After all, they'd never had the experience.

Zhong's resourceful colleague and a few others began an action, without the involvement of any trade union, to demand higher wages. The ringleader of the strike was also Sichuanese; he'd been working in Guangdong for a decade. Zhong started talking with workers on the assembly lines, encouraging them to strike. People were unhappy with the way things were, and didn't need much persuasion, although some feared reprisals and didn't take part, including Zhong's wife. (She was worried about his role in the strike, but didn't try to dissuade him, though she carried on working.) Eventually, more than a hundred workers joined the action. Initially, there was no response from the management at all, which worried the strikers. There were rumours that the company might begin firing people. It is illegal to strike in China; the right to do so was removed from the constitution in 1982. Gradually, most of the strikers returned to work, leaving just a few behind. The strike ended on the third day.

'The head of the company, Mr Fan, was away during the entire strike,' Zhong told me. 'Everyone who took part was anticipating some kind of verbal response from him. But when he returned, he met with the strikers and out of rage, he slapped one of them. We couldn't believe our eyes – he really slapped our colleague. I didn't know such a thing could happen.'

Everyone was obviously infuriated, Zhong recalled, and their support for the assaulted worker led to discussions about further stoppages. In the end, Mr Fan decided to pay compensation to him. He didn't quite know what to expect from the workforce and he was very concerned about further 'unrest'. But once workers calmed down, the management resumed their offensive. 'After that, we saw the relatives of the strikers dismissed one after another,' Zhong said.

Things remained quiet for a while, but Zhong grew more and more unhappy. Over the next ten years, the workers' situation slowly deteriorated. Wages stagnated and living costs rose. He wanted to send more money home to his parents and he couldn't. By the mid 2000s, he was still earning the same humiliating wage he'd started with: 700–800 yuan per month. Friends kept telling him to quit, get another job. He requested an increase again, and was turned down again. He was losing hope.

In 2008 there was a fire and Zhong lost a colleague. The company behaved as if nothing had happened. Meanwhile, working conditions continued to worsen. The company still changed the rules as they pleased. In January 2008, China's Labour Contract Law was instituted, but Zhong's company applied the new rules only to the skilled workers, not to the casual labourers recruited from the countryside, whose real wages were lower than those stated in their contract, since many were working twelve hours a day instead of the eight they were paid for.

Starting in July 2008, the company began laying many workers off, and the wages of those who remained declined. The company claimed this was necessary, because of the recession. Half of the company's 15,000 employees hailed from Anhui, Hubei, Hunan, Henan and Sichuan, and most of these were laid off. The company used wage decreases to encourage 'voluntary departures' – that is, resignations. The decreases were so drastic, workers were forced to leave.

In 2008, the workers' anger turned to action once again. Hundreds of them organized a spontaneous strike, the second in the history of the company. Caught between lowered wages and layoffs, they hadn't much left to lose, and needed to fight back. Many, including Zhong, felt that the company would have to yield to their collective strength, and began persuading everyone to join the strike. Once again, Zhong's wife did not join him, and he felt that their marriage was also 'going through a crisis'. As Zhong and others stood outside the factory, trying to dissuade coworkers from entering, his wife walked past him without a word. The strike lasted a few days. Instead of backing down, the company dismissed some of the strikers. Others strikers left because the situation had become intolerable. The company declared: 'Those who want to leave can leave. Those who stay mustn't complain.' Wages were decreased as planned. Those workers who remained became more docile.

Many small firms in the area were going bust in early 2009. Many bosses packed up and fled. Workers of a bankrupt company nearby tried to seize the machines because they hadn't been paid, but the local government sent the police to stop their action. Eventually, the government itself compensated some unpaid workers, but they never prosecuted the companies.

Layoffs at Yin Yu Lights continued throughout 2009. Most of the laid off workers were Sichuanese, 3,000 of them from Jianyang. Some who lost their jobs followed the lead of hometown contacts and went to work in the shoe and garment industries in Zhejiang and other provinces. Many returned to their home villages.

After February 2009, the company began to encourage its less skilled, rural migrant workers to quit, giving out leaflets that said 'The crisis is lasting. If you can find better work, you are advised to leave.' About 8,000 employees took their advice.

Zhong eventually left because the company cancelled his year-end bonus, labour insurance, and the food and accommodation that they'd included in his original compensation package. He felt completely betrayed. Some of the 100 security staffers left for the same reason. They believed that this was the way the company got rid of the workers who had made demands – not through direct dismissal, but by viciously breaking the labour laws until workers simply quit.

Zhong was as bitter toward Guangzhou as he was about Yin Yu Lights: 'I have no roots in that province, and I will never become one of them. In Guangzhou, it's impossible for us rural migrants to move *hukou* there. You don't qualify because you can't afford to buy a house. All I could afford was thirty yuan for a temporary residency permit. You'll always be temporary, no matter how much you give them.'

3

Dust and Heat: Black Mines in the Yellow River Region

When I push open the gate, I feel like a fish returning to water ... I close my eyes to enjoy this carefree moment. It's as if I've never seen such bright sunshine. Each time, I turn back and say to the fate behind me: 'Sorry! I'm up here again!' Above ground, there is fresh air, green fields, mountain streams, men and women in clean clothes ... all with flesh and blood, in front of my eyes. With a darkened face, I sigh and say, 'How beautiful! Kill me, but I'll never believe that anyone wants to give up all of this!' How I envy you – the street sellers, the butchers, the paperboys on bicycles, the office clerks ... You are really lucky people. If you don't think so, come and try my work – and I don't ask you to do mining all your life. I'm asking you to try it for just one day.

– Zhang Kai, ex-miner, 'A Day in the Life of a Miner'

From Chengdu, John and I headed for Taiyuan, capital of Shanxi province, northeast of Sichuan. Shanxi's western border is cut through by the Yellow River that traverses nine provinces, and the region is generally called East of the River (*He dong*). Taiyuan was one of the centres of Chinese imperial power, cradle of the Tang dynasty (618–907 AD) and the birthplace of Wu Zetian, China's only empress. The Tang era was one of glorious expansion and free-flowing commerce, and Taiyuan was at its heart – and the words 'Taiyuan merchant' (*Jin shang*) became a synonym for wealth and fortune.

Shanxi was also a major battlefield during the Second Sino-Japanese War. Following the surrender of the Japanese invaders, a large part of rural Shanxi was an important base for the Eighth

Route Army of the Chinese Communist Party as the CCP prepared
for civil war with the Kuomintang. It is hard to see this magnificent and tumultuous past in the humble, aged look of its capital
today, stained as it is with the smirch of coal dust. This province is
home to China's largest coal reserves, yet it has become an interior
backwater, with its per capita GDP lagging behind the national
average. Nevertheless, no Shanxi, no coal. China has about 34,000
coal mines. More than two-thirds of them are small mines producing 10,000 to 30,000 tons of coal a year. Shanxi produces 500
million tons of coal each year – a quarter of the country's supply. It
also has one of the highest rates of mining disasters in China.

In our soft sleeper (*ruanwo*, a type of sleeper in a four-berth
cabin), we were finally able to get some rest. As we'd booked the
cheaper upper bunk beds, we couldn't sit at the table next to the
bottom bunks, so we ate our snacks in bed and started to read. Our
Sichuanese cabin mate, Zhang, introduced himself. He had worked
in Taiyuan but now lived in Chengdu. As we passed the barren
fields of impoverished Shaanxi province, on the way to Shanxi,
Zhang gradually told his story. 'Years ago, I was a coal miner in
Taiyuan,' he said. 'Have you heard much about mining work?'

I told him I'd read a piece of 'labour literature' (*dagong wenxue*,
stories written by workers) called 'A Day in the Life of a Miner',
written by Zhang Kai, an ex-miner, who described miners as
cicadas, struggling in the muddy underground, all longing for the
sunlight above ground. Zhang said no, miners were more like the
donkeys that pull the millstone – they worked their hearts out.
'Mining was truly tough and dangerous work,' he added. 'We had
the possibility of death before our eyes every day when we went
down the shaft.'

Zhang had been recruited in Chengdu by a Sichuanese who
sent a group of job seekers to work in a mine on the outskirts of
Taiyuan. The recruiter was looking for anyone from the villages,
and no previous experience was required. Mining was like the
army: If you're willing to fight and prepared to die, you're ready
for the job.

Zhang and the other Sichuanese men were picked up at the Taiyuan train station, a grey, grim-looking building – as uninspiring as the rest of the town – and a typical rendezvous for all the migrants coming here to work in the mines and construction sites. People sat on their luggage in front of the station; some were collected within thirty minutes and others waited for hours. Zhang and his companions were sent in a van to a state-owned mine miles from the town centre. He remembered the dust in the air as they travelled the bumpy road.

'There were hundreds of workers in that mine. The recruiter gets a good fee for getting us there,' Zhang said. 'He also gets a regular payment – docked from our wages – from the company, which only uses workers from the countryside, like us, without exception.'

Zhang knew that the coal they produced was for the consumption of the entire country. He had no idea how much of the profits were shared between contractors and the company, nor had he any control over the production process. He and other migrants were simply the tools, sent down that mine every single day.

'I thank my stars when I think about it now,' he said. 'I'm so lucky to have got through it. I survived. Many miners died in there.'

'So you voluntarily left the job?' I asked.

'Yes. For this, I have to thank my wife, who saved me from that hell. I met her on the train – in fact, this very railway – on my way back to Sichuan for the Chinese New Year. She was a hotel receptionist in Taiyuan. When I told her that I work in the mine, she frowned. She told me candidly that a mine is not a workplace for humans, that if I want to live and have a good life, I shouldn't stay there. No one had ever told me that – the honest truth. I continued to see her, and on the next New Year she came to visit my parents. She changed my way of thinking completely ... If I hadn't met and married her, I would have stayed in the mine.'

It is estimated that there are over five million miners in China's coal industry, half of them migrant workers, mainly working in the Yellow River region, the northeast, and northwest. There are fifty coal-producing countries worldwide. China is the biggest producer, the source of about a third of the world's coal, followed by the US, India and Australia. And the country's production has continued to grow, almost tripling in the past five years. China is also the world's biggest coal consumer, and will soon become the world's biggest user of coal-derived electricity – nearly 70 percent of its electricity comes from coal. Coal mining is one of the most profitable businesses in the country.

At the same time, China accounts for 80 percent of all coal mining fatalities in the world. The death rate from mine accidents, according to China's own State Administration of Work Safety (SAWS), is 50 times higher than in the US, the world's second-largest coal producer. This is mainly due to poor management and the lack of proper safety mechanisms in the mines. While the industry prospers, the occupation has become the most deadly in China.

On average, nine miners died each day in China during 2008, the year of the Beijing Olympics, leading to a nationwide cover-up. Just before the Games began, a miner was killed in an accident in Shanxi. It was a politically sensitive time and the authorities were worried about 'bad press'. Two reporters in Shanxi took advantage of the situation and accepted bribes from the mine owner to cover up the accident. Seeing that profits could be made, another twenty-six people took a chance and posed as reporters. They approached the mine managers and asked for bribes, threatening to report the death. Meanwhile, on 14 July in the Lijiawa mine in Yuxian near Zhangjiakou, Hebei province, thirty-four miners were killed in an accident and ten journalists and forty-eight officials took bribes totalling $381,000, to help suppress the news, though this particular cover-up was exposed after eighty-five days. But the culture of cover-ups in the mining industry is deep-seated, and many cases have been discovered in which con men posed as reporters and extorted money from mines where there had been accidents and deaths.

The year before the Olympics, 2007, official statistics listed 3,800 deaths from mining accidents throughout the country, and the real figure was probably much higher. The list of deaths from mining accidents goes on and on: 105 miners killed in an explosion near the town of Linfen in Shanxi on 6 December 2007; 57 miners killed in the flooding of the Xinjing Coal Mine in the Zuoyon county of Shanxi in May 2006 (the village chief and the local CCP general secretary covered up that disaster in exchange for bribes, and were subsequently removed from their posts); 47 dead in a gas explosion on 5 November 2006 at the Jiaojiazhai mine run by Xuangang Coal and Power Company, a subsidiary of Datong Group, again in Shanxi; 69 miners killed in an explosion in two mines in Shanxi on 19 March 2005, and so on. According to even the most conservative estimates – official statistics – 45,000 miners have died on the job since 2000. The lessons from these disasters are never learned.

The extremely dangerous nature of coal mining work, and the recruitment of large numbers of rural migrants, are both direct results of the nationwide privatization drives of the reform era. Since the 1990s, in order to boost profits in the coal mining industry the central government has handed a large part of China's coal mining over to private companies. Many small and medium state-run coal mines have shut down or been contracted out to private businesses. Privatization and deregulation of the industry have created around 17,000 small 'black' (illegal) coal mines and these account for a third of China's total coal output. Quite a few large-scale state-run coal mines have also been contracted out.

As the industry became privatized, contractors sought to hire the cheapest possible labour, and rural migrants became the mainstay of the workforce. Today, there are about two million workers, most of them migrants, employed in private coal mines where there is no government supervision. To maximize profits, mine owners speed up production to far above average levels, send down more miners than permitted by law and neglect to provide safety equipment and procedures. These mines are where the majority of accidents occur.

Zhang described how President Hu Jintao came to visit a mine near Datong in Shanxi at the beginning of 2008. Although it wasn't the one where he'd once worked, Zhang, who had friends still employed in the mines, read the news of Hu's visit with great interest. The president had urged the miners to work hard, even through their holidays, and be as productive as they could be *while staying safe*. Zhang's miner friends all took this with a grain of salt. 'Everyone, including Hu Jintao, knew what this meant: Increase production, period,' Zhang said. The country needed a lot of coal to last through the crisis, and even at the expense of the miners' safety, it would have to be produced more quickly. Three days after Hu Jintao's visit to Datong, nine workers were killed in a gas explosion at a mine in Shaanxi province. Not much fuss was made about that in the national press – as if miners' deaths were an everyday occurrence in China. But at least, Zhang noted, no newspapers would dare boast about Hu's visit again.

The majority of accidents involve 'black' mines or mining practices, where safety has been previously compromised by corruption and collusion between local officials and the businesses that run the small private operations; afterward, mine employers and local officials work together to cover up the deaths. In Shanxi alone, there were 3,000–4,000 'black' mines and more than 10,000 local officials involved in illegal mining.[1]

Huang Yi, spokesman for the State Administration of Work Safety, admitted in 2010 that coal-mining safety laws were rarely implemented. The heaviest fine specified by law for safety violations was two million yuan; so far, not one coal mine had incurred this penalty. He added that neither had any official been sacked for allowing illegal mine operations.

In the past few years, as 'black' mines have been the focus of attention in safety violations, the local government in Shanxi has begun to close down these small privately run mines or merge them with large state-run mines, to improve safety levels.

However, state-owned mines, which are the largest ones, can be just as unsafe. Although these mines are under the supervision of provincial authorities, they are not integrated into any national plan and have few safety infrastructures in place. As Huang Yi himself admitted, one third of all safety equipment at the major state-owned mines is obsolete and in need of replacement. Managers at state-owned mines are just as concerned about profits as employers in the private mines, since they, too, have to follow the production-driven model adopted in the entire industry. Moreover, many state-owned mines contract their production out to private operators – in the late 1990s especially, mine shafts in the state-owned mines were contracted out in order to improve profitability. Mine managers sign agreements with the private contractors operating the mine shaft, not with the workers, who are recruited by the contractors, usually in their province of origin. Working terms and conditions are also controlled by the contractors, who – just as in the small private mines – decide how much they will pay the workers and how a big a cut they'll take.

Han Dongfang, director of the *China Labour Bulletin*, has said that the safety level in the state-run mines will only improve if the miners themselves are allowed to play a key role in safety management and engage in collective bargaining with their bosses over pay and work conditions. At present, in Shanxi as elsewhere in China, no workers are entitled to take part in the discussion of safety issues or to negotiate their terms of employment.

While it is true that the Shanxi government's current action to forcibly close and merge small mines could curb corruption among Shanxi officials, it will not address this most important reason for coal mining accidents, namely that no mine workers have the right or opportunity to defend their personal interests with regard to work safety, let alone wages and benefits or working hours. So long as they have no voice, to employers in both state-owned and privately operated coal mines they will be little more than mining tools that breathe, as Han Dongfang put it. He doesn't think that Shanxi's provincial government has recognized these fundamental issues of workers' rights, and as a result, he doubts that the present much-publicized restructuring measure will bring about any real improvements. For now, worker safety in the mines remains only a promise.

*   *   *

Zhang decided to quit mining work for good after months of persuasion by his then fiancée. She told him she didn't want to marry a man whose life was in constant danger. She wanted to be a wife, not a widow. And so he quit —that is, he simply did not return to the mine after the Chinese New Year. He now runs a small business trading steel products. Steel is a rich industry in Taiyuan, and there are many stainless steel companies from which he can purchase products to sell in Chengdu. He sees himself as a rare case of success among ex-miners: 'I gained from my social networks and personal connections built up over the years of rail travelling and working between Chengdu and Taiyuan, and I managed to set up my own little trade.'

Taiyuan, in the heartland of China's heavy industry, continues to be the work destination of many Sichuanese and migrants from neighbouring provinces. About one quarter of its population of four million are migrants, most of them without *hukou*. But Zhang has moved on from that life of insecurity, degradation and danger. Thanks to his new venture, he managed to save up for the first holiday of his life: He took his wife to Yungang Buddhist Cave, west of Datong, a three-and-a-half-hour bus ride from Taiyuan that cost them only eighty-eight yuan each. He had heard that the cave is one of the earliest masterpieces made possible by migrant labour. The largest Buddhist cave in China, it was built by the Turkic Toba people during the Northern Wei Buddhist dynasty, 386–534 AD. The capital of that era, Datong, today is a mining town with some three million people – a town known to be polluted and in need of an environmental clean-up. The Datong Coal Mining Group, the third-largest coal enterprise in China, is based here, Zhang told his wife. During the bus trip, songs of the Mongolian singer Tenger played in the background. One was a morale-boosting song for the peasants:

> Every day, hope fills every day of our lives …
> Every day, sweat rolls down my face …
> As long as green mountains last,
> we'll always have wood to light our stoves …

When they finally arrived at Yungang, sixteen kilometres from Datong, they were stunned by its magnificence. These caves are the earliest (built in 453 AD), the grandest, and the best maintained of the three major Buddhist cave sites in China. Fifty-one Buddhist grottoes are skilfully carved into the sandstone cliffs. Each cave is illuminated by daylight, revealing the wrinkles of age – the cracks and lines between the carvings. The scale of the caves speaks of the 40,000 craftsmen who created them. And they were migrant labourers, not only from other regions in China, but also from Central Asia and India. This visual experience, Zhang said, enlightened him.

But his friends and all of those who continue to work below ground are still in darkness; the tunnel in front of them is still far too long. For them, life itself – let alone the pleasures in life – is never taken for granted. Not long after I left Taiyuan, I heard of another mining disaster, an explosion in the Tunlan Coal Mine owned by the Shanxi Coking Coal Group in Gujiao, fifty kilometres from Taiyuan. Seventy-eight miners were killed. No mining bosses have been penalized.

A few months later, when I was in Xiamen, the southernmost city of Fujian province, on China's southeast coast, the issue of coal miner deaths arose again. I was in a cab when the tragic news of the death of eleven coal miners in Shanxi province was announced on the morning radio.

'Every two weeks you hear about miners dying!' exclaimed the driver, Xiao Dong. His eyes narrowed in anger. Xiao Dong was one of the many Henanese migrants driving cabs in Xiamen. Henan, with 103 million people China's most populous province, and also underdeveloped and poor, is one of the largest sources of migrant labour in the country. Xiao Dong had come to Xiamen from one of Henan's thousands of coal mines, where more than 130 million tonnes of coal are produced each year. Henan's coal is concentrated in the west, where 138 million tonnes were produced in the first three quarters of 2011. Coal mining is one of the main sources of revenue in this otherwise largely agricultural province. Small and private mines have been operating for years there, with a high rate of accidents and deaths. Xiao Dong's anger at the tragedy in Shanxi was sharpened by painful memories of his own life down a private 'black' mine back in Lugou, a village in Henan. 'When is the government going to do something about it?' he cried.

Xiao Dong and I kept talking. He was taking me to the public security department to sort out my visa. He explained why he knew just how those eleven miners' families must feel. Seven years before, a relative of his had left Henan for Shaanxi to work in a mine near Xian, the provincial capital. There were no other options around and he needed to bring in an income for his parents. He sent money home regularly, every month, for eight months. Then one day, his parents received news from the recruiter, who came from their village, that there had been an explosion in the mine and their son had been killed. He gave no details. The parents were devastated. But being so far away from Shaanxi and having no resources at hand, they could do nothing but hold a decent funeral for him. 'In the old days, the authorities suppressed these things. The bastards!' Xiao Dong cried. 'We didn't see it in the news then. He just died. Like dust, vanished. Didn't seem to matter to anyone apart from the family.

'Now, the government can't keep the truth from the world. You see, we've been hearing about thousands of deaths of miners in the past few years!'

Xiamen is a sunny city whose bright surface says little about its dramatic past. Traditionally known as Amoy – the Gateway to China – it was established in the mid-fourteenth century, and at the end of the Ming dynasty, in the mid-seventeenth century, when the Manchus were gradually taking over the country, it became a centre of anti-Manchu forces. The legendary Ming prince Koxinga led the resistance here before fleeing to Taiwan, at that time an unremarkable island. Xiamen became an entry port for the imperialist powers after the seventeenth century, and following Britain's invasion and China's defeat in the Opium Wars (1839–1842), it was designated by the Treaty of Nanjing as one of the five Chinese ports where the British had the right to reside and trade. Later on, France, Germany and the US entered into similar treaties with China and tried to expand their influence in Xiamen. But the British maintained a dominant presence – their centre of operations was the island of Gulangyu, just a ferry trip away from Xiamen – until the Japanese invasion in 1939.

Xiamen was one of the starting points of China's sea trade and coastal development. But Xiamen's –and Fujian's – maritime activity was put on hold during the collectivist period of 1949–1978, when Cold War containment made Fujian a strategic frontier across the Taiwan Strait. Agricultural production became the province's mainstay, even though less than 10 percent of the province was arable. Under Mao, Fujian received less than two percent of the nation's capital investment. Just prior to the beginning of reform and opening up in the late 1970s, Fujian lagged far behind other coastal provinces, ranked twenty-third among thirty-four in GDP.[2] But in 1980, Xiamen's close relationship with international capital was dramatically revived by Deng Xiao Ping's government, which made the city one of China's five Special Economic Zones (SEZs).[3]

In the past decade, the government has attempted to create the impression of growing wealth in the Haixi (West of the Strait) region, of which Xiamen is the centre. The city's rapid development, physically visible in its high-rising construction projects and well-established transport system, has been based on a huge pool of migrant labour from all over the country. Today, 80 percent of the city's population comes from outside the province – 60 percent of them from Henan, and others from Jiangxi, Zhejiang, Guangxi, and Yunnan. Most of these migrants work in the construction and hospitality industries.

Xiao Dong's apartment was in 'Henan village' – a low-rent neighbourhood on the outskirts of Xiamen, miles from the city's palm tree avenues and shopping malls – inhabited by migrants from his province. Xiao Dong called it their ghetto. Later I went to see him in his room, behind a fish restaurant among run-down blocks of flats crammed in narrow alleys. Some laundry was hung on the tiny balconies. A few women sat on benches in the street, waving their fans and chatting in a dialect that I assumed was Henanese. There was a distinct feeling of a small, closely-knit community. I learned that Henanese migrants also tend to concentrate in specific trades and industries.

Xiao Dong, his wife, and their daughter and son shared their apartment with another Henanese family of three from their own village. His wife is in her early thirties and also comes from his village. They'd met years ago and decided to come to Xiamen together for a new life. Their shared apartment was the only place they could afford: 200 yuan per month. They had one bedroom – for all four of them – and the common living room. The couple they lived with – the man was in construction; the woman was a domestic helper – had a young daughter. Sharing a flat with people from the same village was very common there, Xiao Dong told me. This evening, he had invited his best friend, Luo, to join us. Luo came into the flat and put on a pair of slippers as if he'd done it many times before. Then he lit up a cigarette, smoking and walking up and down Xiao Dong's concrete floor. He and Xiao Dong are like brothers. He, too, was from Xiao Dong's home village and worked as a cab driver in Xiamen. He often came here for a drink with Xiao Dong after work, while Xiao Dong's wife was still out working, as she was this evening, as a cleaner on the night shift.

Xiao Dong pointed to a picture of her on the TV set that sat in the corner of the five-square-meter room. She was slim, with black hair to her waist, and wore a pair of dark sunglasses. In the picture it looked like a really sunny day. 'That was taken on our little trip to Gulangyu during the first year we arrived in Xiamen,' he said. 'It was the first holiday we'd ever had in our lives.'

Xiao Dong and Luo had been in Xiamen for more than a decade. Their families were among the first group of forty peasants who left Lugou village, which then had 1,000 residents, in the late 1990s and came to make a living in Xiamen. Both were already married when they came, lured by the stories told in Lugou of Xiamen's better environment and higher living standards. Like most Henanese migrants, they brought families with them and planned to settle for the long term. Luo said that none of them wanted to go back to farming the land. His family of six owned only two *mu* and were barely surviving.

Coal mining was the only nearby industry in which young people could find jobs. Back in Lugou, Xiao Dong worked in the mine run by the village chief, which he described as 'the worst job of my life'. He earned just two yuan (18p) a day, slaving in pitch darkness down a black tunnel, day in, day out. Young miners lost their lives in there, he said. Most were killed in gas explosions. He never knew how these accidents happened, and no one had inquired about them. He and other miners felt angry and frightened when their coworkers were killed, but there seemed nothing they could do. They were just kids and needed to keep their jobs. He remembers that after each death, the mine would stop operating for a few days, and then go back to business as usual. The families of the victims would bury them, holding a funeral in the village. Villagers were sympathetic and all came to attend the funeral and shed a few tears. No one outside the village knew anything about it. No one ever visited as a result of the deaths. And their work simply continued.

'Even if you don't get blown up in there, there are many other ways to die in a mine,' said Xiao Dong. 'Did you hear about Zhang Haichao, a villager from my province? Last month, he volunteered to have an operation to open up his chest to prove that he was suffering from fatal pneumoconiosis.'

Pneumoconiosis is an occupational lung disease caused by the inhalation of dust, often from coal mines. Your risk of getting pneumoconiosis depends on how long you have been exposed to the dust. The symptoms are coughing and shortness of breath, and there is no specific treatment for the disease, but no further exposure to dust is essential. The coal mining industry is the biggest cause of pneumoconiosis, which is recognized as the most deadly occupational disease in China. Each year, around 57,000 miners nationwide contract the disease and 6,000 miners die of it. According to official figures, about 600,000 miners are now suffering from the disease.

Zhang Haichao was twenty-eight when he got pneumoconiosis. He was fit and well before he started working at an abrasive-materials factory in Xinmi, not far from Zhengzhou, the capital of Henan, where he comes from. On the job, he inhaled a huge amount of dust every day. In the second half of 2007, he began to cough and felt short of breath.

Zhang had a checkup at Xinmi Centre of Disease Control and Prevention: They told him he had pneumoconiosis. When he asked for a formal diagnosis, Xinmi Centre informed his employer that he needed a second checkup to confirm the disease. But Zhang's employer refused to release information on Zhang's work and working conditions– for two years, until he discovered it in 2009.

Because of this, Zhang was unable to obtain a formal diagnosis from the Xinmi Centre. Instead of dropping the matter, he put pressure on the city government to intervene, and they did. Xinmi Centre had to produce a diagnosis – but this time, they produced a false one, saying that Zhang had tuberculosis. Eventually the truth came out: the Xinmi Centre had colluded in covering up Zhang's disease so that his employer would not have to compensate him.

By this time, Zhang Haichao's illness had plunged him deeply into debt. He had spent nearly 90,000 yuan (£8,252) of his own money on all the medical costs – and had a three-year-old daughter and parents to support. Zhang decided that he must do something to prove that he had the disease. So he went to a hospital and requested to have his chest opened up.

When his surgeon uncovered the truth, there was a public outcry. Questions were asked: What kind of a society is this where hard-working people are so mistreated, where a worker's health is so abused, and where he must then risk his life on the operating table to prove he needs medical help?

The spread of news about Zhang Haichao's case, now all over the country, gave hope to other workers suffering from the disease. Many began to go public about their condition and to demand justice from employers and the authorities. At the end of July 2009, 119 workers from Hunan province, all suffering from pneumoconiosis after drilling and building Shenzhen's skyscrapers for a company that failed to provide prevention facilities or on-site safety training, while the local government failed to inspect or monitor working conditions, staged a mass sit-in and other protest actions outside the Shenzhen municipal government, demanding compensation. Their campaign grew in strength, and the municipal government eventually agreed to pay a compensation of 14 million yuan.

But there are numerous cases of migrant workers becoming ill with pneumoconiosis and not being able to win compensation. One of the main reasons is that to qualify for compensation workers are required by their employers to get an occupational disease diagnosis from a government-designated hospital. Unfortunately, to qualify for such an examination a worker must provide the hospital with his labour contract, and many workers haven't got one. In Shanxi, Zhongguang Wei was diagnosed with pneumoconiosis after working as a driller in a coal mine in Datong for six months. He had become too ill to continue working, but was unable to claim compensation because his employer had given him no contract, and that meant no official diagnosis. He then tried suing the company; his suit has not been successful. Currently, he's using a microblog to publicize his situation and try to win support for his case.

In February 2011, in Wuwei city, Gansu province, 124 miners diagnosed with pneumoconiosis were unable to get compensation for the same reason – no contract.

'At least my job in Xiamen isn't dangerous,' said Xiao Dong. He felt fortunate compared with the miners – he would never go back to that world again. 'I am not earning much, around 2,000 yuan per month. A lot of this will go toward living expenses and child-rearing in an expensive city, but I am safe and well here, with my family.'

Luo also talked about how he detested mining work, because of his memories of horrible deaths suffered by miners in his village. For him, working as a miner was a choiceless choice. He'd got out of it ten years before and gone to work outside of Henan as a lorry driver, which was better paid. The job had been easy enough to find – in fact, the previous driver, a villager about to take another job, had passed it on to him. Driving a lorry across the country wasn't bad, Luo said; you got to travel and see new places. He used to drive long distances, for days on end, transporting bricks for various brick kilns from province to province, sometimes going from barren Yanchuan county, in rural Shaanxi, all the way to Vietnam. Even he was struck by the poverty of those rural communities he'd seen deep in the interior. In Yanchuan he'd seen children with dirty faces walking around empty streets and felt really sorry for them. Where are their parents, he'd wondered, why didn't they take care of these kids? Some children came up to him and stared at him curiously, as if they'd never seen an outsider before. One of them had mud on his red little cheeks. 'I had seen poor children in our villages in Henan, but these kids up north were something else,' Luo said. 'I don't know what will become of them. No one seemed to care about them or provide properly for them.' On another occasion, he'd even attracted a crowd of Yanchuan's villagers – by eating meat in a noodle shop. People very rarely ate meat in those villages – some had never tasted it. Someone from outside of the province eating meat in the noodle shop was bound to draw much attention.

But though life in Xiamen was much better than in such places, it was difficult being a migrant worker even there. Local drivers, who were much more familiar with the city's labour environment and practices, had a much easier time finding work at cab companies and were better equipped to demand fair treatment.

In 2008, the local cab drivers succeeded in organizing a spontaneous strike against the vehicle-hire fees, though arrests of strikers were made that August. Some migrant taxi drivers have also taken part in collective action, as they did in strikes in Guangzhou in the winter of 2008, which mobilized 10,000 drivers. They followed news of drivers' strikes in other parts of the country too, saying that all drivers had long been exploited by taxi companies who monopolize the market by controlling the fees. In January 2011, two thirds of Guangzhou's taxi drivers struck again against the vehicle-hire fees, the biggest action since 1989. Some migrant drivers also took part, Luo said, but noted that migrants, primarily concerned about surviving and supporting their families back home, aren't easy to organize. They tend not to see beyond immediate, personal gains, and don't want to rock the boat.

Xiao Dong agreed: Their generation of migrants was burdened with the past and their origins, but the next generation would be different. They would have better education and better resources in their hands, and would be less fearful than their parents.

'This is why I'm going to give my daughter the best education, why she's going to learn about the world,' Luo said of his four-year-old. For now, Luo and his wife had to leave her in the Henan village nursery all the time, because both of them worked every day of the week. The nursery, set up by Henanese migrants, provides Henanese parents with low-cost child care. Luo spent twenty yuan a day to send his daughter there. Because of her parents' situation, she was the only child who stayed at the nursery on Sundays. 'But although we spend little time with her, we know she's doing well and learning things fast,' Luo said.

Xiao Dong didn't want his son to stay in the village either. He wanted him to join the army – considered a good start to a career. However, too many parents want the same thing for their sons. Only those who can afford big 'red envelopes' (bribes) can get their sons admitted. Xiao Dong was told it took 50,000 yuan (£4,584, $7,939), which he could never afford. He said to me, 'Now do you understand what the People's Liberation Army (PLA) meant when they said they are there to serve the people (*renmin*)? They meant, to serve the RMB (*renminbi*, the Chinese currency).'

Several months later, I received a phone call from Xiao Dong while I was travelling on the train to Beijing. He wanted to visit his home village in Henan province, and wondered if I'd like to join him. Henan (the name means 'south of the Yellow River') is located in China's central plains, and more than a thousand years ago it was the centre of Chinese civilisation. But heritage cannot always feed people, as the writer Lu Xun observed in the 1920s. Henan today is lagging behind the rest of the country: Its infrastructure is underdeveloped, and its economy is still dependent on agriculture and limited coal reserves. It is one of the most impoverished provinces in China. I told Xiao Dong that I would be more than interested to visit it. 'Let's meet at Yuzhou bus station two weeks from now,' Xiao Dong said. 'Yuzhou is the nearest town to my home village.'

During the twelve-hour rail trip to Zhengzhou, Henan's capital city, I'd heard endless warnings about the place from people in all walks of life. 'Beware in Henan!' they said. 'There are many cheats and con men in that province.' 'Don't get yourself into trouble!' I wondered about this commonly held negative attitude toward Henan and the Henanese.

I was soon to see that the reality of Henan is rural poverty. The province is the most populous in the country, and the majority of its 100 million people (a figure that does not include the 21 million who have migrated to all parts of China) are peasants. On our way to Lugou village, the views were all of peasants farming wheat and sweet corn on small plots of land in coal dust–covered villages. The average per capita annual income for a peasant in Henan is around 3,851 yuan. Half of the province's rural revenue comes from money sent home by its migrant workers. (If it were not for these remittances, the per capita income gap between these Henanese villages and Xiamen might well be more than ten times what it is.) It is obvious that those who have not left home to find their future elsewhere will be permanently trapped here, as Xiao Dong put it.

Poverty has also been the cause of Henan's deadly AIDS epidemic, which in 2008 became the leading cause of death by infectious disease in China. Throughout the late 1980s and the 1990s, AIDS began to spread most widely in impoverished villages in Henan, where peasants augmented their income by selling their blood, for as little as 45 yuan (£4, $6.4) per 800cc, at unsanitary blood collection stations sanctioned by local authorities and run by private businesses.

In 1992, when the national media was infatuated with Deng's ethos of 'economic progress', the ability to bring in cash became the only criteria for assessing an official's capabilities. Henan's government actively promoted a local economy 'dependent on blood plasma', in which local health departments (whose officials often had dealings with the pharmaceutical companies looking to buy cheap plasma) and *xuetou* (literally, 'blood heads', those in charge of blood sales) mobilized peasants to sell their blood.

Local authorities advertised the sales with such exhortations as 'Sell your blood and get rich; it benefits your health and keeps your blood pressure under control.' Some *xuetou* went right into the fields to recruit peasants for these drives. Thus encouraged, poorly informed villagers flooded into blood stations. The officials, collecting their blood cheaply using substandard practices and sanitation, profited; the villagers became infected with HIV. The *xuetou* sold their contaminated plasma to pharmaceutical companies in the cities, who used it to manufacture all types of health products, then sold them on the market. In 1993 and 1994, one local official even led a delegation to the US to discuss setting up a US pharmaceutical company in Henan, where there was plenty of cheap plasma.

Although this plan didn't materialize, the growth of blood stations in China continued, with local health departments and businesses taking the lead in setting them up.

AIDS was first found to be disseminating through hospital blood transfusions in 1984. In 1988, Sun Yongde, a doctor in a disease prevention unit in Hebei province, called on the authorities to address the serious problem of AIDS-infected transfusions. These warnings fell on deaf ears. The authorities didn't do anything to control the spread of AIDS, and continued to reap profits from the plasma economy.

In the 1990s, all over China blood stations were sprouting like spring bamboo. In Henan, there were 400 stations, and 117 counties had been affected by AIDS. Zhumadian, Zhoukou, Kaifeng and Shangqiu, all prefecture-level cities, were the areas worst affected in Henan. In their villages, the majority of working-age men and women had sold blood and had died or were dying of AIDS. The elderly people who remained couldn't keep up the farms and had to find other ways to bring up the grandchildren left behind by their parents. In Shuangmiao, a village of 3,000 residents, 90 percent of young and middle-aged people, about 1,500 people, had sold blood, and 800 of them had been diagnosed HIV positive. The others were too afraid to get tested.

Even then, the government denied that AIDS was spreading and maintained a nationwide cover-up. Few Chinese knew about the tens of thousands of people who were dying of the disease.

It took years for the government to recognize the scale of the problem and allow the media to cover it. By the end of October 2009, health ministry data showed 319,877 Chinese people confirmed to be living with HIV/AIDS, up from 264,302 in 2008. The ministry noted that the real figure was probably nearer to 740,000,[4] which is the official estimate of people with HIV/AIDS in the country to date.[5] Chinese AIDS activists believe there are more than 800,000 people living with the disease.

AIDS was one of the first things that Xiao Dong mentioned when we began to discuss Henan's rural poverty. We had met as planned at Yuzhou, where I got off the bus from Zhengzhou, Henan's capital. Yuzhou has twenty-six townships and a population of 1.2 million, and is seen by national and international businesses as one of the best investment cities in Henan. Xiao Dong took me for a walk along the main street in town. When we passed the massive city government building, he pointed it out to me: 'Look at the grandeur! Look at the style! Who says there's no money in Henan? They're not stingy when it comes to the officials' playground!' He looked furious, and said that the Yuzhou he knows is one of corruption and a 'bitter gap between the stinking rich and the rottenly impoverished'.

He stopped on the side of the road and waved at a well-built man in his forties who was stepping out of a black car. He introduced the man as his friend Da Cai (literally, 'Big Talent'), also from Lugou village. Da Cai worked as a coal dealer (*mei-fanzi*), transporting coal and renting out land for coal sales. He greeted me politely and offered to drive us to the village, 20 kilometres from Yuzhou town centre.

So we came into Lugou, Xiao Dong's home village. Lugou is part of Fanggang township, a collection of fifteen villages with a total population of 40,000. Lugou village is tiny, with a population of 1,000. It was once an impoverished place tucked deep in a mountain valley, but it had been relocated here where living conditions were better, thanks to its enterprising migrants. Da Cai recalled the tough times in the old days when his parents lived by growing sweet potatoes. His father used to go up to the mountains and bring stones back home to sell. Each of the five brothers in the family had only one *mu* of land. They all gave up farming and rented out their land, except the youngest, who was willing to farm only because he was partially deaf and there wasn't much opportunity for him elsewhere.

Da Cai smiled and said they used to live on tasteless ground wheat. Xiao Dong reminded him that things were already improving slightly in the early 1980s, when the villagers began to eat noodles made of better-quality flour, called Eight Five Yang Noodles, which everyone loved. The name of the noodles came from the local saying 'Eighty-five percent' (that is, eighty-five percent of the flour production goes into their diet). Xiao Dong still remembered how good those noodles tasted the first time.

As we spoke, the entire Fanggang township appeared before our eyes. It looked stained with layers of black dust from the coal mining operations that surrounded it. Coal had always been the only industry here, and almost every young villager in Fanggang had done mining work at some point in his life. Since the nation-wide privatization of the coal mining industry began in the 1980s, as part of the era of reform and opening up, and state-run mines were contracted out or sold to private businesses, 'black' mines had mushroomed: A small private mine with an annual production capacity of 30,000 tonnes can be highly profitable to its owners and lucrative, too, for local officials. These black mines imposed harsh working conditions and openly employed child labour. It was commonly known in the villages that people not only toiled their hearts out in the mines but also died in them. Recently, because of the extremely high death toll, most of these private mines were finally closed down, too late for the families who lost their sons. There is now only one major, state-owned coal mine in Fanggang, although the conditions are harsh there too. Da Cai said that some of the local officials, including the village chiefs, are still profiting from the business in one way or another and helping to run it, mostly as shareholders.

Da Cai was once a miner here. He detested the work like everyone else. He left Lugou in 1996 among the first wave of young villagers who headed out to work in Guangdong province and later Xiamen. Xiamen was a much smaller city then, just starting up as a special economic zone. Like Xiao Dong, Da Cai worked there as a cab driver and eventually bought his own cab. He made about 300,000 yuan (£28,000) in total between 1996 and 2003 and was seen as a success among the Henanese migrants. 'But being an outsider in Xiamen, you just don't get connected to the latest information,' he said. 'You are isolated, quietly making your little bit of money. You miss out on opportunities. You wouldn't even know if people were talking about picking up gold off the street!' In 2003, he decided to go back to his hometown, where he felt that opportunities were improving thanks to all the incoming investment. He was sure that there was money to be made and that it was the right moment to return.

One day, I followed Xiao Dong around Lugou's centre, where he'd grown up. It was really just a few streets. A few women sat on small stalls peeling fruits for their children. There were no high-rises like those in Fujian – no sign of material improvements brought by migrants. But when I asked about this, Xiao Dong disagreed instantly and pointed to the bottom of the lane: His basic one-storey farmhouse had recently been renovated and now had a new front gate.

The village was surrounded by wheat fields. To the right, there was a small lane where a few carts pulled by buffaloes went slowly past, hauling crops. We walked through the fields to the back of the village, toward a wide valley. When we came to the top of a hill, Xiao Dong pointed at a huge black hole, narrow and frighteningly deep. 'Look down there,' he said to me. It was the private coal mine where he and others had once worked. It wasn't in use anymore, but there was no fence around it, no sign warning people not to walk into it.

Staring down at it, I couldn't see anything inside. It was pitch dark.

He told me that it was a thousand metres deep, going all the way down to the bottom of the valley, and could accommodate hundreds of workers. This was where he would go below ground every day, he said. It was the passage to Hell. 'We're going to Hell,' he and his coworkers would say each day before setting out for work. You never knew if you'd come back alive.

Xiao Dong stood silently at the top of that hill, looking down the valley and taking a deep breath. After work, he and his friends used to stand in this green field and gaze at the bamboo forests from the cliff. They spent a lot of time here. We strolled toward his three *mu* of wheat, planted beyond the woods. 'All this wild grass around,' he said. 'This little plot of land looks deserted, doesn't it?' It did – it was hard to see much growing on it. He used to earn less than 1,000 yuan (£91, $145) annually, after deducting the cost of fertilizers. Like some of the other villagers who have migrated, he has left the cultivation of the land to a friend, who shares half of the farming income.

One of Xiao Dong's other friends, Chai, who was driving us around in his cab that day, came into the fields looking for us. He walked through the wild grass surrounding the plots of land. Then he pointed to his own land a few metres away: only 0.75 *mu*. This was what they were given per person in his household. The amount of land had been allocated at random, and neither Chai or Xiao Dong knew why they were given so little, but Chai said that was the reason he'd left farming to drive a cab in town.

With living costs rising and produce prices falling, it's not surprising that villagers are always seeking new sources of income, or that some are prepared to do anything for cash. Blood sales to biomedical companies continue in many of the villages surrounding Lugou. Most peasants remain unaware that the collection stations are illegally run, unmonitored, and unsanitary.

When Xiao Dong and I met with Da Cai the next day, Da Cai told us about a woman in Zhangde village, five kilometres from Lugou, who had resorted to selling her blood. Everyone knew of her, he said. She had sold to an unsafe blood station, contracted AIDS and died in one year, still in her early forties, after passing the disease on to her husband. Da Cai added that since there were no clinics in the village, the sick woman had sought help in the hospital in Yuzhou, but there was nothing they could do, and for her husband, who was dying now, it was the same. There is no treatment available here, Da Cai said, and the man couldn't afford to travel to a bigger city to seek help. The couple had had no children, a good thing, since they'd soon have been orphans. In the village, no one would go near the sick man, as people had no knowledge of how AIDS is caught or how to prevent it. Some thought that they might become infected merely by entering his house. They kept away from him, as if he were already dead.

'As long as villagers have to sell blood to survive, officials will go on profiting like hell,' Da Cai said resentfully. 'Zhou, the former mayor of Yuzhou, is one such hated official. He was caught in a huge corruption case – he was paid ten million yuan for every one of Yuzhou's construction and infrastructure projects. But you know, Zhou was never punished. Instead, he was moved to Xuchang to work as the deputy head of a department. All that happened to him was the nickname he won among us: Zhou One Thousand – one thousand corruption cases.'

'The village is finished,' Xiao Dong murmured to Da Cai as we drove past the fields. 'There's really nothing left here, is there? No one owns anything except the village chiefs, still profiting from the coal sales.'

As we drove away from Lugou back to Yuzhou, Xiao Dong looked out the window, and couldn't seem to take his eyes away from the black dust–covered farmhouses that were fading away into the distance.

It was around this time that Dr Gao Yaojie's autobiography, *The Soul of Gao Yaojie*, was published in Hong Kong. Dr Gao, now eighty-five, is a leading AIDS activist from Zhengzhou, Henan. She was a gynaecologist for twenty-one years and a professor for sixteen years before becoming a rights advocate for women and children's health and the village poor in 1990. *The Soul of Gao Yaojie* details her work in Henan villages, where she educated people on HIV/AIDS prevention and provided support for orphans of the AIDS epidemic in Henan. It documents her tremendous contributions to awareness about the disease in China and globally, and her powerful critique of the official national cover-up in China.

She had known for twelve years that AIDS in China was a public health disaster created by corruption and government incompetence. The authorities, she said, were warned about the spread of the disease three decades earlier, in the late 1970s. Having witnessed the misery of the infected peasants, she set out, without connections or financial resources, on a long battle with the authorities. From the mid 1990s to 2003, she focused her energy on proving that there was an AIDS epidemic in Henan.

She visited more than a hundred villages all over China and witnessed the spread of the disease. She found that the Yellow River Region, the centre of the 'plasma economy', was the worst affected. The degree of the catastrophe deeply shocked and saddened her: 'I've seen whole families wiped out by the disease ... I saw six victims buried in one day when I visited.'

Dr Gao's investigations revealed that AIDS in China was mostly spread through blood sales and transfusions and that peasants were the major victims. *The Soul of Gao Yaojie* was published in English in 2011, but the Chinese edition from 2008 was never circulated in China itself, except in Hong Kong, where it had been published. And although the AIDS epidemic has since been recognized by the authorities, publications on the subject remain censored. Those who want to expose the catastrophe and cover-up to the public must do it in a clandestine way. Yan Lianke, the Henanese author of the banned novel *Dream of Ding Village*, based his book on the three years he spent undercover as an assistant to an anthropologist in order to witness how villages had been destroyed by AIDS. Eventually, he had to fictionalize his work in order to be published.

Dr Gao fled China in 2009 after years of harassment and persecution by the Chinese authorities. She first left Henan, travelled to Beijing and Chengdu, and eventually reached a village in Guangzhou, where she stayed while college students helped her type up her work and looked after her. She reached New York in 2010.

Dr Gao said she had to leave China in order to write further about the AIDS disaster. 'Following the arrest of an activist, Tan Zuoren, who fought for justice for the Sichuan earthquake victims, I felt uneasy at the possibility of my own arrest ... I didn't want the material and information that I had to become lost like "a stone in an ocean" ... I wanted to reveal my information; I want the public to know the truth.'

She now lives in exile, in the US. I spoke to her to learn more about her experiences. The first thing she told me was what hurt her most when visiting villages in Henan: 'As we entered one of the villages, we heard a child crying inside a house. "Come down! Come down!" the voice said. When we walked in, we saw a young woman who had hanged herself from the beam ... Her body was hanging stiff ... At her feet was this two-year-old boy, crying his heart out, biting his mother's feet and asking her to come down. This young mother and her husband had sold blood in the village and both were infected with AIDS. Her husband had died six months previously. Being alive had simply become too painful for her. A month after her death, her boy also died.'

These were villages devastated by 'reform and opening up' and the anarchy of the market. Villagers had no proper health care, not even now, when they were dying, and no information about the outside world. When Dr Gao visited one infected villager and gave him medicine, he asked her, 'Did Chairman Mao send you?' He didn't know that Mao had died thirty years before. He kept asking the same question. Dr Gao was saddened and didn't know how to answer him, and simply said: 'Why don't you take some medicine and drink more water ...'

Dr Gao told me that the AIDS deaths are not merely statistics: 'They are real names and faces. They are desperate cries and endless new graves. The question that every AIDS victim asked before dying was, "What are my children going to do?" or "What's going to happen to my parents when I die?" '

Impoverished Henanese peasants will travel a long way to sell blood, as far as Shanghai, or Urumqi, the capital of Xinjiang Uighur Autonomous Region in the extreme west, or Guangzhou and Hainan provinces to the south. Qi Cheng began to sell blood at the age of sixteen. He went to cities all over Henan, from Kaifeng, Zhumadian, and Zhengzhou to Xuchang; he sold his blood a thousand times – literally. Sometimes he sold 700 to 800 centilitres three times a day. With his blood earnings over fifteen years he and his wife had built three houses and paid off the 10,000-yuan penalty (although they still owed the village committee 3,900 yuan) for violating China's birth control policy. But when Dr Gao visited, both husband and wife were dying of AIDS, leaving behind four children and an elderly mother.

At that time there were an estimated 10,000 blood stations all over the country. Today, underground blood stations are still operating not only in Henan but also in the provinces of Hebei, Anhui, Shandong, Shanxi, Yunnan, Guizhou, Hubei, Hunan, Guangdong, Guangxi, and Heilongjiang.

When Dr Gao visited Sichuan, she met Li Bing, a peasant in a village in Zigong who went to sell blood in Hubei and was infected with AIDS. 'When he was dying, he called and asked me to adopt his six-year-old and eight-year-old children,' she told, 'When he realized that I was nearly eighty, he burst into tears.' She also investigated the situation at Gongmin village, one of the most infected areas in Sichuan. There, those who migrated to other provinces for work and became infected with AIDS through selling blood are leading a hopeless life of extreme social isolation and discrimination, with death the only way out.

Dr Gao told me, 'The infected people in China live in scattered communities. For fear of discrimination, they haven't come out to register themselves, and so it's hard to find them. There are a large number of these hidden, infected people.'

While media reports on AIDS were banned and journalists were barred from entering affected villages and arrested for reporting the disease, Dr Gao never ceased to try to raise public awareness, self-publishing her investigations. To inform the rural population about the high risks of selling blood, she wrote *The Prevention of AIDS* and printed 370,000 copies herself; she issued a newsletter, *Knowledge for HIV Prevention*, which she disseminated in many villages. Afterward, large numbers of patients came to visit her in her home, to seek help and advice.

Dr Gao achieved her aim of making known the existence and severity of the epidemic. Since 2003, international attention has pushed the local authorities to recognize the disease and send out medical teams to the thirty-eight most affected 'AIDS villages' in Henan. But Dr Gao saw this as only a partial victory: 'Even today, there are no reliable figures on the number of AIDS-infected people in the province and how widely the disease has spread.'

After 2003, she focused on publicizing information on *how* AIDS spread so widely: 'By this time, the authorities acknowledged the existence of AIDS, but insisted that it was spread through drug use and sex ... They want to make the disease sound like a dirty disease, caught through a bad lifestyle ... They talk about migrant workers infected with the disease through sexual contact when working outside of their provinces ... but in fact this is a small minority. Evidence proves that AIDS was spread via blood [sales and transfusions] in most cases.' She argued that, even today, blood sales and transfusion are still the main way of spreading the disease, and that the authorities are responsible for this process.

Dr Gao talked about Zhou Fenglin, a nineteen-month-old child, who was infected with AIDS through a blood transfusion in August 2005. His father, Zhou Hongqiang, said, 'Ten years ago a four-year-old child died of AIDS through transfusion in this same hospital. Why is history repeating itself? The blood disaster has not been stopped!' In 2006, after his son died, Mr Zhou attempted to sue the hospital, but the court wouldn't take up his case. In Ningling county, in Henan, over 100 people were recently found to have been infected via blood transfusion.

Meanwhile, this part of the cover-up continued. Dr Gao said local authorities have used five main methods to keep the truth from public knowledge since 2005: overt bribery; unsolicited gift-giving; bribery through promotion; threat and libel; 'education' of activists through labour, detainment or imprisonment. Leading AIDS activist Hu Jia spent a total of 214 days during 2006 and 2007 in detention and under house arrest. He was sentenced to three and a half years in prison by a Chinese court in April 2008, for 'inciting subversion of state power'. Li Xige from Henan was infected through a blood transfusion administered when she gave birth to her child, who later died of AIDS. She, too, has become an activist. In 2006 she went to Beijing and asked the central government for compensation. Instead she was detained for nearly a month and since then has been put under house arrest and still faces criminal charges for 'inciting assault on a state institution' – that is, petitioning the authorities in Beijing.

Dr Gao herself, of course, suffered much over the years from harassment and intimidation by the authorities. Her family had been intimidated into keeping their distance from her. They realistically feared being implicated and becoming the target of persecution. Her husband once burned her research material for fear of reprisal from the authorities. And, most saddening for her, her son was sent to beg her on his knees not to travel to the US to receive the Vital Voices Global Partnership Leadership Award for her work in 2007. All AIDS activists, particularly those working in the most affected provinces, who campaign for action, organize, and seek financial and legal support for AIDS victims remain at high risk of arbitrary detention, harassment, and imprisonment. Even violent assaults against them, organized by local officials, have often been reported.

The government never ceased monitoring Dr Gao's movements and communications with the outside world until she finally left China in 2009. Her family was also under surveillance. 'My son and daughter and my seven siblings and their children, altogether forty family members, were all subjected to monitoring and harassment. When I left China, their phones were being monitored … I have a sister in the US. She's retired and is looking after her grandchild. Her phone, too, has been tapped. I've never taken part in any political activities … My crime, according to the authorities, is that I "damage Henan's reputation".'

But thanks to years of campaigning by these activists, the Chinese government has finally acknowledged the severity of the problem. China's State Council issued a statement on 16 February 2011 warning of the wide spread of HIV/AIDS in some areas, saying that the situation was grim: 'The disease in some areas and population groups has become highly prevalent and many HIV carriers and patients have not yet been discovered.' Although the authorities have pledged to bring the spread of the disease under control by 2020, poor policy coordination and local corruption remains a barrier to real progress.

In rural China, blood stations still operate. 'They have gone further underground, and people continue to sell blood to them and get infected,' Dr Gao told me. 'In January 2010, it was found that a billionaire in Hunan has made his fortune by running numerous unsanitary blood stations. Local officials were involved in the scandal. In May 2010, hundreds in Hubei were found infected with AIDS through selling blood.' And these were only the reported cases. 'The infected blood plasma continues to be circulated … and the number of people infected through transfusion has increased.'

In January 2010, over eighty people were infected by blood transfusions in a single hospital in Hubei. These eighty people have passed on the disease to their families.

Amid the anarchy of the blood sales, certain underground blood stations were even found to have recruited peasants to work outside their villages and then detained them for their blood. Dr Gao spoke of one such case: 'In Ji County of Henan, Mr Xu Yubao was deceived into travelling to work in Kaifeng city. When he got there, he was locked up in a factory and his blood was taken every day until he passed out … When he was finally released, he went home and died, leaving two children behind. I spent three to four years trying to seek justice for his family, to no avail.' In Henan, these victims are called blood slaves (*xue-nu*). Their plight has received no attention from the authorities.

I remember the day I watched the National Day celebrations in Tiananmen Square. I saw the Henan float rolling through the parade among the thirty-four floats that represent the provinces of China. While the well-dressed Henanese on the float waved happily at the audience, the faces that came into my mind were those in Henan's villages.

4

The Dark Kilns: Brickmaking in the North

Xiao Zheng picked me up at the train station in Tianjin, a port city eighty kilometres east of Beijing and one of the four provincial-level cities in China. We were heading to Beihuaiding, a new-looking village built of red bricks, in Ninghe county, a few kilometres outside of Tianjin. Xiao Zheng, in his forties, had a friendly brown face, weathered by the sun, and a gold tooth that shone every time he smiled. He showed up in a Honda driven by his friend Chen, a local cab driver. A man I knew in London, also named Zheng, who had migrated from Beihuaiding, had sent Xiao Zheng, his best friend, to meet me here and show me around.

I'd met my London Zheng eight years before, when I visited the lettuce farm in Selsey, in West Sussex where he was part of a team of Chinese migrant workers. I used to visit him and his coworkers in their caravan during the summer, and we'd had some good times talking and drinking together. In the winter, he had a job in a salad-processing factory next to the farm that produced all types of packaged salad lunches for the supermarket chain Tesco. He was extremely hardworking, but was laid off as cheap Chinese labour began to be replaced by workers from Eastern Europe. He then went into catering, toiling in the kitchen of a Chinese takeaway, working hours that left no time for any social life. He also lived in constant fear: fear of an immigration raid and deportation.

He'd left Beihuaiding and his wife and daughter seven years before. He once farmed the land, growing sweet corn, but the income it brought was insufficient. Xiao Zheng had tried to persuade him to invest in his own fishing trade, but Zheng was much more ambitious than that. He dreamed of building a new house for his family – of giving them a good life. He heard villagers talking about going abroad to work and decided to go himself. But he wanted to do it well: The only destination worthy of his investment of money and time was Britain, where, he'd heard, work was easy to find and money quick to earn. He approached an agency in Tianjin's city centre and applied for a business-visitor visa for the UK. Within a month, he'd received the visa and was ready to set off.

As Chen, Xiao Zheng and I drove into the rural suburbs outside of Tianjin, the city landscape gave way to rows of semi-deserted farm houses and small brick kilns. Little other industry can be seen along the way. Suddenly, it felt as if we were already a long way into the countryside. Then a huge building marked 'Le Gou' ('Happy Shopping') came into view. It was odd to see a warehouse of this size in the middle of a run-down rural area. 'That's "Tee-see-co" shopping mall, built not long ago,' Xiao Zheng explained enthusiastically. Tesco.

Tesco, founded in 1919, is now the world's third-largest multi-national retailer and, in 2005, it became the first UK-based retailer to reach profits of over £2 billion. It has branches in fourteen countries across Asia, Europe and North America; China is still a relatively new market. Most of Tesco's stores in China are based around Shanghai, but the company is looking to expand to other areas. Tesco also outsources some of its garment and textile manufacturing to places like India and China, and has profited from the low costs of production in those countries. Chinese companies producing for Tesco include the Hong Kong–based Gatex Industrial Company, which manufactures knitwear, and the fabric makers Fountain Set Group, also Hong Kong–based but with factories all over China.

As we drove, Xiao Zheng talked about how villagers in the area mostly grew cotton and sweet corn, but because their land holdings were small, the crops didn't bring in much income, so many of them, men and women, had begun to supplement their income by working in small- to medium-size textile factories nearby. In recent years, many villagers had started up their own new ventures, such as breeding freshwater shrimps and running huge fishing ponds for Tianjin residents to enjoy during weekends. Xiao Zheng pointed out one of these ponds alongside the road, the size of a large swimming pool but quite deserted, as it was a weekday.

Beihuaiding, with a population of a few thousand, still depends mainly on agriculture for its revenues. Those who are working in the factories still don't earn enough to make ends meet. The surrounding brick kilns employ only cheap migrant labour. Young people in the village were leaving. Xiao Zheng said that many of them paid an application fee of five to six thousand yuan to agencies — some of them travel agents, others registered as trading companies — to arrange for travel to South Korea. That, added to the plane fare, which the fee did not include, was a large amount of money for any villager, but the migrants hoped they'd be earning that money back within two months and then be able to start making much more money than they could in China. People began migrating to South Korea on tourist or short-term visas (which they then outstayed) in the late 1980s, when South Korean factories and building sites were short of workers. Today, Chinese make up more than half of South Korea's 200,000 undocumented migrant workforce and are the most targeted migrants for arrest and deportation. 'Who can stop them?' said Xiao Zheng. 'They will be earning eight times more over there. Even middle-aged people like me want to go try it out there.'

I thought about Zheng in suburban London. He'd led an isolated life since joining the Chinese catering trade in the middle of an affluent English town. He has had no one to talk to except his Cantonese-speaking boss and the Malaysian-Chinese chef. His life has been dominated by work and the fear of losing it. On his precious day off, all he can do is hang around a tiny local casino — not because he particularly likes gambling, but because there is no other social space where he can feel safe. Could life in South Korea be any better for a migrant without papers?

Many Chinese peasants choose South Korea because the travel arrangements are cheaper (compared with travel to Japan, the US and Europe) and there are more opportunities for employment, via well-established Chinese migrant communities there.

'Our villagers choose to go to South Korea also because the South Koreans are ethnically closer to us,' Xiao Zheng noted.

Not so in London, where Chinese immigrants make up only 1.5 percent of the city's population of seven million and are largely split up into culturally and linguistically diverse enclaves.

'Zheng told me everything about England. Heavens, it shocked me,' Xiao Zheng said. 'I'd never imagined that foreign workers would be paid half of the local wage rate in an advanced country like the UK. He told me that happened to him in a number of jobs over there. And they worked him to the bone! And they didn't pay him for overtime. I was truly worried about him. He's a soft-hearted man, you know; I didn't know if he would be able to cope with such a harsh life in England.'

Beihuaiding village is centred around a bustling food market where friendly, noisy vendors display huge amounts of shrimp and fish in their stalls. Villagers gather around the market to chat as well as buy. They don't usually have visitors from outside, and it's easy to draw a crowd if you are differently dressed. 'Where are you from? Who are you looking for?' one after another of them asked me. Xiao Zheng and Chen led me from the market into the residential part of the village, neatly divided into lanes of red brick houses. Xiao Zheng told me that most of these houses have been built by bricks produced in the nearby kilns. 'These kilns basically made our village,' he said.

All five of the kilns in the Beihuaiding area are owned by the village chief, Li Xiangguo, known as the richest man in the village. 'Our governor, our native emperor (*tu huangdi*),' said Xiao Zheng. He had no confidence in the county elections, for which candidates were appointed, calling it the worst of jokes, and believed that the village chief had bribed his way up to his position and then used it to accumulate more wealth. Although these allegations could not be verified, the villagers were clearly angry at the contrast between his lifestyle and their own.

'The bastard lives in such luxury,' said Chen. 'He has such a huge beautiful house.'

'And five expensive cars!' said Xiao Zheng. 'Why does anyone need so many?'

'So he can drive a different car each day,' replied Chen.

'When one man gets his way, even his hens and dogs go to heaven,' Xiao Zheng said, laughing. This Chinese proverb, '*Yirendezhi jiquanshengtian*,' expresses neatly the idea that once a man has wealth and power, all those around him will benefit.

Of course, all those around the village chief are not the villagers but the chief's cadres. Village administration mirrors those of towns and cities, that is, it includes many posts that are not necessary and are a waste of public money. Villagers believe that those who fill these 'superfluous' posts are all associates and relatives of the chief. It infuriates them to hear these people called cadres and to have to pay their salaries out of the public purse.

And the number of these local 'cadres' continues to grow. When the communes of the late 1950s and 1960s were finally abolished, the government, without consulting the peasants, immediately turned the land into 92,000 townships and gave the townships the power to run their own finances and map out their own administration. Local bureaucracies were established and built up by bringing new 'cadres' into the fold; from 1979 to 1989, the number of people on China's government payroll increased from 2.28 million to 5.5 million.[1] As capital investment shifted toward the cities, thanks to the economic reforms of the 1980s, local bureaucracies ballooned with new cadres added to help manage finances and increase revenues. By 1997, the number of people on government payroll had reached eight million, and since then has increased further.

The cadres also make up much of China's economic elite. As Xiao Zheng noted, local elections are not run democratically: the candidates are appointed, having their own sphere of influence in the local area. They maintain that influence through bribery, favouritism and other manipulative measures – common practice in local politics. Their position as cadres brings them power and wealth.

'Socialism with Chinese characteristics' has meant that half of China's wealth has gone to the top fifth of the population, while the bottom fifth receives just 4.7 percent.[2] In 2011, the 'Hurun Rich List', an index to wealth creation in China first compiled in 1999 by Rupert Hoogewerf, a Durham University graduate and chartered accountant, and two students from Shanghai's Donghua University, showed that 30 percent of the top fifty were delegates to the CPPCC (China People's Political Consultative Congress). 'Despite the continuing global financial crisis, 2011 has seen a record year for China's rich,' Hoogewerf wrote. Liang Wengen, with $11 billion, topped the list.

China's wealth gap was obvious to everyone. Xiao Zheng could even cite statistics from memory. 'You know how much the rich spend in this country?' he sneered. 'More than four and a half million yuan (£388,080, $621,315) a year per person! No idea how they could spend so much!'

'Probably on golf holidays in Hainan province?' replied Chen, disgustedly. 'They wear luxury watches, drink luxury wines, and smoke the best imported cigarettes.'

Chen looked down at the cheap local cigarette in his own hand, Red Tower, eight yuan a packet. Deng Xiaoping's favourite cigarettes cost 800 yuan, that is, £79, per packet. 'Lesser Panda [another expensive brand] would be too tacky for their taste,' he said.

'Our village chief is one of them,' said Xiao Zheng, shaking his head. 'Asshole!'

Xiao Zheng took me to one of the nearby brick kilns. He said that normally the kilns wouldn't allow strangers to enter, but as he, a villager, was escorting me, it wouldn't be a problem. He would bring me in as 'a friend on holiday' – I could even pretend that I was an overseas trader interested in buying bricks.

So, along the dusty country road we drove. There were sweet-corn fields on both sides and they seemed to expand forever into the distance. As the roads got bumpier, Chen drove faster. Ten minutes later, the lanes grew narrower and the bushes taller, blocking a full view of our surroundings. I could see heavy smoke coming out of long, high chimneys a mile ahead. The smoke got thicker as we approached. The lane became dustier and I tried to wind up the window. I could see dots moving in the distance – straw hats. As we pulled into the site, I heard the voices of men and women. Suddenly a whole camp of labourers was before us, working with their heads down, under straw-roofed work houses. I felt as though we had entered another world.

When Chen parked the car, I could see many people in the work houses turning toward us and observing our movements. Behind the concealing bushes was a vast field; I couldn't see the end of it. Laid out across it were thousands of rows of muddy bricks. In the distance loomed the high brick-burning tower. It was an over-whelming sight. The sound of machinery seemed to drown the noise of people, though there were 150 workers at the site. The workers were divided into three areas: some making bricks in the work houses next to us, some burning bricks in the distant tower, others loading and unloading bricks in the field and laying them out to dry.

I counted more than twenty women carrying heavy, wet, muddy bricks bare-handed from their work house to the carts, loading them up to be taken to the tower. The workers in this section were mostly women, in fact, because this part of the brick-making process was the least strenuous. I approached them. They told me that they and their co-workers at the other four kilns were all from Sichuan province. One woman, whose face was tanned and worn, stopped to talk. She had her black hair tied back and was wearing a thick pair of gloves and a plastic apron around her waist. She said that they had been part of a group of more than fifty from a village near Chongqing city, a two-day train trip from the kiln. They'd been recruited by a Sichuanese who knew one of their villagers. He told this acquaintance that he needed a large group of workers and that the job would include accommodation in the brick kiln. She had been part of this group.

The woman said that she was in her mid forties and had a ten-year-old daughter, now being looked after by her parents. Her husband was also working in this kiln – right now he was at the brick-burning tower. 'There was no money to make on the tiny bit of land we have. No jobs in my village. I had to leave. I've been working here in this kiln for two years. I work and live here, and I go home for a visit in the winter.'

It was the first time she'd ever worked in a brick kiln, and in the beginning she had found the work physically very demanding – much more so than farming. And her movements were confined to the site for the entire year. She found the isolation difficult. 'We can't ever go out,' she said. 'Not allowed. We just stay in the kiln, all the time, from the spring to the beginning of the winter. I have no idea what's happening outside every day,' she added, trying to smile.

A teenage worker drove past on a three-wheeled cart full of muddy unburnt bricks. He was half the size of the cart and only sixteen, and had come here with the men and women from the rural outskirts of Chongqing. His face was smeared with mud and so was his pink T-shirt, and he zigzagged along the lane on his cart, heading toward the king-size kiln at the top end of the site.

Xiao Zheng approached. 'We may be attracting too much attention. Let's move to the other side.'

So we got back in the car, which we'd parked a few feet from the work houses. We drove down the lane and turned a corner arriving at the second section of the site, where workers burn the bricks: the stage called *chu-yao*, 'out of the kiln'. There were always two workers on each shift. Those who had just got off their shift were resting in one-storey shacks provided by the kiln. We walked toward a shack, and Xiao Zheng told me that this was the migrants' sleeping place. There was no door, and I put my head in and took a quick look. I was utterly shocked by what I saw. So was Xiao Zheng. I had not imagined that the workers' 'sleeping place' was literally there.

The migrants were very friendly and invited us to go into their room. There were a dozen layers of bricks inside, and ten workers – they all looked middle-aged, and were in sleeveless tops and shorts, as it was very warm that day – had made beds on top of the bricks with pieces of board. There was a light bulb hanging down from the old ceiling. There were mosquitoes buzzing around, and the 'sleeping places' were covered by mosquito nets hung from the ceiling. Towels were being dried on a piece of string across the room. Baskets in which the men had stored their food were placed next to the refuse bins.

'A sleeping place,' Xiao Zheng murmured again. He and the other villagers only lived three miles from this kiln, but had no idea what kind of life the kiln workers – all migrants – lived within the compound. I could see the embarrassment on Xiao Zheng's face, the shame at having a guest witness this reality. 'Li Xiangguo,' he kept saying. 'That bastard.'

But the Sichuanese workers were hospitable. 'Sit down, sit down,' they welcomed us, despite being worried about their employer seeing them. (Although he didn't seem to be around that day.) One of the men, a Mr Chen, pushed aside his belongings and made space for me on his brick bed.

As I sat down, I saw packets of painkillers by the bed. Mr Chen must have brought these from home in Sichuan, I thought. Unable to leave the site to see a doctor, he would have to rely on painkillers no matter what caused the pain. I had a thousand questions that I wanted to ask him, but I hesitated to begin.

'Where are you from?' Mr Chen asked me instead. He handed me and Xiao Zheng a cigarette each. 'We never have any visitors here, you know.'

I told him, and asked him the same question. Mr Chen said he and fifty of his co-workers had come from villages near Zigong, a town in Sichuan. He was a farmer, growing wheat, sweet corn and soy on the plains. But with no more than 1.5 *mu* of land per head, no one in his village could survive, especially with the rapid rise in costs over the past decade. They only made 200–300 yuan (£18–27, $31–47) a month, and taxes were heavy, even though investments in rural infrastructure, including health and education, had failed to produce any improvements. Mr Chen's wife had left to work in a garment shop in Zigong, and he'd chosen to leave Sichuan altogether. He had been here now for nearly four years. He went back home every year during the winter for the Chinese New Year break. There he could live with his wife for three months, and come back to the kiln again in the spring. What was it like for him to be apart from his wife for the rest of the year? I imagined it must be difficult, because from the way he was talking about home, he seemed very concerned about her health and well-being. But I also got the impression that, for many couples in this situation, survival is the main issue: They can sacrifice their personal feelings for the sake of securing a livelihood for their family.

Mr Chen and the others in this 'sleeping place' worked loading carts of bricks into the kiln. Half a tonne of coal was needed to burn a thousand bricks, which took three hours. They were paid by the cartload of bricks burnt (each cart held one hundred bricks), earning roughly 50–60 yuan a day (£4.80–5.80, $7.9–9.5 a day) – at least triple what they'd earned back in their home village. But this is not the wage they receive – the labour contractor (*baogong-tou*) skims off a regular payment for his intermediary role. 'We have never been told how much he is taking from our wages,' said Mr Chen as he lay atop his 'bed', the dim light flickering above. 'We just know that we must accept whatever terms there are. We are not in a position to bargain for anything.'

Mr Chen and the others work nonstop for nine months each year, from March through November, returning home to Sichuan in December to be reunited with their families for the winter and the Chinese New Year. (Brick production, like most other manual and seasonal work in China, pauses in the winter.) Often, Mr Chen worked the morning shift, from four a.m. to noon. Sometimes, he did double shifts when the workload was heavy – usually once or twice a week. When they weren't on shift, the men often gathered in their shacks, playing chess and drinking tea. That was the only entertainment they had. Like the women in the work houses, they weren't allowed to leave the site, on the grounds that they were 'not familiar with the local surroundings and might get lost.' But the workers believed that the real reason was to stop them from leaving their jobs.

Brick production is a profitable business in China. Its history can be traced back to 3,800 years ago in Xian where burnt bricks were discovered. Today, China produces 54 percent of the world's bricks. The bricks from the kilns in Beihuaiding are mostly consumed by the construction industry in the surrounding villages and the Tianjin area. The brick industry employs mainly migrant workers, as a cheaper and easily accessible workforce. At many kilns, including Beihuaiding's, contractors openly use child labour.

Our visit to the shack was interrupted by noises outside. A man peeked in and told me, 'The owner's father wants to meet you.' That was a surprise. We'd all thought that the boss wasn't around that day, and hadn't realized his father was. And I'd assumed that it would be all right for me to follow Xiao Zheng and his friend Chen into the work site – there'd been no security around to stop us.

So my conversation with the Sichuanese workers was abruptly ended. Xiao Zheng, Chen and I left the shack, and were led by the messenger into an office at the top of the lane. It was large and nicely decorated, with an executive's desk in the middle – a sharp contrast with the workers' humble shacks. There were press cuttings and medals hung on the notice board, but as I was about to take a look, a man in his eighties walked up to me and shook my hand. He was friendly – in fact, too friendly. 'Can I help you with anything?' he asked politely. He must have become suspicious of our visit. I told him I was a tourist and a friend of a Beihuaiding villager. Xiao Zheng also walked up to shake his hand and introduced himself. The old man smiled and said nothing. He remained civilized, but soon escorted us off the site.

On our way back to Beihuaiding, Xiao Zheng and Chen began talking about the village chief again. Xiao Zheng whispered, 'The profits of the kilns aren't enough for him to spend.'

'Wait until the next county election, when the asshole will bribe the whole village again!' Chen responded, spitting out from the window to show his contempt.

On our return to Beihuaiding village we went to meet Lan, the wife of my London friend Zheng. During the seven years her husband had been away, he'd sent home a total of 600,000 yuan ($95,259). When Lan opened her front gate to us, I saw a house in the classic quadrangle pattern (*siheyuan*), newly built with bricks from the kiln we'd just visited. This was the fruit of Zheng's seven years of hard labour in Britain. At the same time, I knew, Zheng had paid for it in more than money: He had missed seeing his daughter grow up. When Lan sent him pictures of her high school graduation ceremony, Zheng was shocked to see a young woman of eighteen, and though she had her mother's large black eyes, high cheekbones and heartwarming smile, he didn't immediately recognize her. When he left Behuaiding, she'd been a kid, one who always needed attention from her parents, forever asking questions and wanting answers, eager to learn. Even at the age of ten, she'd said she wanted to study English one day.

Lan was expecting me and shook hands with me when she opened the front door. She had been a housewife all her life, though when Zheng was at home she used to help with the farm work. When their daughter was growing up, Lan had begun to feel the need to improve their income, and had discussed the options with Zheng. She'd encouraged him to give up farming. She had hoped he would find decent work in their area, instead of going abroad. But when he came home one day to announce his decision to leave for England, she hadn't said a word. Zheng had told me once in London that he no longer felt close to Lan. He said that when they talked on the phone, she often asked him about his work and when he would send money home. When the money was delayed, she would question him about it. Zheng wished that she would sometimes ask him how he was, how he felt living alone, and whether he had made friends. Year after year, they communicated only by phone, and in the end, the calls no longer consoled him.

Lan didn't appear happy. She looked exhausted. After all, she had raised their daughter all on her own. She seemed subdued, and kept quiet when she led me into the sitting room. I looked for a place to sit down, but there were no chairs or sofas, just two beds. The sitting room was bare. The place didn't look like a family home. Possibly she had not had time to buy the furniture yet – the house had just been built.

Lan also looked uneasy, as if she didn't really know how to talk with a visitor. Xiao Zheng, who hadn't seen her for a long time, also stood there looking confused, and then coughed embarrassedly.

I handed her a suitcase of goods that Zheng had given me to bring to her. She nodded, looking awkwardly thankful. I was trying to make sense of her uneasiness. Perhaps it was because it has been seven years since she'd seen Zheng, and seeing his friend reminded her of their long-lost marriage.

'Let's go out to eat,' she said. She was in a hurry to leave, but we were all glad to get out for some fresh air. Xiao Zheng suggested a fish restaurant nearby that had a huge aquarium. When we got there, everyone gathered around the tank to select the dinner. I was no fan of the local seafood: Those river crabs and shrimps (*pipi-xia*) were incredibly intimidating. After being cooked alive these creatures still look raw to me, and I dreaded the thought of a *pipi-xia* clenching its tail while being chewed in my mouth. But these were all Xiao Zheng's favourite dishes.

As we sat down, Lan told us that a week ago her daughter had begun work as a secretary in a private firm in Tanggu town, about an hour from Tianjin. It was her first time away from home, and the job was demanding; she had already begun to work overtime. Lan worried about whether she could cope on her own. Today was her day off, and Lan had been to see her early in the morning. She'd brought her bags of food and a rice cooker, and taken her out to lunch – a good, three-dish Tianjin meal – in Tanggu town centre. They'd always been very close, especially after Zheng left for England. All they had was each other, and there were days and nights when they'd cried on each other's shoulders. Over the years, they'd become used to Zheng's absence. For Lan, it was like being a single mother. She had organized her child's life and coped with day-to-day problems while Zheng, the absentee father and husband, sent them the money to survive.

Lan cracked open a piece of crab. I watched her eat. She urged me to take a piece from the dish, but I had to say no and quickly moved the rotating platter until the crab was out of my sight.

Xiao Zheng toasted everyone, taking one cup of rice wine after another. Chen also enjoyed drinking, so they started to do drinking fists.

Halfway through the dinner, I realized Lan hadn't said much at all. I tried to tell her something about her husband. 'Zheng is living in a place called Aldershot, half an hour outside of London,' I said.

Lan nodded. She lowered her head. Why didn't she ask me about him? What the town was like? What he did after work? Who he socialized with?

'He finds the place quite dull and lonely,' I continued. 'It's an affluent area, but very quiet.'

She nodded again. 'Let me wish you good health,' she said, and raised her cup and toasted everyone. We all raised our cups. Now Lan, too, began emptying one cup after another. Xiao Zheng, who always liked a drinking pal, encouraged her.

So we all carried on merrily, with rice and sorghum wine, through the evening. After a while, I didn't feel so anxious about Lan's silence anymore. I toasted her, and she toasted me back.

Xiao Zheng was looking drunk – he'd had more than six cups of wine, and six bottles of beer. As he relaxed, he started to ask more personal questions. 'Why did you never invite me to your house, sister?' Xiao Zheng asked Lan, 'I grew up with Zheng.

We're like blood brothers. But you keep a distance from me. It's not nice!'

'Ay, brother, don't speak like that,' Lan answered quietly, smiling embarrassedly, then frowning. 'I don't invite men around my house because I want to avoid gossip in the village. You know villagers gossip about other people's marriages. Keeping a good name is important.'

'But you should not forget the people closest to you!' Xiao Zheng persisted, sounding emotional. He obviously felt quite strongly about not ever getting invited to visit her, and finally he had the opportunity to tell her so. 'It's not nice,' he repeated.

Lan didn't know how to respond to his complaint, but asked gently, 'How have you been? Still busy with work?'

'Yeah, busy. I'm planning to set up my own trade and not work for others anymore,' Xiao Zheng said, downing another cup of wine. 'I'm looking for people to be my business partners.'

Chen, already drunk, butted in: 'You never want to put your feet on the concrete floor [*jiao ta shidi*, that is, be realistic and persistent]. It's good to have dreams, but big dreams don't always materialize!'

'Not true,' Xiao Zheng liked a little debate during his drinking sessions. 'Zheng had big dreams. He went abroad and he made money, didn't he!'

Lan nodded quietly. She looked feverishly red, from the alcohol, but she was beginning to relax. 'You know,' she confided, 'on that day when Zheng left home, we didn't say a word to each other. We just wanted to get on with it. It was as if speaking would only bring us pain. He took his luggage out of the house and we walked silently to the bus stop. We said nothing. I saw him onto the bus. But the moment he was out of sight, I started crying. And I couldn't stop for hours.'

I met Xiao Zheng again six months later, in Shandong province, south of the Yellow River that links other central provinces such as Shanxi, Shaanxi and Henan. It is here in the Shandong plains that the river completes its long journey across China. Indeed, the region owes much of its character to the Yellow River. At one time, Shandong was one of the poorest regions in China, suffering from unpredictable floods, which over the centuries claimed tens of thousands of lives. However, it was also here in the river delta that China's oldest agricultural society developed, and so the delta region is known as the cradle of Chinese civilization. Today, the province isn't doing badly, according to official data: It ranks first in production of cotton and wheat, along with other crops, and is rich in natural resources like oil and petroleum, and those industries form a significant part of Shandong's economy. In 2010, the officially reported GDP for the province was 3.98 trillion yuan, the third-highest in China, after Guangdong and Jiangsu. But not everyone in Shandong has benefited from this growing wealth.

I was in northern Shandong to visit a large brick kiln where many Sichuanese migrants work. Brick production is an important industry there, and many kilns are concentrated in northern Shandong as they are in southern Hebei. These kilns always recruit migrant workers from Sichuan, Hebei, Henan, and other provinces. I called Xiao Zheng and asked him to meet me and accompany me. After working in Hebei all his life, and with friends working across the neighbouring provinces, he was well-connected and familiar with the construction and brick industries not only in his home village but also in the surrounding region. Northern Shandong was four hours' journey for him. He told me he wouldn't mind helping me and would also bring a resourceful friend, Mr Qi, with him.

Our rendezvous was the train station in Dezhou, a prefecture-level city in northern Shandong. When I got there, the station was quiet, and looked half derelict. I waited outside. A few middle-aged women were selling local snacks, *jianbing*, the Shandongese fried pancakes with chives and eggs inside. Five minutes later, Xiao Zheng and Mr Qi walked out of the station and greeted me. Mr Qi, in a grey suit, looked in his late forties. He was as tanned as Xiao Zheng and had deep wrinkles on his forehead. He shook my hand, asking how my trip was. He had a much stronger Hebei accent than Xiao Zheng; he sounded as if he were constantly chewing his words. He had very easy-going manners, greeting me warmly as 'older sister' (*da-jie*), although he looked older than me. Xiao Zheng saw the puzzled look on my face and explained instantly, 'We call women "older sister" as a way of showing our respect.' Qi nodded repeatedly.

Qi was a maintenance worker and repaired machinery at Dong Sheng, the brick kiln we were going to visit in Gaoyan village. He said that Dong Sheng, like many brick kilns in China, had been contracted out. It was theoretically owned by the villagers and meant to be used for the village, but it was actually run as a private enterprise by a local businessman. There was no way to defeat the alliance between the corrupt village chiefs and the businesses, Qi said. Today Dong Sheng is the largest kiln in northern Shandong and supplies the construction industries over a large part of the region.

Qi knew the area like the back of his hand. 'These villages along the Yellow River, not far from the border between Shandong and Hebei provinces, are a complete wasteland, where even birds don't lay their eggs,' he said. 'And who cares if nothing grows here? It is a forgotten place.' Along the river are the hidden 'black' brick kilns, the *hei zhuanyao*. As with black mines, this colloquial term refers to private kilns that operate secretly without following any labour rules, kilns with harsh regimes that exploit workers. In some of these *hei zhuanyao*, both on the border between Shandong and Hebei and in Hebei and Shanxi, even slaves had been found, as in the 2007 Shanxi child labour scandal.

The three of us took a bus together from Dezhou to Wudi, a town at the northern tip of the province, known as 'the county of plums' – plum cultivation there went as far back as 200 BC. Qi told me that the name Wudi came from a very old legend: Once there were flowers, called sugar di, bright yellow and fragrant, growing everywhere in the town. These flowers were much loved by the villagers, but one day they were all swept away by a sudden flood, just like that. *Wu* means 'nonexistence', and *Wudi* means 'The sugar di flower is no more'.

Officially, Wudi was part of the so-called Yellow River Delta development zone. In November 2009, the State Council of China endorsed the Development Planning of the Yellow River Delta High Efficiency Eco-economic Zone, to 'increase the support to the development and construction of the Yellow River Delta' with the stated aim of cultivating 'the new economic growth hub and urban development zone of the economic circle around the Bohai Sea'. The region had officially become part of the 'Bohai Economic Rim', an economy based on heavy industry and manufacturing, including the hinterland surrounding Beijing and Tianjin as well as areas in Hebei and Shandong. 'The region has gone through major changes in economy and infrastructure,' the state media claimed. 'This emerging region is rising as a northern economic power-house that rivals the Pearl River Delta in the south and the Yangtze River Delta in the east.'

However, little cash has been put into the area to further its development plans. Wherever we looked, infrastructure was notably lacking, as were public facilities and basic conveniences. Even roads were poorly maintained. There was little industry around. The area remained largely agricultural: Of its population of 430,000 people, around 370,000 were still eking a meagre existence out of farming.

The bumpy bus trip from Dezhou lasted an hour but seemed never-ending, with lifeless views of vast maize fields on both sides of the road. It was early evening when we finally got to Wudi. There were two main streets in the tiny town centre – a few dumpling shops and restaurants were open, but the streets were almost empty. Qi said it was too late to go to the brick kiln, so we checked into a cheap hotel, which I paid for, although Xiao Zheng and Qi both insisted they wanted to pay for my room. It was a male pride thing. The hotel restaurant looked like the best in town, Xiao Zheng said, and so we dined there. Over dinner, Qi looked as if he were getting ready to tell me something. He said, 'One of the reasons for my visiting Gaoyan village tomorrow is to claim the wages they still owe me for my maintenance work last year.'

'What?' I was surprised.

'Yes, sister. I'd like to at least try to get my money.'

'How much do they owe you?' I asked.

'A lot. They still owe me half of my wages for last year – for six months of labour!' That came to nearly 5,000 yuan, and Qi had not dared to return alone to claim it, for fear of reprisal, possibly violent reprisal.

I began to picture the different ways that tomorrow's visit to the kiln could pan out. Would the boss yield to our collective pressure and release the money? Or would he turn nasty and hire thugs to get rid of us – as in the stories I had heard so many times before? Brick kilns were notorious for not paying workers properly – and were also notorious for resorting to violence when workers demanded owed wages.

'Do you think you have a chance of getting your money back?' I asked.

'Probably not much chance, but I should try,' Qi said. 'I wouldn't go back to the kiln if you and Xiao Zheng weren't with me. I wouldn't do it alone, just as you shouldn't visit the kiln alone.'

Many local brick businesses and factories are still run by village officials and protected by organized criminals. Corporate violence has been reported by campaigning organizations like China Labour Bulletin, which has described how enterprise bosses frequently employ thugs to harass, beat up and intimidate workers who complained about nonpayment of wages or harsh working conditions. Migrant workers are often the main targets, since they are the most vulnerable. In August 2008, a group of Henanese migrant workers in a kelp-processing plant in Rongcheng city, in Shandong's Weihai prefecture, demanded their back pay. The boss hired local gangsters to beat them up and threatened to kill anyone who refused to accept the company's terms, which determined that the workers should wait till the company was ready to pay them. There was also the horrifying story of Wang Chao, a migrant worker from Sichuan who had his left arm chopped off by a group of thugs hired by a Nanjing construction company when he demanded wages owed to him and his colleagues. That company was a subsidiary of a state-owned company, China State Construction Engineering Corporation.

I asked Qi if he was worried about a violent response from the kiln bosses.

'Of course I am,' he said. 'That's why I will not be confrontational. I will be nice and polite, and reassure them that I'm not there to make trouble for them.'

Next morning Qi showed up in a clean white shirt and a pair of suit trousers with a black belt. 'Dressing up for the occasion,' Xiao Zheng teased him. 'For the negotiation table,' Qi shot back.

It took another hour by bus to get to Gaoyan village from Wudi. When we finally arrived, Qi sighed at the mere sight of it. It was like a desert, truly in the middle of nowhere. There was a vast barrenness in front of us – and behind us.

'Look around. What a wasteland, right?' Qi said.

'Looks like nothing grows and nothing comes from here,' Xiao Zheng said.

There seemed to be little infrastructure or industrial progress either. Qi said the area was thirty years behind the national pace of reforms and opening-up: 'It's difficult to find this left-behind place even on the map of Shandong.'

We walked on, hoping to flag down a cab to take us to the kiln. But there was no sight of any vehicle. Finally, ten minutes down the road, we saw a cab and got in. Qi directed the driver as we went, until a small stream with wild grass on both sides came into view. We got out of the cab and crossed the stream. As we walked on into the grassy field, to my relief a large sign with 'Dong Sheng Brick Kiln' in red characters appeared in the distance. 'Just follow me into the kiln and don't ask questions yet,' Qi said.

We entered the work site, and it was completely obvious that we were outsiders. The workers loading bricks in the distance stared at us: Who would ever come in here if they weren't coming to sell their labour? To the left of where they stood was a castle-like three-storey building with smoke pouring from the roof; Xiao Zheng said it was the brick-burning tower. Both he and I were stunned by its size – a kiln even larger than the one in Beihuaiding. We followed Qi to a one-storey building a few feet away to the right of the kiln; this looked like the office. A middle-aged man with a shaved head, wearing a white vest and blue jeans, smoking a cigarette, came out of the office and recognized Qi instantly.

'What are you doing here? How's it going?' the man said, with a false grin.

'I'm doing fine, thanks,' Qi answered confidently, with both his hands on his belt. 'I'm just dropping by with a few friends.'

'Dropping by?' the man raised his voice slightly, looking us up and down. 'All this way to Gaoyan village? Dropping by?'

'Yes, dropping by,' Qi repeated. 'My friends wanted to visit Wudi and the surrounding area.'

'Is that so?' the man turned to look at me again. 'You are interested in Wudi?'

Not knowing how to respond, I just nodded.

'And, by the way,' Qi didn't wait long to get to the point. 'I would like to talk to you about my *issue*.'

The man was taken aback for a second. He looked at Xiao Zheng and me uncomfortably, and said to Qi, 'Come into the room to talk.'

Qi followed the man into the room that we thought was the office. Ten minutes passed. I tried to look through the window, but couldn't see through the green mosquito net that covered it, even from a few feet away. The workers in the distance were still loading bricks and no one was watching us now.

'I think we should go in,' I said to Xiao Zheng.

'Don't worry. They won't do anything to him. It probably wouldn't be OK if he'd come here alone. The man in charge wouldn't have been so reserved. They never like people asking for wages. But because we are here, Qi will be all right.'

I looked around. There were hundreds of rows of unburned bricks laid out on acres of land, all covered with plastic sheets. This was a vast place with a huge amount of work to do and everyone minding his own business. The disappearance of one person would not draw any attention. If Qi had been alone and the bosses had got tough, no one would have known what happened to him.

Five minutes later, I started to worry again and urged Xiao Zheng to go into the office with me to find Qi. He hesitated, then agreed. We knocked and went in. Inside the tiny space, three square metres furnished with a desk, two chairs, and an old electric ceiling fan, the man sat facing the window, chatting with Qi about how the business had been doing in recent months. He ignored our presence completely. Xiao Zheng and I stood there, listening, not saying a word (and I didn't think Qi would have wanted us to). 'We are taking losses at the moment,' the man said to Qi quietly, shaking his head. 'Business is in decline.' There was no mention of Qi's wages.

A few minutes passed. Qi waved at us to indicate that it was time for us to leave. Qi and the man both got out of their chairs, and the man politely handed him a cigarette, as a good-will gesture, and escorted the three of us out of the room.

As we walked away, I asked Qi if he had gotten his wages.

'No. He said if I come next time, he will have the cash for me. But not now – not my half year's wages. I expected this, actually. These bastards. I knew I wouldn't get the money back. But just a try.'

Qi had decided to put it behind him. It was no use fighting the kiln bosses, he murmured. He simply didn't have the resources. 'I could only use you and Xiao Zheng as an excuse to come here,' he said to me, shaking his head.

He tried not to show he was depressed, and suggested that we take a walk around the kiln. As he had told the man in charge that we were visiting the area, we'd been given special permission to tour the site. Qi led us up the side stairs to the roof of the brick-burning tower, built in the shape of an ancient city wall. On the roof were chimneys with huge amounts of smoke coming out, making a great deal of noise. We stood looking down at the bare-chested men loading and unloading bricks nonstop on the ground floor. We could also see the entire vast field of unburnt bricks. Then Qi pointed to the small shacks in the righthand corner of the site and said, 'That's where the workers sleep.'

'Where do the bricks go?' I asked. And Qi told me about Fu Huacheng, the wealthiest man in Wudi. The number one. A 'local snake' (*ditoushe*), a phrase that signifies an embodiment of the local powers that be. Fu, he said, controlled and monopolized all sales from the kiln. The kiln was obliged to sell half of its products at a discount of 20 percent to the 'snake', who acted as the kiln's protection front. Out of 30 million bricks, 15 million had to go to him at that special price. 'There is no way round it,' said Qi. 'Even when a kiln isn't doing well. This man is so influential that no kiln owner dares to say no to him. He controls the majority of brick production in this area and beyond – as far as Tianjin.'

Like the rest of China's economic elite, Fu was not only wealthy but also politically well connected. His son-in-law ran a number of state-owned tobacco factories in the area. In fact, most brick kilns have this same criminal involvement. The local snakes work with the local authorities – black and white paths to the same gains, as people say. Many kilns, like this one, have party officials as their shareholders and local snakes as their guards.

As we walked to the workers' shacks, Qi told me that many workers have migrated here with their entire families. Parents brought their underage children with them, he said, and instead of going to school, the kids worked with their parents driving the brick carts. We saw a few women workers washing their clothes in a sink outside the shacks. Through a door, I could see a number of workers still in their teens. Unfortunately, neither the women nor the children were willing to talk.

Qi said that this kiln had always employed underage workers, who put in long hours for less pay. I asked how the kiln bosses continued to get away with this, even after the scandal in 2007.

'When public security officers visited once in a while as part of their local patrol, the kiln boss would lay out a good feast to shut them up, or "flatten" them, as they call it,' said Qi knowingly.

Xiao Zheng laughed. 'What a familiar story,' he said.

Some workers do quit – for the same reason that Qi did. A group of Sichuanese were owed six months' wages. They demanded payment; the kiln delayed endlessly. Eventually, the workers decided to throw down their tools. Their strike was easy to organize, because they all came from Sichuan and worked and lived together as a community. Thanks to this solidarity, their action stopped production completely. The kiln boss was furious, not only because he'd lost money but also because he felt he'd lost face, from having such a 'disobedient' workforce. He asked the labour contractor to replace all of the Sichuanese with new workers. That was easy enough for the contractor to do. He sent all the Sichuanese to Taiyuan, and brought in migrants from his own province, Hebei. These workers were much more docile. Not a peep out of them.

As we were speaking, the well-tanned Mr Yu walked up. Qi whispered to me that this was the labour contractor, who worked at the kilns, where he did supervision, and at recruitment sites in Hebei and other provinces. He was frowning at the sight of us. Maybe he sensed trouble.

Yu recognized Qi immediately. 'What's the matter?' he said. 'What are you doing here?'

'Just looking around. My friend here' – Qi pointed to me, improvising – 'she's from Taiwan and she might move up here to do brick kiln business. If you want more business, talk to her.' Xiao Zheng and I looked at each other and tried not to laugh.

And it worked. Yu began bowing to me repeatedly, trying to sound hospitable as he said, 'You like it here in Gaoyan village? Have you been to see other kilns yet?'

He told me he came from Chengde, a prefecture-level city in Hebei, and had been in the brick business for more than a decade. He eagerly exchanged contact details with me and said he looked forward to 'future interest' from me.

I knew that the workers here had to pay the recruiters a minimum of one tenth of their total wages, on top of the money the recruiters made directly from the kiln owners. Yu bragged that his annual income was around 300,000 yuan (£27,000, $47,628) – which would support a very comfortable life in Gaoyan village or even back home in Chengde.

'My workers can earn up to 3,000 yuan per year if and when the workload increases,' he continued. 'Better than what they can get working on their land.'

I nodded. He had no idea that I knew how often those wages were paid late – or that sometimes they weren't paid at all.

'Would you like to come into the room for some tea?' he asked me. But Qi was eager to leave the site, as the manager had just come out of his office again. I promised Yu that I would at another time, when I returned to visit Dong Sheng brick kiln again.

5

'Bad Elements': The Uprooted and the Permanently Impoverished in Shandong

Shandong had seen another kind of exodus besides the migration of poor peasants: the migration of the 'enemy class' of the poor peasants. I learned about this when I went back there a few months later on a personal mission: to accompany my mother on her trip 'home' – or, more accurately, her home province, which she'd left more than sixty years before.

Today, she lives in Taipei, the capital of Taiwan, retired after a career as a preschool educator. But she was born in Gaolu village in 1942, to a landowning family that also owned a variety of businesses in the village. Gaolu is located within the precincts of Rizhao, a prefecture-level city, in the south of the Shandong Peninsula. The Civil War had great impact on this region's economy in the late 1940s, when the CCP first began to experiment with land reforms. The idea was to abolish the landowning class by confiscating privately held land and distributing it to the landless peasants. The first, sporadic trials were made in small sections of the country, such as Shandong, where there were larger numbers of landowners. These early reform measures resulted in a small peasant economy before the People's Republic of China was established in 1949. Later, the Land Reform Law, promulgated in June 1950, would transform this private peasant ownership into public ownership.

In the 1940s, my late grandfather – we called him *Gong-gong*, Granddad – owned five *mu* of land in Gaolu village. *Gong-gong*'s father, my great-grandfather, had been a large-scale landlord.

In his late life, he sold most of his land to provide medical treatment for his sick sons. He himself died of tuberculosis when my grandfather was only fourteen. The loss of his father had led my grandfather to want to study medicine and become a doctor. He had his first glimpse into that world when he was seventeen, from some Western missionaries who came into the village to teach basic medicine and preach. Following his teacher's advice, he travelled all the way to Shanghai to buy books on medicine. He memorized the entire medical dictionary and became a self-taught pharmacist. Eventually, he opened a pharmacy in the village, naming it Qinghua Great Pharmacist. As my mother recalled, our grandfather loved his medical equipment and used to carry a medicine bag around, giving villagers vaccinations. He also set up a post office, a bakery and a textile factory.

'Then, in 1945, the CCP began to gain ground, after two decades of civil war against the Nationalists,' my mother told me. During the war, the CCP had won wholehearted support from the peasantry, who had seen them as much more determined than the Nationalists to fight the Japanese. Sick and tired of the corrupt Kuomintang, peasants hoped the CCP would restore what was theirs and change their destiny. By 1946, the People's Liberation Army had grown to 1.2 million troops and had taken over one fourth of the country. By late 1948, they had captured the northeast. Everywhere they went, they gained control in the countryside much earlier than in the cities. In Shandong, Nationalist troops were stationed all over the province, but in early 1947, everyone in town was talking about the Communist army coming in. My mother's family began to prepare to flee, fearful of being punished when the troops took over their land.

In mid 1947, when my mother was six, the family left the village. 'Your granddad took all of us with him on a route away from Gaolu one night. I didn't know why we were leaving; children weren't told. I didn't have time to say good-bye to anyone. Your granddad was carrying only a small suitcase. We walked in the dark, through the woods. We were taken to a village called Baytuan, where we stayed with our relatives for about a year. It was only later that I realized that our home in Gaolu was taken by the Communists and that was why we had to flee.

'When they came, they turned our land into a school, and my eighty-year-old great-grandfather, who didn't want to leave home, was beaten to death,' my mother said. This family story had been retold over and over again since we were kids. But we were always spared the details of what actually happened: Had her great-grandfather refused to hand over the land? We will never know.

At the time, my mother and her family were warned by the Baytuan villagers not to travel in a large group, so Granddad left for Qingdao alone. Next he arranged for his eldest son to travel there to join him. And then Grandma, my mother, and her other two brothers:

'That day, your grandma bought our pass tickets and took us, together with her beloved younger sister, to travel from Baytuan to the fishing port Shijiusuo. There was no bus, train, or any other vehicle. We travelled on foot. I remember the roads being very rough... There were a lot of other people walking together with us during the night. When the sun rose, we hid ourselves in a small inn. When the dusk came, we started walking again. I still remember the fear when your grandma warned me not to cry or make any noise. "The wolves are around us!" she said. I was so terrified!

'When we arrived at Shijiusuo, your grandma and young aunt were crying bitterly. I saw people gathering around them asking what had happened. Then I was told that my second-older brother had gone missing! He had walked too fast and lost himself in the middle of nowhere. Your grandma was devastated. By chance, he'd walked right into the camp of a Communist troop. They took him in, but didn't know what to do with him when they were leaving the area. A childless couple nearby asked to keep him. Eventually, your grandma was able to locate him through some other villagers. This was why we stayed in Shijiusuo a few days longer than planned.

'On the night of departure, we all sneaked onto a little boat that was only able to accommodate twenty to thirty people. There was a terrible smell on the boat – I wasn't sure what it was. Could it be someone's vomit? I myself almost vomited. Everybody slept on his own luggage through the night. I felt so frightened. We arrived at Qingdao in the early morning. Your granddad was there to meet us at the port and took us to a flat on Jiangsu Road.'

We were standing right in front of the port at Shijiusuo while my mother recalled her escape on a boat. Fish and shrimps were piled up along the side of the road. Villagers were working busily on hundreds of small fishing boats. Today, Shijiusuo is also a national centre for sailing competitions. It has expanded and become part of Rizhao city. I focused my camera on my mother and the fishing port that had given her a new life. She didn't feel like lingering at the scene of that escape, though. 'Let's leave. Something smells badly here,' she said, frowning.

During the family's stay in Qingdao, Grandfather became a doctor in a navy hospital, the Shandong Sanitation Hospital. His job was to provide medical care for the people who had fled their hometowns during the ongoing, fierce Civil War. The family home on Jiangsu Road was a single very crowded room. 'Your granddad lived in the hospital dormitory, away from us. I remember he was in a blue navy uniform every time I saw him. He was very handsome.'

As a former landowner, Granddad was always a loyal supporter of the Kuomintang (KMT), although he didn't join the party. He was never a very political person. But he continued to serve as a doctor in the Nationalist navy after leaving Qingdao and continuing his flight from the PLA. By then the Nationalist troops were facing defeat everywhere, and after losing their capital, Nanjing, to the CCP, they retreated to Canton, then Chongqing, and finally Chengdu. By the end of 1949 they had been chased out of the country.

Following the defeat of the Kuomintang, my mother's family left Qingdao on a navy ship. They docked in a town called Dinghai, in

Zhejiang province in the south. They spent a year there, waiting to
see the turn of political events. My mother remembered the town
canal, where people did their clothes-washing and cleaning. Often,
there was a water shortage and they had to set out buckets to catch
rain for drinking. She was sent to a Dinghai primary school. One
day, a year later, the family was put on a navy ship again. This
time, they weren't sure where the ship was taking them. 'Hainan
Island', they'd heard. But the ship eventually turned in the direction of another island, called Taiwan. No one had any idea what
Taiwan was like. But my mother's family repeated what they'd
been told by others on the ship: It is an island where birds don't fly
and flowers don't grow. On seventeenth-century maps of China,
Taiwan was called Yizhou, 'the barbaric land'.

Their first stop on Taiwan, in that autumn of 1949, was a navy
base near Kaoshung, the second-largest city on the island. The
family was lodged in the Navy's First Hospital, where temporary housing had been prepared for the new arrivals. My mother
remembered playing in the fields outside the hospital every day.
'We chased after dogs and pigs, dug up sweet potatoes, climbed
trees to pick fruits, caught butterflies and other kinds of insects. I
didn't go to kindergarten. That was my kindergarten.'

The family stayed in Kaoshung for a few months and then were
moved to Magong, a town in Penghu, an archipelago belonging to
Taiwan, where another navy hospital was located. Magong was a
pretty town full of shops selling beautiful coral and precious stones.
My mother said, 'I saw my first flowers in Taiwan there – I never
knew flowers before. I thought they were beautiful. Your grandma
liked them, too.'

They lived in the navy dormitory in a military harbour called
Tse Tian Dao. There were long stretches of clean, white sand. It
was like having a beach outside their house, my mother recalled,
and the children used to do a lot of swimming. Many navy families
shared a big yard, which became their social venue. But Grandma
rarely went out to chat with the neighbours. She stayed indoors,
thinking about the family she'd left in China. Her youngest sister

had not come with them to Taiwan, because the family didn't want to be burdened with 'too many mouths to feed'.

That was the story of how my mother came to an island that her family saw as a temporary shelter and that she hasn't really identified as her 'home' until recently, although she and her family became part of Taiwan's so-called Mainlanders – the political term for the Chinese elite who emigrated with the Kuomintang regime, who became the ruling clique that controlled the state apparatuses on the island.

The Kuomintang began making preparations for taking over Taiwan in 1944, following the resolutions made in the Cairo Declaration in 1943, in which the island was promised to Chiang Kai-shek in return for his cooperation in fighting against the Japanese. Taiwan was treated as a war prize, just as it had been when it was given to Japan by the Treaty of Shimonoseki of 1895, beginning a period of Japanese rule that lasted until 1945. The Taiwan Investigation Committee was formed in 1944, headed by Kuomintang general Chen Yi. The administrative body of the committee was staffed only by Chen's own personnel. The Kuomintang government administration and the police took over posts occupied previously by the Japanese colonizers and maintained a state bureaucracy that completely excluded the Taiwanese, and was similar in nature to the Japanese government-general. The Taiwan Office of the Chief Administrator differed from the representative system of provincial governments in China. The Chief Administrator was given administrative, legislative, judicial and military power, with a position equivalent to the governor-general during Japanese rule. The Kuomintang also took over and monopolized former colonial industries. The monopoly worked through a system in which the members of the Government's Confiscated Property Commission controlled and directed the operations of the commission by creating a new series of subsidiary commissions, each devoted to a specialized category of enterprise or property. Within each commission, management committees were formed to control enterprises, and then transformed into a board of directors.

Under this hierarchy, the commission that oversaw the confiscated companies ran them as private enterprises. Through this official-merchant monopoly structure, the interests of the new elite were fully secured. The Kuomintang used the resources and wealth of the island to ease crises on the mainland. The new Kuomintang government was soon nicknamed by many Taiwanese the New Government-General.

Between January 1946 and February 1947, the Taiwanese had their first taste of the Kuomintang rule: The monopoly system made corruption very easy, and that worsened inflation. Taiwan being used as a supplier for the mainland also led to a shortage of rice and a dramatic rise in prices. Both rice and sugar prices became much higher than those in Shanghai and Hong Kong. As the unemployment rate increased sharply, ordinary islanders were finding it harder and harder to survive. As if this were not enough, the Taiwanese had to tolerate the corruption and brutality of the Kuomintang army.

The 28 February Massacre began with a street incident in Taipei involving the Monopoly Commission staff and a female Taiwanese cigarette vendor. Their violent behaviour toward the woman enraged the crowd. During the confrontation, one man in the crowd was shot dead by the commission staff. This sparked off a series of island-wide city uprisings beginning on the morning of 28 February 1947. People rallied to demonstrate their anger against the presence of the army and police and their brutal intervention in people's everyday lives, and against unemployment and the imposition of a system of inequality that favoured Mainlanders over the islanders.

When more Nationalist troops entered the island from Keelung and Kaohsiung, on 8 March, the bloodshed began. The troops went into Taipei, and from 9–13 March, Taipei was a killing field. My late grandmother, my father's mother, remembered Taipei's Danshui River becoming a river of blood. Estimates of the number of deaths vary from 10,000 to 30,000, or more. The massacre marked the beginning of the Kuomintang's rule of White Terror on the island, during which thousands were imprisoned, persecuted, and executed for political dissent. The native Taiwanese became a subordinated majority, just as they had under Japanese rule.

In the following four decades, the only way a native Taiwanese could take a job in the civil service was by joining the Kuomintang. The KMT aimed to expand its youth membership by recruiting in schools and colleges, via the party organization Educated Youth (*Zhiqing*). My father, a native Taiwanese, was pressured to join and recruited into the party by the headmaster of Beidou High School, where he was a student. When he went to study at the University of Politics in Taipei, he was granted a Sun Yat-sen Scholarship (available only to Kuomintang members), which enabled him to study in the US.

To this day, my father has not forgotten what the Kuomintang dictatorship was like in those days. He remembered that once the Party wanted to punish him for having recommended that they recruit an outstanding political science student named Lu Xiuyi, because twenty years later he was found to be studying Marxism and in the early 1980s was singled out as a 'Communist spy'. (Lu Xiuyi later became a politician working for the pro-independence opposition.)

My father's parents had been teachers during Japanese rule. Like many native Taiwanese, at first they welcomed the island's 'return to the motherland' after Japan surrendered, but the brutality of the Kuomintang regime soon disillusioned them. Their resentment and anger became part of the deep social division between natives and the Mainlanders. There was little social interaction between the two groups then, and no intermarriages except between Kuomintang soldiers (who later retired in Taiwan) and native women. Taiwanese men rarely married Mainland women. My father, however, met my mother when both were studying in the US. As students, they felt free and were able to break through the social barriers and disparities that might have separated them in Taiwan. Although my parents said there was no real objection from either of their families to their marriage, nevertheless the families have always felt hostile toward and kept a distance from each other.

One thing I remember most clearly about growing up under the Kuomintang dictatorship was the military education and anti-Communist indoctrination in our schools. We were given compulsory lessons and training by military instructors who exercised their authority independent of the school administration. As adolescents, we were trained to use rifles and told that 'recovering China' was a historical mission. As teenagers, we were crammed with the idea that China, a country we'd never seen in our lives, was our motherland. 'Recovering China' was the Kuomintang watchword throughout the Cold War period. Every day, when we entered the school grounds we were forced to bow to Chiang Kai-shek's statue inside the gate. We were forbidden to speak our own dialects or languages at school; only Mandarin was allowed. Speaking the native Taiwanese languages in public was generally frowned upon and treated with contempt. We were made to learn and memorize China's history instead of Taiwan's. Children grew up not knowing anything about their island's history of colonization and resistance, that is, they were educated as native children had been during the Japanese rule. In my youth, therefore, I secretly rejected the notions of 'roots seeking' and returning home that were trumpeted by Mainlanders, as expressions of a reactionary nostalgia encouraged by the Kuomintang's anticommunist, 'reunificationist' propaganda. When I entered the university in the late 1980s, nothing had changed, and the first student demonstration that I took part in was against the military presence in our universities.

Despite the 'recovering China' ideology, the return home to China has taken decades for many. When the Kuomintang regime established itself in Taiwan, it declared martial law, maintained that China was the enemy state, and operated under Cold War policies that closed off any form of transportation or communication between the island and the mainland. For many years, there was no postal service between the two countries. My mother's family had ambiguous feelings about this situation because they still had relatives in China. The precious letter they received once a year from their aunt and cousins in China was sent to a mutual friend in Hong Kong and redirected to Taiwan from there. But one letter a year hardly seemed enough.

Things began changing in 1987, when civil movements for democratization and against the Kuomintang's quasi-colonial rule created so much pressure on the ruling clique that they were forced to loosen their grip on Taiwanese society in order to survive. Martial law and the cross-strait travel ban (imposed only by Taiwan's government) were lifted, and Taiwan's people were finally permitted to travel to China – albeit only via a third country.

In 1989, I travelled to China for the first time, alone, though not out of loyalty to family ties so much as curiosity about whether life was different under a self-proclaimed socialist regime – and also as a rebellion against the idea, force-fed to me throughout my life, that China was an 'enemy state'.

I had actually kept my travel plans a secret, worried that my parents might be too concerned about my travelling alone and might stop me from going. When I arrived in Hong Kong, my transit country, I wrote them a postcard, saying, 'I'll be in China and will be back in a week. Don't worry.' As a student, I couldn't afford to stay longer, anyway.

All excited, I arrived in Guilin city, Guangxi province. I'd chosen Guilin because of its reputation for a peaceful environment and beautiful landscape. All true. It was a tranquil place and there wasn't much traffic. I was really impressed with the way people relied on bicycles as their main transport. The sight of cyclists riding leisurely along wide green avenues shaded by oak trees was refreshing. The air was crisp and fresh – much less polluted than Taipei's. I found the simplicity of the town's culture appealing and admired its social atmosphere. I enjoyed watching people playing chess in the alleyways and listening to people chat and socialize in parks. As the travel ban had just been lifted, there was a lot of curiosity on China's side of the Strait too, and it was easy to attract a crowd wherever I went. Local people, men and women, were eager to talk, and ask questions about me and my hometown. In the Friendship Store, the boys behind the counter giggled and asked, 'Where are you from?' 'What is it like over there?' 'Is Taipei prosperous?'

I went on a four-hour cruise down the Li River to Yangshuo, a small city in Guilin's prefecture. I stood on the deck, gazing at the karst mountains along the river. Another traveller, a man with very curly hair that he admitted was permed – unusual for a Chinese male in those days – was there, taking photographs with an old camera. He told me he lived in suburban Beijing and was on holiday from his job as a technician in a state-owned firm. He asked me what life was like in Taiwan. Then he said that Deng Xiaoping had initiated economic reforms and that these might lead people out of their 'economic stagnation'. He waved his camera in front of me, smiled and said, 'I wouldn't be able to afford this without the economic reforms.' 'Yes, some people probably have already benefited,' I said. We exchanged addresses and corresponded with each other, through Hong Kong, for a year or two. In his letters, he talked about buying an apartment in his area and about his future travel plans. He said he might be going back to Guangxi again; he liked visiting rural areas on holidays. He also told me that he was planning to get married soon, to a colleague of his. A few months later, in his last letter, he told me that the company had made him redundant. I haven't heard from him since.

Just before the train pulled into the Qingdao station, two police officers came walking up and down the aisle of my carriage with their detectors, checking to see if anyone might be carrying explosives. I was travelling to Qingdao to meet my mother, still on her 'roots' journey, to help her look for the flat where she and her family had lived for a year after fleeing their village in Rizhao. She wanted to see it again with her own eyes. The traditional view in Chinese agricultural communities was that people should remain home and not travel far. Loyalty to your hometown was both expected and valued. But this has changed dramatically and irreversibly in the past three decades in China. Peasants are forced by circumstances to travel anywhere to bring in a higher income, and the ability to do so is now seen as an achievement that the family can be proud of. China's peasants have become migrants cut loose from the land. The value that they bring to hometown and homeland is rooted in their transience.

Most Westerners know Qingdao as the home of the Tsingtao Brewery and the Olympic sailing competition of 2008, not as a cheap-labour economy, though this apparently booming city depends on low wages for its prosperity. Qingdao, with a population of over 8.7 million, has a GDP of 42.3 billion yuan and ranks tenth among China's top twenty cities in terms of prosperity and growth. This is where most of the development in Shandong province is concentrated. According to Jiang Daming, the governor of Shandong, the creation of a high-end manufacturing industrial zone is the priority here, and most of the budget of 1.6 trillion yuan made available to initiate the scheme has been allocated to an infrastructure-construction programme. In 2009, 335 key construction projects, representing a combined investment of 337.4 billion yuan, were initiated in Qingdao. The unspoken truth is that most of those toiling away to make this city a success are migrants, mainly from Hebei province and the northeast, working in construction and the tourism-led service industries.

Qingdao, like so many of the cities I visited, has a dramatic history. In the late nineteenth century, the Germans adopted it as one of their deep-water navy ports. Kaiser Wilhelm expanded Germany's sphere of influence in China by using the murder of two German missionaries during the Boxer Rebellion as his pretext to demand a concession from China's Qing rulers. Wilhelm spoke of a 'yellow peril' and threatened to declare war. The weak Qing imperial court ceded the city – and the right to build railways in Shandong – to Germany on a ninety-nine-year lease. In 1919, at Versailles, the city was given to Japan as a reward for Japan's support of the Allies in the First World War. For Shandong's people, that was the most humiliating page in their entire history. One of the demands of the May Fourth Movement was 'Give back Qingdao!' The city was returned to China following the Washington Conference of 1922.

It was midnight when I arrived there. My mother had checked into a four-star hotel in the old district of town. At her age she felt entitled to comfort when she travelled. I benefited from that – she'd booked a double room.

When I got out of the cab, she was standing there waiting at the front door of the hotel. Typically, she rushed over and paid the fare for me. It was good to see that she hadn't changed in three years. She was smartly dressed in a silk top and black skirt. Her short hair was still black and shiny. At sixty-eight, she was still active and full of energy.

As we sat down on our beds in the hotel room, face to face with each other at last, we chatted as we had every two weeks on the phone, as if distance didn't matter. I suppose we'd got used to living in different parts of the world a long time ago. She told me what the family was doing and relayed apologies from those who couldn't come to see me in China – especially my hardworking younger brother, a postgraduate from a university in Britain. She said he hadn't been able to get even a few days' break from the management, who clearly overworked him. As they said, if you threw bricks from a window and hit ten passers-by, nine of them would be MAs. Competition in Taiwan was fierce, and with the economic downturn, jobs were hard to keep. As for my father, well, my sister had gone on holiday to Sweden, and pleaded with him to stay home and look after her pedigreed cat.

My mother was eager to tell me her adventures. She couldn't wait to see the home she remembered here, and had begun her search by herself, at midday. 'I went out and started looking for Jiangsu Road immediately after I put down my luggage,' she told me. The apartment she had lived in was a five-floor building with a spiral staircase in an open central yard, and she had walked down the street trying to locate the house in her memory.

'At first I didn't see anything that resembled it in the slightest. I thought to myself, The flat is just gone! I felt desperate. I walked to and fro along the street and everything seemed wrong. How could it be, though? I tried so hard to bring back my memory. Think! Think! I said to myself. Finally, near the end of Jiangsu Road, I found something – the iron net covers of some basement windows along the right-hand sidewalk. A trivial thing, but it brought back my memories! Every day when I came home from school, I would walk past those iron nets and curiously peep through the windows. But I still could not find our flat.

'I remember it being really warm in the summer ... My two brothers took a straw mat to sleep on the roof. They sometimes brought me with them. And I remembered the first fruit we had. Your grandma called it foreign sweet potato. "Come and eat the foreign sweet potato," she said. In fact, it was a banana.'

There'd been a little surprise at the end of her search that day. 'Do you know what I saw at the end of Jiangsu Road?' she asked as I unpacked my suitcase. 'A Shandong chive-pancake vendor! I pointed to the pancake and asked the seller what it was called. "*Ha bing*," he answered. Yes! *Ha bing!* That's right! *Ha bing!* I remember that's what it was called when I was a kid.'

The next morning, to avoid the hassle of finding transport, my mother asked the local travel agency to send us a guide. As we headed toward the Qingdao beach, the guide introduced herself as Xiao Niu – literally meaning 'little cow'. She reminds me of Gong Li, the well-known actress, who also comes from Shandong. 'Shall we ask her if she's interested in getting acquainted with a Taiwanese boy?' my mother whispered to me in the backseat, already thinking of matchmaking her with my then thirty-one-year-old unmarried brother. 'Qingdao is the fourth-largest port in China,' Xiao Niu recited from memory, in her soft, elegant voice, as we looked out the window at the crowded beach.

She was telling us how the city had been chosen to host the sailing events of the Olympics, and I could immediately see why: It is a deep-water port with beautiful white sand. Xiao Niu seemed to want to carry on quickly with the tour, and asked the driver to take us to the Buddhist temples on Lao Mountain, half an hour away by car. Along the way, we saw Qingdao's semicolonial history clearly written in the Bavarian red-roofed buildings, the churches, and the enclaves of European-style villas in various parts of the city, especially those facing the beach, which now house the new rich created by the money the government is putting into the development of the city.

Our driver, Mr Wu, happened to be a migrant from Hubei. He'd been working for the tour agency for five years. He said that housing costs were rising like mad as the city was gentrified by incoming investors. 'It's been taken over by the new rich. They have jacked up the price of real estate here. For us outsiders, even renting is really tough.' Xiao Niu chimed in and said that she certainly couldn't afford renting a place of her own, and was living with her parents. She added that most college graduates of her age were in a similar situation. Yet she tried to be content. 'I'm quite lucky, really. At least I have a regular job. I studied hard to pass the exam to work as a guide.'

Later in the afternoon, when the tour ended, I offered to accompany my mother back to Jiangsu Road. We walked slowly along the street in this old district of west Qingdao. The air was unusually crisp. The trees on two sides of the road had grown to form a beautiful shade, leaving only a crack of the sunlight shining through the leaves in the middle of the road. My mother decided to look for the school that she had attended at the age of six. It was quite easy to find; it was the only one on Jiangsu Road. Its name had been changed to Qingdao Experimental Primary School, the words lettered in gold on the wall facing the street. At the front gate, we could see a wide flight of stone stairs leading up to a new, handsome-looking building. 'I know it's the right place, although somehow it doesn't look or feel like it. But I still recognize it. The entrance. The location…' My mother sighed thoughtfully. 'Aren't human memories untrustworthy? The little school that stayed in my memory for these sixty years is just different from the school in front of my eyes.'

As we sat down to a plate of Shandong dumplings in a café near the school, she recalled the old days: 'I remember the nicknames people used to call me at school – *Hsiao-sha-gua* (Little Nut). All of the school kids were well dressed and neat, but I guess I wasn't. I wrote on toilet paper with a pencil of the poorest quality. I remember my young aunt always sharpening the pencil for me, because it broke so easily. I was the only one from the countryside. I used to feel so inferior to them. I felt like hiding myself at school. I never paid attention to what the teachers were saying … and in fact I did not understand what they said at all. I didn't know anything; I might have been the last in my class. I remember my eldest brother holding my hand, helping me to write with a brush pen. God, school was not a happy place.'

Next day my mother was eager to go on to her birthplace in Rizhao. *Rizhao* literally means 'the sun shines'. For over six decades, Mother had lived with a blurred memory of its beauty – a spacious place with green fields and, of course, sunshine. During our two and a half hours on the bus from Qingdao, she spoke little. Only once she turned to me and said, 'You know, Rizhao is well known for its environmental projects. It uses solar power.'

After passing through a lifeless, concrete-coloured town centre with neon lights slowly lighting up, we finally arrived at Rizhao Cinema, our stop. A fiftyish man with grey hair walked up to us and shook my mother's hand and introduced himself: Grandma's adopted son, Mr Lin. Then he introduced us to his son Fulin, a serious-looking man dressed in a black suit, a successful banker in Rizhao. Fulin took us to the parking lot and helped us load my mother's bags of gifts into his car. When we arrived at our hotel in the town centre, we found everyone from the family in Rizhao in the lobby waiting for us. Mr Lin and Fulin walked us into the marble-floored hall, and a frail-looking woman in her eighties, with a hairpin in her white hair, came up to my mother. She held up her hands.

'Judeh!' she cried.

'Auntie!' said my mother, warmly embracing her. 'It's been a long time!' There was more curiosity than sadness in their faces. It had been sixty years and I wondered if they really did recognize each other. (My mother told me later that in fact she had not recognized her aunt.) She was my great-aunt (*gu-po*), the one who had looked after my mother when the parents were busy, back in Gaolu. She had told my mother children's stories, and sometimes taken her along on her stroll into the centre of the village.

Great-aunt and my mother couldn't let go of each other's hands and couldn't wait to tell their stories –about how they had separated, about how my great-aunt had decided to stay behind, how she'd got married and coped with hardship in all these six decades. The stories of their entire lives. But where would they begin?

Each of the fifteen family members was watching this reunion intensely. They were all dressed well for the event. When the two women embraced, they all remained silent, just as I did. They all looked unsure what to do. Some went up to my mother, waiting to shake her hands. Others nodded and smiled politely to me, without a word. Perhaps everyone was wondering the same thing – how do you express emotions appropriately to a family member you know so little about? The only thing I'd heard about my relatives in Shandong was that my great-aunt was supported by her two daughters. The only thing that these relatives had heard about my mother was that her husband was a politician – and they'd got my father's name completely wrong. Everyone was overwhelmed by this long-awaited reunion, but the only people here who had ever met in their lives were my mother and her aunt.

I was more confused than anyone else, and was particularly unsure how to address the family: the titles for different family members are extremely complex in Chinese, and I'd never had the opportunity to use all these titles in Taiwan. Every Chinese person knows that relations on the female and male side of the family are addressed differently. But distant relatives and their descendents present more difficult problems. For instance, an uncle on your mother's side is called *jiu* or *jiujiu*, and your grandfather's brother should be addressed as *jiu-gong*. But I didn't have any idea what to call the son or daughter of a *jiu-gong*. Most complex is when you are not related by blood but by adoption. How was I to address Mr Lin's son and daughter? And what about his son-in-law? Or my great-aunt's daughter and her husband? Let alone their son? Instead, I tried to memorize all their names, although generally it's considered impolite to address your elders by their first names.

This emotional first meeting was followed by a glamorous dinner in the hotel itself. My great-aunt and my mother led the way to the dining room, walking in front of everyone, and I followed after the rest. I stood around at the back, politely waiting for the others to find their seats next to their immediate family members.

Cold starters of cucumbers and garlic squid were served, although no one really paid much attention to the food. Their eyes were all still on my mother and her aunt, who were talking about *Gong-gong*'s character as they remembered it. 'Your father was a good man,' Grandaunt said sorrowfully. 'People knew he was a landlord who employed labourers, but they didn't know he was also a decent man. You wouldn't remember when the Japanese came in the late 1930s... Back then, the villagers were all terrified. No one knew what kind of trouble the invaders would bring. Our family owned many houses, and the local officials lent them to the Japanese, to placate them. But the Japanese still wanted your father to work for them. During the invasion, some landowners did become *han-jian*, "Han traitors."[1] Your father was not that kind of man. He didn't want to collaborate with the invaders – that was the last thing he'd ever do. But you know what the Japanese were like – they'd coerce you into working for them. So your father went into hiding, staying in different houses around the village. Even then, he didn't forget to bring his medical box with him.'

The main course arrived: steamed prawns, Four Happiness meatballs made with chilli pepper and rice wine, spicy crab, Shandong tofu, about twenty delicious dishes in all, with every kind of meat under the sun, either steamed or cooked Shandong style.

Grandaunt was whispering to my mother. My mother told me

later that Grandaunt was apologizing to her for having been a village bully when she was young. As a landlord's daughter, she'd been a spoiled child, as she described herself to my mother, and an arrogant teenager. She had treated her sister-in-law, my grandmother, badly too, and now regretted it.

As we ate, Grandaunt's son-in-law, Li Yi, kept piling expensive cigarettes – Su Yan brand, a few hundred yuan a packet – in front of me, a typical friendly gesture to a smoking guest.

Mr Lin's son-in-law was a local official in the transport department. From the humble way everyone addressed him, I could see he was the pride of the family. He wore a suit and was polite and dignified. He toasted me with sorghum wine, and drank it up. Everyone cheered. He said he'd be visiting London on a business trip the next year, and handed me his business card. I hadn't brought mine, so I scribbled my contact details on a piece of paper and handed it to him. He then asked me curiously, 'Do you belong to the blue camp or the green camp?' In Taiwan, the 'blue camp' is the pro-unification, pro-Kuomintang faction, and 'green camp' is the pro-independence, pro-opposition group. The colours refer to the flags of the Kuomintang and the Democratic Progressive Party. 'Neither,' I said. My mother had suggested that I avoid talking politics with the relatives, and I tried to divert the conversation to Chinese communities in Britain. But he was persistent and started to critique the greens.

My mother's cousin Xia, my *biao-yi* (now I knew how to address her, but I will call her Xia), smiled at me warmly and asked what type of Shandong food I liked most. 'Miangeda,' I said. She laughed, because miangeda, a local soup made of flour and vegetables was what people cooked to use up leftovers. Xia told me she was a nurse in a hospital ward. Her husband, a doctor, ran his own clinic. They led a busy life as members of Rizhao's urban, professional middle class. He earned 3,000 yuan a month (£254), Xia slightly less. Their joint income would be enviable in the eyes of many in Rizhao. They could cover the cost of a full education for their only son (who was home that night reviewing his lessons); they'd even considered sending him to a university abroad someday. During summer holidays, they were able to send him on excursions all over China. But the couple weren't content.

Xia's husband Li Yi sighed and said that Rizhao's average income is only three fifths that of Beijing – they were still far below the middle classes of the capital. 'We don't have the same consumer power as in Beijing!' he said. Also, they felt overworked: their income didn't reflect the effort they put into their jobs. They would have liked to work less and earn more, improve their quality of life, enjoy themselves – maybe take a holiday abroad – not just save up for their child's future.

Even so, the couple's relative affluence had given them self-confidence; they were comfortable sharing memories of the past. They described how China's social upheavals had transformed their lives, from the land reforms in the 1940s to the economic reforms since the late 1970s. Over a span of sixty years, they had gone from descendants of landowners to migrant proletarians to urban middle class.

Xia saw nothing wrong or regrettable in her mother's decision not to go to Taiwan with the family. Her mother, on the contrary, still dwelled on these memories. Grandaunt explained with much sorrow in her eyes that the choice between leaving her hometown and parting from her family was the hardest she'd ever made in her life. She had just married her husband and had a baby daughter, and was too afraid to leave China, even with them. Change is always frightening, she said, still holding my mother's hands. Going to a new place, leaving everything behind isn't easy. How could she raise her child in a strange island she knew nothing about? The unknown had been too much to contemplate. No matter what happens, they'd thought, this is home. Her voice grew fainter as she recalled what did happen. A few years after her family's departure to Taiwan, she had been singled out as a descendant of the landowning class and paraded down the street in Rizhao. It was the most humiliating experience she'd ever had. And although her husband was a poor peasant, he was never able to join the CCP, because his wife's ancestry branded everyone in her family as counter-revolutionaries.

One evening, Xia cooked miangeda and Shandong dumplings for us and invited us to visit them in their apartment. It was a nicely decorated three-bedroom flat in the centre of town, with a pretty balcony where she grew plants. Over dinner, she told me that her grandfather had been the wealthiest landlord in the village – something the family in Taipei had never told me. He had owned more than a hundred *mu* of land, a huge amount, while many peasants were starving. No wonder the Revolution had viewed him as an enemy.

In the aftermath of the Revolution, there were movements to 'de-class' the descendants of landlords, who were set apart from the rest of society, denied access to proper education and public life. Class, instead of being determined by ownership of the means of production and the relations of production, was seen as a static entity that could be passed down from generation to generation, as *hukou*, one's household registration, is today. In the practice of ideal Maoism, the only way to declass the descendants (including the most distant descendants) of the enemies of the Revolution was to deprive them of education and means of livelihood.

During the Cultural Revolution, Mao singled out nine categories of enemies: landlords, rich peasants, counter-revolutionaries, the criminally inclined, rightists, traitors, foreign agents, capitalist roaders and intellectuals (nicknamed the Stinking Ninth) and described them all as 'bad elements' – a vague category, which also included all persons related to counter-revolutionaries. Xia recalled that children of her background – descended from 'bad elements' – used to suffer a great deal of discrimination. Teachers in primary schools subjected them to public humiliation and verbal abuse and encouraged other students to do the same. In a lesson about land reforms, for instance, Xia would be pointed out as representing the landowning class. The children felt branded for life, and their actions and words were constantly being scrutinized, critiqued and punished. As a child, she often wondered why children were held responsible for the actions of their forebears.

Xia and others of her background had no choice but to leave – not just Rizhao, but Shandong province – in order to escape those who knew them and their class origins. Many people who were affected by the land reforms were leaving for the northeast – the further north, the better. Those who didn't go of their own accord were sent for labour re-education on northeastern farms and mines, where they would learn to repent the wrongdoings of their parents or grandparents. Xia's own brother, as a landlord's son, was sent to Jiamusi city, in Heilongjiang province in the northeast and put to work on a farm and, later, in the mines. Xia's mother decided to send Xia to stay with him, far away from the battle of the classes, where she could find a future. One day she put Xia on a northbound train, on her own, with just a small suitcase in her hand. From the window, Xia waved good-bye to her mother and her hometown. She had been uprooted. She was only eight.

Back then, it was common for people of a 'bad element' to move to another province. It was the only way to raise themselves from their reassigned position at the bottom of the social ladder in a new, revolutionary China.

So Xia began a new life in Jiamusi, near the beautiful Songhua River, not far from Russia. She stayed with her brother, who looked after her and sent her to a school there. He was poor, and was able to take in only Xia. Xia's elder sister, Yun, wasn't able to leave Rizhao, and so remained a peasant all her life.

Xia had been more fortunate, but growing up without her parents wasn't easy. In Jiamusi, she always felt like an orphan, and had to start from nothing, on the same social and economic level as the poor peasants in her village back in Shandong. This was indeed the revolution. But she was determined not to be a victim, not to be defeated. With a strong will, she managed to complete her senior high school education. She befriended local people and developed her own social circle. She also became acquainted with a few other people who'd migrated from Shandong. Now and then, from her mother, she had news of what was going on in her home province. She grew homesick, but even when the Cultural Revolution ended, she feared its aftermath and was reluctant to return home. Finally, in the late 1970s when the era of reform and opening up began, she felt sure things must be changing in Shandong, and decided to return.

Back in Rizhao, Xia tried to rebuild her life. She met her future husband, Li Yi, in a hospital in town where she had started to work as a nurse. Li Yi had had a slightly different experience during the Cultural Revolution, as his family had been 'middle farmers' (*zhong-nong*), the Maoist term for those who had a low income but owned a moderate amount of land, ranked just above 'poor peasants', who had little land, or none. Li Yi's parents owned twenty *mu* of land. They had once owned 100–200 *mu*, but fortunately for them, they had needed money and sold most of it in the early 1940s. As a result, their children were not placed at the bottom of the Maoist classes like Xia and her siblings.

Xia's sister Yun remained poor all her life. Today, she grows tea on a small farm on the outskirts of Rizhao. She's always busy with farm work and doesn't usually come to meet relatives from Taipei nor invite them to her farm. She heard about Mr Lin's son-in-law, the local official in the transport department, and recently asked my mother to 'put in a good word' for her son, so he could get a clerical job. It is common practice for influential people to introduce acquaintances or relatives into jobs in the civil service. Connections are paramount. Yun told her that normally people had to pay a bribe of around 60,000 yuan (£6,000) for such a favour and she wouldn't be able to afford that in her lifetime – she had only a bag of dried sweet potatoes for a gift. She knew that this official appreciated his ties with the relatives from Taipei, and was asking my mother to speak for her.

Although they eventually became much more prosperous than Yun, Xia and her husband had struggled hard through Mao's time. What did they think of him now? Xia had no doubt that Mao had achieved most of his goals for the country. She repeated the official line, 'Mao was 70 percent merit, 30 percent mistakes.' Once again, I heard no resentment or regret in her evaluation of the past. Probably it had been buried by her present affluence. After the reform and opening up, their old inherited class status no longer mattered; the ethos of the Deng era put individual merit above all else. Those who had been victimized in the previous era were now able to discuss openly the mistakes of the old Party line, and Xia and her husband were able to work their way up without carrying the heavy burden of their class origins. They worked hard and became successful in their professions. Having rejoined the better off of Rizhao, they felt positive about the impact of economic reforms over the past three decades: Both of them had benefited from Deng's policies. Li Yi said, 'The economic reforms gave people of our background the opportunity to "flip over" [*fanshen*], to change our lives. It gave us a future!' Both he and Xia expressed great confidence in China's future.

As they talked, I thought of all the peasants I had met so far. While children of 'bad elements' were denied the chance of 'moving up' in the years following the Revolution, the peasants, in theory the vanguard of that revolution, were made to undergo wave after wave of collective pauperization. Were the children of these impoverished peasants just as confident of China's future?

My mother seemed a little apprehensive about our next visit, to Red River village, where Grandmother came from. Grandmother's marriage to Grandfather had been arranged through a matchmaker, the normal practice in those days. There had never been 'romance' between them; in fact, that idea was alien to them. When asked by his children whether he thought Grandmother was pretty in her youth, Grandfather always replied, 'She's all right!' Grandma was a traditional woman who always seemed to be in the background of her husband's dramatic tales. She never talked much, but she was very skilled at household tasks: cooking, confectionery, and weaving – she had made all of her children's clothes, from winter jackets, gloves and scarves to summer wear. She'd been good at these things since she was a teenager.

My mother's cousin and Grandmother's younger brother were still living in Red River village. There had been little contact between them and the relations in Taipei, but I had heard that they were the poorest of the family in Shandong.

The family in Taipei had set up a joint fund for the relatives in China, and my mother had prepared a gift of 5,000 yuan (£423.7), on their behalf for her cousin in Red River village. 'This will keep him going for a year,' she told me. She had no idea what he did for a living. Both my grandparents had visited Red River village in the late 1990s, not many years before they passed away and they must have known something about his life, but they had not disclosed it.

Mr Lin offered us a lift to the village, only five miles from Rizhao's town centre. We drove through thick bamboo forest with deserted farmhouses scattered between. Suddenly Mr Lin stopped the car. We had come to a broken bridge along the shallow river that separated us from Red River. I could still see the cracks that showed where the bridge had broken in two.

'What a nuisance!' Mr Lin clearly hadn't expected this, but he hadn't been this way for years. 'This must be the result of the flood a few years ago. They [the local authorities] didn't even bother to repair it.'

We were forced to change our route. Mr Lin drove for quite a while through some more wild bamboo on a bumpy country lane. Finally a few huts came into view and we knew we'd come to the edge of the village. First we passed pile after pile of bricks, lining the muddy road, waiting to be laid. Then many tiny, single-storey brick houses appeared. There were dozens of piles of peanuts on the ground, and a few middle-aged women were kneeling to sort them. Mr Lin said the peanuts had just been harvested – they were the main crop of the village, which had a population of just a few thousand. As we got closer to the village centre, which consisted of one major lane, we saw more and more heaps of peanuts, blocking both sides of the road. We got off to ask directions to my mother's cousin's place. Mr Lin stopped a vegetable seller, a man wearing only a pair of shorts. He shook his head, looking confused. A woman in her eighties, carrying a half-dead hen for slaughter, walked past, staring curiously at us. This looked like a village with few visitors.

As we asked around, a man whose back was bent at a nearly ninety-degree angle slowly walked up to us. He was in his seventies, and wore a traditional black *zhongshan* – the Chinese tunic suit introduced by Sun Yat-sen – with a dark blue hat to match, and looked like a caricature of a Party cadre circa Mao. He looked around, and then stared at us again with a concerned look on his wrinkled face.

He hesitated, scrutinizing us, then decided to come nearer.

'You are the cousin from Taiwan?' he said to my mother. I looked at him closely. He had thick eyebrows and a long, pointed hooked nose – an eagle's nose, as Chinese people call it – just like Grandma's. He and my mother did not embrace or even shake hands. They had never met in their lives. And they were probably taken aback by each other's visible differences: he looked humble in his old, wrinkled *zhongshan*, and my mother looked self-assured, smart and urban in her black cardigan. They were, in fact, complete strangers, connected only by blood. What did they have in common?

'Come this way,' my new uncle said, leading us through a narrow path bordered with more peanuts on both sides. At the end of the path there were just two or three modest-looking households with unrepaired damaged windows. We walked quietly behind him. Then my uncle pointed wordlessly to a house in front of us. He opened the front gate, which was covered with torn red papers on which words of good wishes had been written (the papers are called a *gualian* and are hung outside for good luck). We were led through a semi-derelict yard that was littered with broken bricks, dirty plastic washbasins, and rubbish, giving the impression that the farmhouse was uninhabited. Across the yard, Uncle pointed to a green door in a one-storey house covered in thick dust. This was where he lived.

The space inside was five square metres. The corners of the walls were covered with spiderwebs. There was a huge Red Cross sign on one side of a bare wall, and the wall was stained yellow, rotting and cracked. A towel hung on a metal wire that stretched across the room. Piles of used goods – half-broken plastic baskets, empty cans and bottles – were scattered on a red sofa, covered in dust. Most looked as if they had been collected from litter.

To the left, big red wall banners said 'Glory and Wealth' and 'An Air of Fortune Fills the Household'. They looked sad yet dignified.

To one side of the door, there was an old-fashioned metal stove that looked so worn and rusted, I wondered whether anyone used it.

'Do you cook, uncle?' I asked him. It was the first thing I'd said to him.

He turned round and smiled without answering me. It occurred to me that he must do his own cooking – he would never be able to afford meals out.

My mother hadn't said a word since entering the house. When I turned to speak to her, I saw that she'd been shocked into silence. She had not anticipated this level of poverty among her relations in China – her parents had never mentioned this cousin of hers, perhaps because his ill destiny, his place at the bottom of society, had brought them shame? It was as if this uncle had been the dark secret of the family.

Now Uncle kept mumbling about things he ought to get for the house, but I couldn't hear him properly. 'I'm sorry there's no place to sit down,' he apologized, pushing the little bench toward my mother. She listened, not knowing how to reassure him or how to disguise her anxiety and confusion.

I looked up, and saw that the ceiling wasn't made of concrete but of an old white tarp. He actually lived under a tarp.

'What happened there?' I asked.

'Ah, that,' he spoke hesitantly. 'The roof was damaged by the bad weather two or three years ago. I couldn't afford to repair it.'

My mother took out a red envelope with 5,000 yuan inside and handed it to him with both hands. 'This is for you,' she said, not able to look him in the eyes. He took it, gratefully. Then she reached into her bag and pulled out two large boxes of dry shrimps that we'd bought in Qingdao, and instructed him, 'You must soak these properly in water. They put chemicals on it to keep it fresh.' Like a child, he nodded thankfully and put the boxes on the sofa – he didn't seem to have any cupboards in the house.

'What are these?' he asked, seeing a large bag filled with layers of clothing. The relatives in Taipei had bought them as a present.

'They are for you, all new, from Taiwan.'

Uncle kept on mumbling to himself about something, but I couldn't hear what he was saying. I looked up, and saw an old clock with a pink frame hung on his filthy wall. Does he ever look at the time? I wondered. Why would he care?

My newfound uncle was truly one of those left behind by the Revolution. His father hadn't actually been a landlord; in fact, he'd been a schoolteacher all his life until 1949, but his job was taken away from him because of his landowning ancestry. He was then forced to become a farm labourer. It seemed sufficiently criminal that Uncle's grandfather had been a landlord. Uncle's 'element' was bad, never mind that it was not of his own choosing. He was never given the opportunity to go beyond a primary school education. His father, the former teacher, had taught him a little about how to read and write. Insufficiently literate, Uncle was trapped in a life of hard labour on a small piece of land. Growing sweet corn was all he could do. I asked him if that was the only means he had had of staying alive all these years.

'I didn't know how to do anything else,' he said quietly. 'Only how to farm the land. That was hard work. That's why my back is like this now.'

Uncle's life had not been changed by the economic reforms, when many of the 'de-classed' were able to make use of new opportunities brought by Deng's to-get-rich-is-glorious ethos. It was as if three decades of tremendous social change had passed him by.

Since Deng's era, Shandong's four cities – Jinan, Qingdao, Yantai and Weihai – had seen speedy development, with generous government budgets pouring in. These cities now account for 72 percent of the GDP in Shandong province. My mother's family in Taipei always spoke proudly of Shandong as one of the most prosperous provinces on the mainland–it was the second province in China to reach a GDP of over three trillion yuan and saw a growth rate of 12.1 percent in 2008, according to the provincial government. This seeming prosperity, however, is concentrated in urban areas. While the people of Rizhao believe their town will also benefit from investment, only five miles away, in Red River village, life is disconnected from the outside world, and not only by a broken bridge.

'Do you have any children?' I asked. Uncle smiled shyly. He had rolled a cigarette, and now he looked down at his old shoes and blew smoke at them. 'No one wanted to marry me. I was too poor.' Poverty had kept him single and lonely. He didn't even have the cash to leave home, to change his life as Xia had.

Knowing that he was now too old to work on the land, I asked him if he received any state benefits. 'No. Nothing,' Uncle said with his head down. 'And you know that we peasants don't get a pension.' Uncle never told us, but I could see from the litter he'd piled up and kept inside the house that he was eking out a living collecting rubbish.

No doubt he felt embarrassed about not even having tea to offer us in his house. He soon suggested that we go to visit Grandmother's younger brother (my *jiu-gong*) and his wife (my *jiu-po*), who were also living here. Uncle slowly led us to a slightly more populated part of the village, with dozens of houses next to each other. *Jiu-po* welcomed us into the front yard, and I could see that her house was twice the size of my uncle's. Sweet corn had just been harvested. The husks had been peeled off and the corncobs hung from a tree branch to dry. *Jiu-gong* came out to greet us. His facial features strongly resembled Grandma's – especially that 'eagle nose' again. 'So you are here,' he said to my mother. There was no warm embrace, but a kind smile on his face, exactly like Grandma's.

Despite their physical resemblance, my mother and her uncle found it hard to find a common language. My usually confident mother didn't utter a word for ten long minutes. I felt like telling her, 'Say something! Ask him how he's been all these years. There must be things to talk about!' But I didn't. I didn't want to pressure her. I got up from the bench and walked around the yard, looking at their harvest.

Another ten minutes passed, and then twenty, mostly in silence. *Jiu-gong*'s son appeared from outside the front door. He looked in his thirties, and came to shake hands with us – the first person to do so in Red River village. I exchanged polite greetings with him.

My mother suggested that we go to have lunch together in a local restaurant. She thought it would be a nice thing to do with them. Mr Lin butted in at this point and said that his car could only take four passengers, which meant that not everyone could get a lift from him. 'Why don't some of us take a cab?' I said. But everyone frowned at my suggestion. Then I understood that none of them wanted to spend money on a taxi. At this point, embarrassed, my mother offered to pay for one. But the idea that a guest would be paying for a taxi ride was too uncomfortable for everyone.

'I don't think everyone needs to go to the lunch,' *Jiu-gong* suddenly said, without a smile anymore.

'I agree,' *Jiu-po* said, 'Let two people go. Mr Lin's car can take two of us.'

Then they started to debate *who* should be the two. They were all being polite and each asked everyone else to go. In the end, only my new uncle and *Jiu-gong*'s son were persuaded to come to lunch with us.

We were the only diners in an empty restaurant at the edge of Rizhao, just three minutes from the village. Inside our own private dining room, I sat everyone down and poured tea. Mr Lin filled the two uncles' cups with strong plum wine and toasted them. For some reason, he didn't pour wine into my cup, as if assuming that I wouldn't drink alcohol.

Uncle drank two cups in one go, and asked for more.

The waiter brought huge dishes of food – fried squid, steamed fish, tofu and spicy chicken– that my mother had ordered.

'Eat, eat!' my mother urged.

None of the men moved their chopsticks. To be polite, I waited.

'I'll have another drink,' Uncle said.

'The food will get cold,' my mother said, 'Eat, eat!'

'When I have enough to drink, I will eat,' Uncle replied, with a proud, stern look on his tired, wrinkled face.

Mr Lin poured him another cup of plum wine. By this point, my mother and I had started to eat.

Uncle took up the cup and had a quick sip, then said to my mother: 'I think I've had enough to drink. You can't drink too much. You have to take things in moderate quantities.'

My mother gave him an annoyed look.

He carried on, 'If you take more than your own capacity, then you are extravagant. Extravagance is no good for anyone.'

Everyone went quiet. What did Uncle actually want to say? We were all trying to read between the lines.

'You are good at lecturing people, cousin,' my mother finally responded with coldness in her voice. She wasn't used to being lectured. She was always the lecturer, being a preschool educator.

'This is not lecturing. I am simply saying what's right,' Uncle said, speaking defiantly.

Perhaps his words were simply a statement of pride. It couldn't have been easy for him to accept not being able to pay for the meal and not being the real host. Though impoverished, he wanted to show that he could still be a cultured man.

When Uncle was finally persuaded to pick up his chopsticks and eat like everyone else, he gave half the rice in his bowl to the younger uncle sitting next to him. 'I can't manage all of this,' he said, 'Let young people eat more.'

Then he sat there, eating his rice slowly, no one knew why. He kept his head down, occasionally picking up a few bean curds from the plate on the table. He did not once look at any of us, or seek a conversation. Sometimes he glanced up, but then quickly looked away, as if to avoid meeting our eyes. His apparent discomfort revealed much more than his infrequent, cryptic remarks.

I turned to my younger uncle and asked if he was still working on the land. He said yes, he grew peanuts, wheat, and sweet corn. He was the only member of the family still tilling the land. He noted that villages like Red River had little to offer their residents, as no one could really live off the production of small plots. He himself was struggling to survive.

The two uncles and my mother didn't talk to each other through the entire meal. I tried to talk, but found conversation difficult in this uncomfortable atmosphere. The only real noise in the restaurant came from the midday TV news broadcast. Loudly and clearly, it transmitted news centred around the thirtieth anniversary of China's economic reforms and opening up. Premier Wen Jiabao said in his speech:

> Our socialist modernization has the economic reforms and opening as its centre ... In the past thirty years, we have realized the fastest growth in the world. From 1978 to 2007, we had an annual growth of 9.8 percent ... People's livelihood has made a huge historical step forward ... The average annual income of a rural household has risen from 134 yuan to 4,140 yuan ... We have by and large eliminated absolute poverty in the countryside.

On the contrary, I knew that poverty was the abiding characteristic of rural China. Even today, 204 million peasants in China – that is, one in six Chinese – live on less than $1.25 a day, the benchmark of poverty set by the World Bank. In countless villages like Red River, the annual income of many rural households very obviously falls well below the figure given by Wen Jiabao. A year before China joined the World Trade Organization (WTO), Gao Hongbin, general director of the State Council Leading Group

Office of Poverty Alleviation and Development, claimed that China had eliminated 'absolute poverty' and met the target of the seven-year poverty alleviation plan launched in 1994, when there were 80 million Chinese living in absolute poverty. But in those years the government defined 'absolute poverty' as living below an annual income of just over 1,000 yuan – officially a level 'sufficient for a person to enjoy basic life necessities', to have enough to eat, adequate clothing, and a place to live. Few of the peasants I met in villages all over China were able to enjoy 'basic life necessities' even with an annual income above 1,000 yuan – and many make less than that. My uncle, for one, cannot afford to eat, clothe himself, or live in a properly sheltered home, and just by walking through Red River, I could see that he was not the only one.

The following day, on my mother's suggestion, Mr Lin took us to Gaolu village, five miles away from Red River. We were coming at last to my mother's birthplace: Her 'old home' (*laojia*) was now minutes away. We were greeted by a large sign: Han Family Gaolu Village. Every resident in this village bears the surname Han or is related to the Han family.

We walked along the main (and only) street in the village, now inhabited by just a few hundred people. Peanut and wheat farming seemed the only occupation; there were no village enterprises, not even a convenience shop on the main street. Like all of the villages around, Gaolu had a humble look – and little infrastructure and few signs of interaction with the outside world.

According to Grandfather, their family home had been built on two sides of the main street and called East Street and West Street. The eastern half had been donated to the church to build a school named after my great-grandfather. Our grandparents lived in the westside yard. But there was no trace of East Street or West Street – not even the name. My mother looked lost as she strolled through the village. Any traces of her old home had been swept away by the flood years ago – the same flood that had broken up the bridge.

'Where is the river?' My mother remembered a river not far from their home. When she was four, her father used to take her up in his arms and bring her to the riverside. There were many children from the village there, and he would sit by the riverbank and let her play with them for hours. We walked down toward the end of the village and found that the river had dried up.

As we were leaving Rizhao city (the only place with transportation back to Qingdao), I kept thinking about the older uncle we'd left behind in Red River village. I thought about his bent back, his frail figure, and the life he had wasted since the years following the Revolution in 1949. With no social network or resources, he'd been unable to change his destiny, not even when the tide turned in Deng's era. It pains me to know that he will die a lonely death.

On the evening news back in Qingdao, they were still trumpeting the three decades of economic reforms that had transformed China. They applauded the past thirty years as the biggest achievement in Chinese history – despite the fact that it was exactly through Deng's initiatives that China's peasants had been given short-term leases on minimal plots of land controlled by unelected Party leadership in the villages. It was under Deng that the peasants had suffered the most severe level of corruption and random taxation. Will history record that one day?

In autumn of 2009, prior to the thirtieth anniversary of the economic reforms and opening up, China's rulers, headed by President Hu Jintao, announced a new policy. In order to increase productivity and release wealth in the countryside, boost domestic consumption and help China through the global financial crisis, the government would allow China's 800 million peasants to sell the rights to the land they tilled. In other words, peasants could lease their land to businesses and agricultural enterprises, turning land rights into another commodity to be circulated on the market.

Many fear this new policy, when it comes into effect, will bring back big landlords and make poor peasants poorer – that rural social relations will revert to those targeted by the 1946–48 land reform. It will increase the number of peasants who own no land and further widen the wealth gap in villages. It may also legitimize the illegal land grabbing that developers have practiced in large parts of China's countryside over the past three decades. Although the proposed policy has not been formally implemented, the concentration of land rights in the hands of the few is, unfortunately, a growing trend under government plans to tap into rural resources.

Meanwhile, the exodus of impoverished peasants continues. An increasing number in rural Shandong have been compelled to leave their homes to seek a livelihood elsewhere. They are taking greater risks, borrowing heavily, going abroad and putting their destiny into the hands of unscrupulous agencies. They will travel wherever the promise of work leads them. Belonging nowhere, they are now the 'rootless' in China.

6

The Factory of the World: Recession in Guangdong

Guangzhou's train station was a depressing sight. It was nearly midnight and the day's waves of travellers had receded, leaving a tidemark of litter on the concrete floor. The place was filthy and cold. Many of the city's jobless migrants had come to spend the night here. They arrived in groups of seven or eight, men and women from Guangxi and Yunnan, mostly in their thirties and forties, pulling their heavy plastic bags of personal belongings and clothing across the station floor. They'd search for a corner and sit down, leaning against their bags. Some dozed off quite quickly, weary after a long day spent walking around the city looking, in vain, for any sign of work. Others had their eyes wide open, on the watch for security officers.

These migrants had not been able to return home after the last round of layoffs. Some had lost their jobs weeks before but stayed on in Guangzhou because they hadn't been paid and couldn't afford to buy even a bus ticket home. Others had lost their jobs that very day, and since their accommodations had been provided by their employers, they'd became homeless immediately. They certainly couldn't afford a private rental – the cheapest single room in this city cost about 400 yuan per month, that is, half of their previous monthly wage. So they clustered here, sleeping on the station floor until morning, when police and the station staff would chase them off. But as soon as night fell again, they'd return to the station and find corners to sleep.

There are three to four million migrant workers living in Guangzhou, which has a total population of ten million. Many of those I saw sleeping at the train station, as well as those who might have left for their home villages after a few nights on this floor, were first-generation migrant workers who had come to Guangzhou believing they'd find higher wages and abundant opportunities. Guangzhou was meant to be a life-changing experience. As many of them told me, most of them had been working there for over ten years, and had devoted the prime of their life to this city.

Guangzhou, the capital of Guangdong province, became one of China's important trading centres in the mid eighteenth century, when Guangzhou became one of the country's major trading ports. Because of its supposed receptiveness to change and exposure to outside influences, it was seen as the most Westernized city in China. Despite its image, the decades of political upheaval and the transfer of power from the Chinese Nationalists to the CCP had not brought much improvement to people's lives. Before the 1970s, a number of urban housing projects were launched in Guangzhou, but slums still existed alongside urban centres. At the same time, Guangdong's proximity to Hong Kong and easier access to international media meant that even during Mao's era, when the country was closed, people in the province were able to get a glimpse of what life was like outside.

Today Guangdong has developed into China's largest provincial economy, with a GDP surpassing three trillion yuan. It is the centre of China's export-led manufacturing industries. Its Pearl River Delta region, comprising nine prefectures – Guangzhou, Shenzhen, Zhuhai, Dongguan, Zhongshan, Foshan, Huizhou, Jiangmen and Zhaoqing – and the autonomous regions of Hong Kong and Macau, has been China's biggest magnet for international capital since the reform and opening up began in the 1970s. When Deng Xiaoping announced the decision to open China to the world market at the third plenary session of the Eleventh Central Committee, on 18 December 1978, three cities in Guangdong – Shenzhen, Zhuhai, and Shantou – became as a group the first of four Special Economic Zones (SEZs) to pilot the reforms. Guangzhou later joined the list as one of the first mainland cities to be opened to the world market, and set up its free-trade zone in 1992, with major industries including international trade, all types of processing industries, and computer software. The SEZs quickly began pulling international capital to the region. As the government stated, special zones meant special economic systems and policies. SEZs are listed independently in national plans and enjoy provincial-level authority on economic management. Perks for foreign capital include tax incentives for foreign investors and greater independence in trade activities, and the option of setting up a Chinese–foreign joint venture, a partnership, or a wholly foreign-owned business. In the SEZs, goods are produced mainly for export. Apart from these reasons, the region's proximity to internationally invested Hong Kong was a great advantage. Wang Yang, secretary of the CCP's Guangdong provincial committee and now one of the future leaders of China, proudly claimed in late 2008 (when he paid tribute to the reform and opening-up policy) that Guangdong has sustained an average annual growth rate of 13.8 percent over the past three decades. Further, it has a minimum of 60,000 factories, which produce some $300 million worth of goods per day, and accounts for around 30 percent of China's exports and a third of the world's production of shoes, textiles, toys and other commodities.

This sounds like a success story, for sure. However, it has been a success story for some, not for all. In early 2007, the government announced, 'Guangzhou has become the first Chinese city to reach a per capita income of $10,000.' But later, it was found that this figure had not factored in the 3.7 million migrant workers living and working in the city at the time. This blatant exclusion underscores the reality that Guangzhou's seeming prosperity is far from prosperity for all. In the past decade, the city's wealth gap has continued to widen. In November 2011, a survey conducted by Guangzhou Society and Public Opinion Research Centre found a great deal of class polarization in Guangzhou. The majority of the low-income interviewees revealed a high level of dissatisfaction with the gap in income and living standards. You can sense the huge disparities as soon as you enter this city, and when migrants first come here to work they are overwhelmed not only by the vast transport system and its endless traffic jams, the thick fumes and suffocating air, but also by the visible inequality – the most ruthless part of Guangzhou's urbanity – between the haves and have-nots. In Guangzhou, you see the upper middle class buying in world-class shopping malls, dining in restaurants run by famous chefs, and drinking in luxurious wine bars, spending a manual worker's two months' wages in a single night, while beggars wait outside for the few yuan you can spare and migrants wander in the middle of the night in search of a corner to sleep in.

But there is no lack of places for them to work. Together, automobiles, petrochemicals, and electronics and information technology, now account for over 40 percent of Guangzhou's industrial production. Major multinationals like Apple (supplied by Foxconn), Sony, Motorola, and Toshiba manufacture most of their products in Guangzhou. The city is one of the major bases of automobile manufacture in China. It is also where the petrochemical multinationals are concentrated: Shell, Total and Du Pont all operate here. And the list goes on.

Migrant labour is what makes the export-led manufacturing empire possible. The wages of migrant workers here are around one twelfth of working-class wages in the UK. Not only do migrant workers have few social rights –thanks to the institutional exclusion and segregation made possible by *hukou* – in practice they also have few labour rights, as those supposedly given them by law are violated and abused by their employers. Since the migrant labour force is seldom organized, workers find themselves fighting injustice alone. Some find no way out of situations of harsh exploitation. And sometimes, in their isolation and extreme despair, they find the most tragic way out. Since 2008, the number of these migrant suicides, final protests of victimized workers in the Pearl River Delta, has increased.

In 1988, Foxconn Technology Group,[1] the world's biggest manufacturer of electronics components and a major supplier to Apple, opened its largest manufacturing plant in Shenzhen, employing 330,000 people. There, besides components for Apple Inc.'s Mac mini, iPod, iPad and iPhone, Foxconn produces motherboards for Intel and parts for Sony's PlayStations 2 and 3, Wii for Nintendo, and Kindle for Amazon, among others. In March 2008, it also produced one of the most notorious worker suicides, when twenty-five-year-old Sun Danyong killed himself after working excessively long hours.

Two workers at Huawei Technologies, also in Shenzhen, killed themselves for the same reason. In fact, six workers have committed suicide at HT in the past two years. Huawei Technologies employs more than 60,000 workers in its factories all over China and abroad, and is one of the best-known telecommunications companies in the country. Chinese 'netizens' have asked questions about this company's aggressive corporate culture – they call it 'wolf culture' – a culture which compelled overworked employees to sleep in their workplace and which they believe has caused the deaths of workers who saw no hope of improvement in their conditions.

In the same year, thirty migrant workers from Hunan province attempted suicide by climbing Haizhu Bridge in central Guangzhou after a local beer company defaulted on their wages. The local newspapers reported, 'The would-be jumpers caused a traffic jam for several hours along the bridge, which has been the scene of many threatened suicides ...'

On 29 July 2009, *Guangzhou Daily* printed this item: 'A twenty-four-year-old university graduate, Liao Shikai, working at Liqun mouldings factory in the Houjie district of Dongguan, Guangdong, jumped to his death on 21 July from his fourth-floor dormitory after being refused time off from work by the management.'

Foxconn appeared in the headlines again in 2010, a year when fourteen of their migrant workers committed suicide. As *China Daily* reported, the first death was of a nineteen-year-old, Ma

Xiangqian, on 23 January 2010. In March, two more workers attempted suicide and one died after jumping from a building. In April, three more young workers attempted suicide and one died. Soon after that, on 6 May, twenty-four-year-old Lu Xin killed himself. On 12 May, another twenty-four-year-old jumped to her death. On 21 May, a twenty-one-year-old worker committed suicide. Two more workers killed themselves, followed by another female worker on 4 August. And on 5 November, a twenty-three-year-old male worker became the fourteenth fatality.

Foxconn's death toll did not stop there. In 2011, on 26 May, a twenty-year-old male worker jumped off a building. On 18 July, a twenty-one-year-old Mr Cai killed himself in the same way. And on 23 November, twenty-year-old Li Rongying committed suicide by jumping off a four-storey building.

Southern Weekly, the only investigative journal in China, in order to find out the cause of these tragedies, sent a reporter to work undercover in Foxconn's plant in Shenzhen. She reported grim working conditions and a harsh labour regime: Employees were compelled to work long hours that left only enough time to sleep and eat; workers were required to sign an overtime waiver (so they gave up their right to refuse overtime work); they were given low pay – only $130 USD per month, so they had to work a lot of overtime to make ends meet. Alarmingly, it is believed by many migrant workers that they aren't likely to find better conditions elsewhere in Shenzhen and the region generally – that region considered by migrant workers to be so filled with opportunities and prospects for a better future.

Foxconn announced profits of $5.04 billion for May 2010. Benefiting from the increasing demand for Apple products, the company accounted for 50 percent of global electronic manufacturing services sales by 2011.

Migrant workers' discontent deepened after the beginning of the global recession. Starting in summer 2007, migrant workers began to leave Guangzhou for the countryside, creating a backflow of migration. Jobs were being lost as factories shut down one after another. The shoe manufacturing industry in Guangdong, for instance, which supplies half of the global demand for footwear, was cutting down large numbers of jobs. About a thousand shoe-making factories in the province shut down in 2007, after laying off 150,000 to 200,000 workers. In 2008, around 10 percent of the 60,000 to 70,000 Hong Kong–owned factories based in Pearl River Delta closed following profit losses, including the many factories that supplied the British company Mattel and the US company Hasbro Inc. According to migrant workers themselves, against the rules set out in the Labour Contract Law, many companies dismissed without notice and without their last month's wages workers who had served them for more than ten years. Company directors fled to avoid paying the wages they owed. According to the Hong Kong–based newspaper *Dagongbao*, in the first ten months of 2008, 15,661 small and medium-size factories in Guangdong either closed down, suspended or relocated their operations. In Dongguan, reportedly 117 factories shut down between September and October, and all of the factory owners fled, leaving more than 20,000 workers without pay. China's State Council issued a notice in early February 2009 requiring companies to notify local labour authorities before any layoffs involving at least twenty employees or 10 percent of staff, but there was no law to penalize companies who did otherwise. The government released figures in April 2009 showing that since 2008 around 25 million migrant workers had lost their jobs all over the country as a result of factory closures and business collapses. In Guangdong alone, it was estimated, several million had lost jobs. According to the Ministry of Agriculture, about 10 percent of migrant peasants had lost city manufacturing jobs and 80 percent of them were now back in the cities trying to find work.

Beginning in 2007, millions of migrant workers had left Guangdong to go back to their home villages in Sichuan, Guangxi, Yunnan and other provinces. But since the end of February 2009, it was estimated, 9.5 million had returned to Guangdong, hoping to find work again. None were sure if there was work to be found, or how long those jobs might last. The nighttime scene at the Guangzhou train station suggested that the situation was not looking good.

I went to visit the factory of Yin Yu Ltd in Heshan, on the southern outskirts of Guangzhou, where Zhong, my new friend in Sichuan, used to work, and where his wife Ying still remained. More than two thousand migrant workers had been laid off between 2008 and 2009 as the company attempted to downsize.

Heshan is an old town, built in 1732 under the Qing emperor Yongzheng. It's surrounded by mountains and according to legend there were many white geese in the old days; *Heshan* literally means 'Goose Mountain'. It's tiny, with a population of 460,000 – a third of the townspeople are known to have migrated abroad, but they have maintained their *hukou* here, and Heshan is also called 'the hometown of the overseas Chinese' (*qiaoxiang*). Since the reform and opening up, Heshan has attracted foreign capital and a number of industries are based there: electronics, textiles, shoe manufacture, printing and others. Yet on the surface, it seemed a tranquil town, the kind of place where nothing ever happens. Modest-looking concrete buildings and a small number of trades on the streets were all that I could see. Yin Yu Ltd is right in Heshan's centre. Founded in 1979, it's the largest workplace in this town, with thousands of employees (although the company's website states only that Yin Yu has 'more than 100 employees'). The majority of migrants here work in its factories, assembling and producing lamps and light fixtures for sale all over China and for export to Southeast Asia, the US and Europe. Assembly workers were on their daytime shift when I arrived, so the streets were empty. The few workers I saw were office clerks, whose ranks included both locals and migrants. I saw a number of them coming in and out of the factory compound.

I noticed one young woman on the street, with short hair and attractive almond-shaped eyes, who wore work clothes that reminded me of a school uniform: a simple white shirt and black trousers. She walked along energetically, with her head up, and looked my way as I watched her. I had the impression that she was outgoing and might be willing to talk. I spoke to her as she passed me, and she was quite willing to stop and talk. When I introduced myself and said I was interested in hearing about her working life, she was immediately excited. She told me that her name was Ling and she was twenty-two, and came from Hubei province. She hadn't gone to university, but had been able to study business administration at a vocational college in her home province. She'd promised her parents that if they supported her during her college years, once she'd graduated, she would find work that matched her new qualifications and skills. When she found the office assistant's job at Yin Yu Ltd, her parents were thrilled. Going to work in an international company in Guangdong was seen as a marvellous achievement. They believed that their daughter would start to bring in a regular income and eventually do very well.

Ling was a talker, the sort who befriends people easily. When I asked her what it was like to live in Heshan, she immediately replied, 'Dull, very dull.' And this was because there were few young men around in the workplace. 'Everywhere you look, you see female colleagues. In the dorm, at the office, and even in the market in town.' Clearly, in Lin's eyes, being in a mostly female workforce had spoiled her fun: 'Since the first week I arrived at this place, I started to think to myself, "God, this is like leading a life of a nun."' I laughed and sympathized with her disappointment.

'Come and have tea,' Ling said after a while, inviting me back to her dormitory. I was delighted that the invitation came so early.

We walked past a street of shops and little beef noodle stores, and headed toward Ling's dormitory, a few hundred metres away. It was a block of apartments with a public square in the middle. As we approached, I realized that Ling would have to smuggle me into the building, which was well guarded by a number of security staff. I didn't see any cameras around, but was quite sure that I wouldn't be able to enter the gate. 'Don't worry. Just follow me,' Ling said. She put on her teenager-like, laid-back, innocent smile, shrugging her shoulders.

'You're female and this is a women's dorm – they won't even notice you,' Ling said. I suspected it wasn't the first time she'd smuggled a friend into the dormitory, and decided it was worth a try. What was the worst-case scenario? Not being able to get in wouldn't be the end of my communication with Ling. So I walked behind her, keeping my head low but acting relaxed. Ling was right – the security staff didn't even look at me.

I followed her up the stairs and through the corridor, now completely empty, as most people were out at work. Ling opened the door to her room, which was tiny but bright – she'd left the window open, letting in the sunshine. She pulled over a wooden stool and asked me to sit down, while she sat back on her metal bunk bed, which occupied half of the room. 'My roommate's at work,' she said. 'She works in the office, too.' On her desk, piled up with instant noodle packets, Ling boiled some hot water in an electric kettle and poured me a jar of green tea. Then she confessed why she was not concerned about breaking the dormitory rules: She was planning to leave the job.

Ling had spotted the company's recruitment ad in one of the labour markets back in Hubei. She'd just graduated and was eager to start work right away and begin an independent life away from home. Her college degree got her the job – for which she believed thousands were competing – at the lowest level of administrative work in the company. She said she had expected basic rights and entitlements, and respectful treatment.

She had been quickly disillusioned. She told me how stressed and overworked she was. From the beginning, she had had to do a huge amount of unpaid overtime, working until 11 pm each day. The overtime was half compulsory: If you refused it, you were seen as unwilling to work hard and would not be considered for future opportunities within the company. Performance was paramount. 'I find it hard to breathe,' she said, describing how anxious she felt on the job every day. 'I have no life.' This, although her job was much envied by most migrant workers on the assembly line, because it was not manual and she enjoyed a relative freedom.

Assembly line workers could never imagine simply walking down the street during working hours. Also, she might hope for a future promotion; her position wasn't 'dead-end' – the assembly-line workers' description for their own work.

But, Ling said, other migrant workers didn't know her job from the inside. The so-called promise of promotion and future opportunities within the company was just a myth, she said. During the five months she'd been there, Ling had never been given a contract, and to date, she hadn't been told when she might be given one. Without a contract, nothing was certain.

This prompted me to ask her whether she would get a redundancy fee when she left. 'No, of course not,' Ling said emphatically. 'They want to give me no choice except to leave without one single yuan in my pocket.'

Ling explained that it was common practice for the company to offer a choice between 'voluntary departure' (*zi-li*) and 'resignation' (*ci-gong*). A voluntary departure doesn't require approval from the management, but you forfeit any unpaid wages. A resignation requires official approval, upon which you receive your full wages. Ling was trapped in a no-win situation: If she chose to plead for approval, the management would certainly say 'no', forcing her to either stay in the job or leave voluntarily without pay.

Ling resented these games of entrapment. 'Life's too short, and I am still young,' she said. 'I don't want to work under this kind of immense pressure and manipulation anymore – I'm not even given the most basic respect.'

What was she going to do after she left?

She said she wanted to set up her own business back in Hubei. The isolated months in Guangdong had made her realize that home was best. What sort of business would she run, I asked. She raised her eyebrows and said she had a wild idea yet to be tried. In Hubei, more and more middle-class people liked to keep pets. The urban new rich not only invest hugely in their one child, they also loved spending money on pedigree cats and dogs. 'I'd like to set up a pet shop,' Ling said, 'There's a demand to be met.' Her ambition was to earn enough that way to lead an independent life: buy an apartment in town and find someone suitable to marry.

Ling got up and walked to the narrow balcony outside her room. I followed her. She stood there, looking out at the balcony on the other side of the building, where women's clothes were being hung to dry. She observed that this was the kind of dormitory where the 'working girls' (*dagongmei*), mostly unmarried women from the rural interior, lived, and she was one of them.

'Look at those apartments,' she said, pointing to the building across the way. 'They are overcrowded, eight workers to a four-square-meter room.' She said she was one of the luckier ones: As an office worker, she was given more spacious housing, a room shared with just one other person. This was the only advantage Ling enjoyed.

The *dagongmei* are mostly young and unmarried and come from rural villages all over China. They have been the preferred workers for these factories, since they have fewer commitments and a strong wish to succeed in the cities – which means that they are prepared to accept the lowest wages. They make up more than 70 percent of the manufacturing workforce in the Pearl River Delta.

Like many young women working away from home, Ling aspired to all the material comforts and new experiences that money can buy. She'd always liked fashion, and since the age of eighteen had followed clothing trends and enjoyed shopping for stylish shoes. In that sense, she said, Heshan had been a huge disappointment – there were no stylish shops. It seemed as if instead the town had been built to suit the spending capabilities of the migrant worker population. It was a sharp contrast to her dream of Guangdong, which she'd imagined was a magnet of consumerism and easy access to foreign brands. Her roommate found Heshan disappointing, too, and had encouraged Ling to go visit Guangzhou with her and shop there together. The temptation had been strong. But at the last minute, Ling had decided against spending her hard-earned wages on a spree in Guangzhou. How could she explain that to her parents, who'd invested every hope in her career? She knew she had to maintain a modest lifestyle in order to save up for her future.

The afternoon passed quickly as we drank tea and chatted. At 4 pm, Ling said she had to return to work. The other women living in this apartment would soon return from their work. I walked back into town with her, thanked her for her hospitality, and said good-bye outside the factory. I saw her walking into the distance behind the gate. The daytime workers would be coming off their shift at around 5 pm. I had made plans to meet with Ying, Mr Zhong's wife, so I hung around watching the few people who passed in and out of the factory. The heat was hard to bear – now around 30 degrees C, in the middle of the summer in late July.

At 5 pm sharp, a flood of workers poured out the front gate. Remembering Zhong's description, I looked out for a woman with short hair. I had no other clues about her appearance. But she recognized me – I was the only one at the gate who didn't look local. Instead of a uniform, I wore a thin blue Kazak dress. She approached me, smiling, looking me up and down as if to make sure I was the right person, then introduced herself as 'Ying, Zhong's wife.'

'I know,' I responded immediately.

Ying wore her hair to her collar and had her work card hanging over her white shirt – her title was 'product control worker'. Her manner was warm but calm; something about it seemed compatible with the woman Zhong had told me about.

We walked along the street, now packed with workers. I suggested we go to a café or restaurant somewhere, to talk and have dinner together. She seemed hesitant, but a few minutes later, she decided it would be easier to talk sitting down. She led me through a busy vegetable market and found a café with plastic tables outside. She picked up the menu on the table and frowned. I didn't want her to worry about having to pay for the dinner. 'It'll be my treat,' I said. 'You're the one who's been working.'

We sat down, and Ying told me that she had been in Heshan since 1996. She'd come from Jintang in Sichuan, known as the home of oranges, as she proudly said. She was only twenty-three then – a young woman with big ambitions and dreams. She'd long heard about Sichuanese doing well in the south and owning their own businesses, and she'd seen them as inspiring examples of success. Ying came from a farming family and had seen her parents – with little education or opportunity to do anything different – live barely above subsistence level. Sick and tired of being poor, she'd wanted to do something with her life. In her early twenties, she'd started looking for work outside of farming, and with her senior high school diploma she'd found a job as a pharmacist in the village. Although it wasn't really a skilled job in those days, requiring little more than paperwork and customer reception, and paid a low wage, she began to understand what it must feel like to have a job that might lead somewhere. And then she saw other young people of her age leaving the village, one by one, heading toward Guangdong.

Ying began to talk with other villagers who intended to migrate for work. One of them had spotted a number of job ads from Yin Yu Ltd, which was recruiting large numbers of migrants at the time. She had heard of Yin Yu many times before, because it was one of the biggest companies in the south that employed Sichuanese workers. In her mind, it was a well-known global company with a future, and she had also heard of Mr Fan, the head of the company. He'd become a legendary figure among many Sichuanese migrants, known not only for his business success but also for his family history: His father had been a pilot working for Chiang Kai-shek. Ying still spoke admiringly of Mr Fan. She'd had conversations with him about work and found him a pleasant, tolerant man. 'And he showed us that as long as we strive, we will achieve,' she said.

It's not hard to imagine how thrilled Ying was when she was offered the job at Yin Yu Ltd. Working for this company was not an opportunity that arose every day, she told herself, so she must work her hardest to make a new life. She started out on the assembly line, like every Sichuanese migrant there. Many of the assembly workers came from her hometown, Jintang, and, as she kept telling everyone, her hometown folks worked very, very hard. 'To climb to the top, you must start at the bottom,' she said to me. Back then, she was paid 700–800 yuan (£64–73.5) per month.

The company and the work soon became her life. One thing she'd never expected to find on her assembly line was love, but she did. She met a coworker who introduced himself as Zhong. He was tanned and well built, exactly her type. He was in his twenties and had also just arrived in Guangdong, and had no relatives or friends there. Zhong was one of the most extroverted people on the assembly line, always speaking loudly and asking questions of the supervisor. She was attracted to his openness and his great sense of humour. When he asked her to go out with him for dinner one night on their precious day off, he said: 'You're not going to find a better-looking man from Jintang, seriously.' He was fun to be with – and Ying found great consolation in his company. He took her to a well-decorated restaurant in town. He'd booked a table. Over their first dinner, they ordered three dishes between them, all Sichuanese – just like right now, with me. She'd chosen her favourite eggplant with chili, garlic spinach, and spicy cashew-nut chicken.

After she met Zhong, Ying had enjoyed her working hours on the assembly line. Zhong would always be there to cheer her up when she missed her elderly parents. He would take her mind off her worries and come up with ideas about where to go on their monthly day off work. On one day off, he presented her with a pleasant surprise: he'd hired a motorbike, and he drove her all the way into Guangzhou. She'd never seen this city in real life. She was stunned by its prosperity – its high-rises, numerous shopping malls and thousands of enterprises. It was then that she was convinced she had made the right decision by leaving home and coming to the south to make a living. It will all be worthwhile, she said to Zhong.

'He used to be such fun,' Ying said to me, sighing as she smiled. A few months later, Zhong proposed marriage and she said yes immediately. All the young women on the assembly line hoped to find a man and get married. Ying had never expressed that wish openly, as they did, yet she was the first to actually do it. She was much envied. When she and Zhong got married, all their colleagues and superiors were invited to the wedding. They held the ceremony in a hotel restaurant in town, and had two hundred guests, all from the factory. Ying said this was the best time in her life – and she'd felt that her work was very much part of her new-found happiness. She felt grateful to the company for bringing her and Zhong together.

It wasn't possible to stay in a company dormitory as a married couple, so they found and rented a room in a small flat in Heshan. She'd enjoyed being a newly married woman, and her relationship with Zhong had given her much emotional strength that helped her cope with the demanding nature of her work. She had her first child, a daughter, six months after the wedding. There was, again, much celebration and encouragement from her colleagues. A number of women from her hometown offered her help, cooking for her after she came back from the hospital a few days after giving birth

The difficult time came when she had a son, her second child. As this was against the one-child-per-family birth-control rules, Ying and Zhong were fined 10,000 yuan –more than one person's yearly wages at the factory. This was a heavy burden on their finances – they were already struggling to pay the rent and send money home to both sets of parents. The couple now had to work doubly hard. They began to take on as much overtime as possible, and the company seemed more than willing to give them the work they needed.

Ying felt that the job had saved them. 'Without it, we wouldn't have been able to pay off the penalty. We wouldn't have survived the difficulties,' she said. But despite being grateful, Ying felt unhappy that her work regimen would make it impossible to visit her parents more than once a year, the Chinese New Year, when everyone went home. Her greatest regret was that her father had died in Sichuan while she was working in the factory. 'I had put my work first, and neglected the needs of my elderly parents,' she said. 'I wish I could turn back the clock: I would do everything I could to bring them to live with me in Heshan – right next to me.' I could see that Ying had never got over her feelings of guilt and shame at not being with her father when he died. It was a natural death and he passed away peacefully, she said with much sorrow. 'But I should have been there.'

Ying is the only child in the family, and after her father died she felt it was her natural duty to look after her mother, who was no longer farming the land and was all alone at home. Ying couldn't bear the thought of her mother's solitude. She took a few days off from work – the first time she'd done so – and went back to Sichuan to attend her father's funeral and arrange for her mother to come to Heshan. She wanted never to be parted from her again.

Her mother now lives with her and her three-year-old son (her nine-year-old daughter lives with Zhong in Sichuan). 'We are so happy together, the three of us,' Ying said. It was tremendous emotional support to have her mother with her. Ying could cope with her schedule now: working till 9 pm every day during the week, and all day on Saturday till 5 pm. She was as passionate about her job as before. Her mother stayed in the flat with her grandson, looking after him and telling him stories about her home village. In the evening, she cooked for the family, preparing Ying's favourite dishes. Ying said she felt incredibly lucky, being able to come back home to Mum's food every night. As an office worker, she can have Sunday off, unlike the workers on the assembly line, who work seven days. On Sunday, the three of them would go out for a walk. Once, they went to Heshan Park, a few miles away. They strolled around and watched people – young and old – dance to Chinese pop music in a group. Ying's mother had never seen this in her village and found it amusing. What's this dance, she asked. Is it Western or Chinese? Ying said it was a mixture.

Ying hadn't mentioned Zhong again, and I didn't feel comfortable asking her what it was like to live away from her husband. Toward the end of the evening, she brought it up herself.

'Many couples got to know each other as colleagues in this factory. They got married, like us,' she said. 'Some of them have stayed together, and others divorced after a few years. Work is on top of you, and you need to make decisions. For me, work has to be the priority. It is my future – it is our future. Zhong chose to quit, as some did, because the company left him no other choice. He wanted to find suitable work in Sichuan. I don't want to go back there. My future's right here, in Guangdong. So we make our choices, depending on what we need to do and achieve in our lives.'

Now they saw each other once a year, during the Chinese New Year. Ying didn't call it 'separation', but that really sounded like the state of their relationship. Ying did not seem concerned about it. Instead, she seemed strong and determined, wanting to carry on what she had been doing: working hard. Ying's passion for her job and determination to build her life in Guangdong has kept Zhong away. It's true that she has set her priorities and put her marriage in second place. When she talked about visiting Zhong in the New Year, she showed little sign of longing. I wondered if she ever thought about him much. As for the children, Ying was content with the current arrangement. Child care by grandparents is always preferable to a nursery. This seemed to work fine, as Zhong didn't seem to mind seeing his only son once a year. I had the feeling he'd given up on trying to put his life with Ying back together, and so had she.

In all of this, I could see how different Ying was from Zhong. She looked to the future for a career – she'd always been ambitious and had wanted to do well since her early twenties. He simply wanted to have a reasonable standard of living.

I was silent as she told me all this. She clearly noticed.

'I would never do what he did – I wouldn't just leave the company,' she said. 'But that's not saying that I don't understand his point. He is right ... We are truly living in hard times.'

She said that there had been three strikes in her factory in the past decade, all over drops in wages, each time 200 yuan less per month, in all departments. This was a considerable amount, considering that the average monthly wage was about 1,000 yuan at this factory, whether from piecework rates paid to assembly line workers or from the hourly rate (5 yuan) made by machine operators. Ying did not want to go into specifics about the strikes, because she didn't want to put the company in a bad light. She simply said that following the last action, the company had got rid of the strike leaders, or in their words, 'those with attitudes'. Recently, the company had hired up to 20,000 workers for lower wages, 5,000 of them through a Sichuanese labour contractor. Labour from Sichuan has always been abundant and easy to recruit; the downside for the employers is that the Sichuanese always come in big groups and are therefore better able to organize. I asked Ying for details about the new low-wage workers in her factory. 'There's nothing more I can say about that,' said Ying. 'People need jobs and they accept the lower wages. Many have brought their families with them. Maybe they will stay long-term, just like me, and like Zhong, once.' Ying said it was the peak of production season and the company was in fact looking for even more workers – there was talk of another 10,000.

'If you put up with it, are flexible and work hard, one day you might get promoted, and you might be working in the product control department, as I am now, earning a monthly wage of between 1,700 and 1,800 yuan,' she said. 'It is up to you whether you accept what they give you when times are bad.'

Not all migrants are willing to bear the brunt of the global economic crisis while multinational companies continue to rake in profits. There is growing discontent among the younger generation of migrant workers, those in their twenties and thirties, who are better educated than their parents and have higher expectations for their present working conditions and future prospects. Sixty percent of migrant workers in China's cities today were born in the 1980s and 1990s, according to the Ministry of Human Resources and Social Security. These young workers' lack of connection with the country's past and their greater aspirations for themselves often give them a fearless approach to coping with 'poor industrial relations'. As they become the mainstay of China's industrial labour force, as they have in the Pearl River Delta, their presence – and certainly their growing militancy – poses a threat to the authorities, who often speak of this generation of workers as 'the new problem of our society'.

That militancy is a well-recognized reality. The number of labour disputes has increased sharply in recent years: China's courts heard up to 100,000 cases in the first quarter of 2009, up 50 percent from the same period in 2008. The number of 'mass incidents',[2] the term used by the authorities to refer to demonstrations, riots, protests and petitions, rose from 74,000 in 2004 to 87,000 in 2006,[3] then to 120,000 in 2008, as the impact of the recession became intensely felt. Faced by job losses and nonpayment of wages in the kingdom of manufacturing in Guangdong, many workers have taken to the streets. Some have taken part in blockades, to put pressure on management to pay them the wages they deserved. *China Labour Bulletin* looked at 100 cases of protests during 2007–2008[4] and found that during that period migrant workers had become more ambitious and militant in making their demands.[5]

The authorities have always known how to deal with these 'mass incidents': The riot police can be called in immediately to 'restore public order', according to the Emergency Response Law of 2007, which was enacted 'to deal with industrial incidents more effectively'. Those who lead these 'incidents' are usually heavily punished. During 2007 and 2008, several labour rights activists were convicted on criminal charges and sentenced to 're-education through labour' (*laodong-jiaoyang*) for up to three years.[6]

Since the first half of 2010, 'industrial conflict' has grown fiercer, and migrant workers' spontaneous industrial actions have begun to gain wider public attention, which deeply worries employers and the government.

Spontaneous collective action has bred a new confidence among young migrant workers. Workers at a wholly foreign owned plant making parts for Honda, in the Nanhai district of Foshan, a city in Guangdong, began a strike on 17 May 2010 that continued until 1 June. They said they couldn't support themselves on the company's basic pay and demanded an 800 yuan raise, better working conditions, and democratic elections for union representatives at the plant. They wouldn't accept compromise offers made by the company.

Their strike inspired workers at other plants to follow suit and eventually production came to a halt at every Honda assembly plant in China. In June 2010, 1,700 migrant workers, mainly women in their twenties – the once 'docile' *dagongmei* – went on strike at a Honda auto parts factory in Zhongshan city, Guangdong, demanding a doubling of their wages and the right to form an independent union. The state-run union did not represent their interests: They wanted their own.

The wave of strikes then spread to Honda Lock, a Sino-Japanese joint venture in Zhongshan's Xiaolan township. About 500 workers took part in the action there, demanding an increase of wages from 1,500 yuan[7] to 2,000 yuan and election of their own representatives. They, too, said they no longer cared to be represented by 'the enterprise union run by employers and the government'. They called the state union, the ACFTU, 'useless' and a 'traitor'. The Honda strikes were followed a few days later by a strike in Guangzhou at Denso (Nansha) Corporation, a car parts maker affiliated with Toyota. Workers demanded higher wages and better benefits, saying that the monthly wage of 1,300 yuan (£120) was too low in a city where their monthly rent averaged 200 yuan. This factory had an annual production capacity of 360,000 units and supplied both Toyota and Honda. The strike suspended it. And workers' action there was soon followed by one in Tianjin, at Toyoda Gosei, also a Toyota affiliate, where 1,300 workers demanded a 20 percent pay increase.

Since the workers' suicides at Foxconn, that company has had to raise the minimum wage for its frontline workers, first to 1,200 yuan, in June 2010, then to 2,000 yuan in October for those same workers, who succeeded in passing a performance evaluation. Foxconn is now making plans for a third increase, including an adjustment of the minimum monthly wage to 1,550 yuan.[8]

The wave of strikes that followed the wave of suicides has won migrants at least partial improvement of their working conditions. The strikers at the Nanhai Honda plant won a 500 yuan monthly pay increase. Their collective bargaining power proven effective, they negotiated a further monthly increase of 611 yuan in 2011 without striking. Workers, now much more confident than before, questioned the effectiveness of the trade union representatives who hadn't allowed them to participate in the negotiation process, expecting them to simply sit and 'observe'. Once again, workers asserted their demand for their own democratically elected representatives to bargain on their behalf.

Thanks to these victories, the authorities have had to adjust their way of dealing with industrial disputes and 'managing labour'. In July 2010, seeing the strength of the strike waves and fearing 'social instability', the Guangdong Provincial People's Congress convened to review the draft of 'Regulations on the Democratic Management of Enterprises' (RDME), a process previously deliberately halted in 2008 because of pressure from business interests. Migrant labour's growing militancy had made the local officials think twice about ignoring workers' demands. The Guangdong Provincial Party Committee now saw the need to 'construct harmonious industrial relations', and added two new chapters to the draft of the RDME, one on 'collective wage consultations' and the other on 'dispute coordination and management'.

For the local authorities, however, the real purpose of the RDME was to prevent large-scale industrial actions like the strike waves of summer 2010. Article 40 of the Regulation forbids workers to begin any work stoppage 'before they have lawfully demanded collective consultation'. The regulations as drafted seemed to be simply an effort to contain labour 'unrest'. In late September 2010, the tide turned against the workers when the RDME was blocked by Hong Kong business leaders, who had lobbied the government against it.

Even so, overall the militancy among the younger generation of migrants has achieved a great deal: Since the 2010 strikes and the subsequent wage increases, workers have demanded similar improvements in wages and conditions all over the Pearl River Delta region. Companies here now fear the domino effect of labour militancy. In late November 2011, waves of spontaneous strikes once again spread across Guangdong province, when more than 10,000 workers in Shenzhen and Dongguan downed tools to protest against the cutting down of overtime work that workers needed to supplement their meagre wages.

To lower labour costs and calm labour 'unrest' in the long term, Foxconn has cut down the workforce in its two plants in Shenzhen from 400,000 to 100,000, and moved its production to interior cities such as Zhengzhou in Henan and Chengdu in Sichuan, where 200,000 jobs will be created by the end of 2011. The company has been received favourably by the local authorities in those two most populous provinces, where millions of migrant workers originated. Due to the rising living costs in the first-tier cities, many Henanese now prefer to find employment closer to home, despite Henan's much lower minimum monthly wage, 750 yuan (compared with 1,350 yuan in Shenzhen, Guangdong).

But the companies' strategy of industrial transfer, as it has increased the demand for labour in the interior, has also contributed to the severe labour shortage reported in the manufacturing industries of Pearl River Delta and Yangtze River Delta regions since early 2010. The trend does not signal the decline of the low-end production that makes up the bulk of China's manufacturing industries. What it does mark is the growth of certain second-tier inland cities and the perception of workers there that migration out of the province isn't always necessary (although the coastal regions are still seen as offering better opportunities in the long term). For instance, many migrant workers now prefer to stay in cities like Chongqing, Sichuan, and Wuhan, the capital of Hubei province, where there's a boom in construction, rather than travelling to expensive Shanghai to do the same work. Shanghai's transportation department revealed in February 2011 that the number of migrant workers returning to the city from Sichuan and Anhui had fallen by 10,000 a day since 2010. In Guangdong, according to the provincial labour bureau, return migration fell short by about one million workers in 2011.

But this labour shortage certainly partly reflects the growth of labour militancy as well. Many second-generation migrant workers have become increasingly reluctant to take up the lowest-paid jobs. Although workers' gains are a small drop that seems lost in the ocean of China's low wages and poor working conditions, they have undoubtedly set a precedent for fighting those abuses.

In recognition of that precedent and its implications, since 1 July 2010 the monthly minimum wage for blue-collar workers has been raised by up to 20 percent in various cities and provinces, including Beijing, Henan, Shenzhen, Shaanxi, Anhui, Hainan, after a two-year delay for the payrise, in order to recruit young migrant workers. In mid July, it was reported that a total of eighteen provinces had seen the blue-collar minimum wage raised. Many cities also saw that minimum wage raised again in 2011. However, the general wage level remains extremely low, because minimum wage in China is currently set (locally, not nationally as there is no national minimum wage) at 40 to 60 percent of local average wage. In Guangzhou, for instance, the minimum monthly wage has been raised to 1,300 yuan in March 2011, still very low compared with average earnings and living costs in the city. Also at the same time, minimum wage has been raised to 1,100 yuan in Dongguan, 950 yuan in Shantou and 850 yuan in Shaoguan. These are all migrant-receiving cities in Guangdong with high living costs. In China today, the average monthly minimum wage for blue-collar workers is 768 yuan (£75.5). Even these low levels of minimum wage have not been met in many provinces.

The rural/urban divide continues. Even the state-run All-China Federation of Trade Unions pointed out in February 2011 that despite recent increases in the minimum wage, the nearly 100 million migrant workers under thirty years of age, who are the backbone of China's industries, are still earning about half the income of urban residents.

Marcelo Justo, a journalist and economic analyst, predicts that this disparity will remain despite official rhetoric about moving the economy toward 'a more balanced model supported both by exports and domestic consumption':

> Growth based on low wages and cheap exports has always had a limit. As development theorists recognize, at a certain moment there has to be a switch from a low-wage export model to one based on high-tech products and a stronger domestic market, for a developing country to move forward to developed status ... But in China's case, it will be a double-track economic route, in which the more developed areas in China move forward toward a more high-tech, service model, whereas the interior will shoulder the low wage export-led economy ... This is already happening and will most probably carry on happening for a long while. Multinationals will be more and more attracted to the latter.

Back in spring 2009, the government was trumpeting news of a recovery. 'Large enterprises' orders have gradually increased, and the demand for migrant workers in the Pearl River Delta region increased again,' read the provincial government website. 'At the end of the second quarter of 2009, the total number of employees in Guangdong had increased by 62,900 over the previous quarter,' declared a Guangdong Bureau of Statistics report.

I was sceptical and wondered what this meant in reality. I went to Dongguan, one of the largest manufacturing centres of the Pearl River Delta, to see for myself. Dongguan, which lies to the southeast of Guangzhou, had been transformed from a largely agricultural area into one of Guandong's 'four little tigers' (along with Nanhai, Shunde and Zhongshan), all cities and industrial centres that have seen rapid development and a large concentration of foreign-owned enterprises and joint-ventures since the era of reforms and opening up. Dongguan is known for its specialized information technology, plastics, and shoe and furniture manufacturing. Its industrial significance was once summed up in a few words by the deputy head of IBM in Asia, much publicized in the Chinese press: 'If there's a traffic jam on the highway between Dongguan and Shenzhen, you'll know that 70 percent of the world's computer products will be out of stock.' Therefore, for decades, Dongguan has been one of the major destination cities for China's migrant workers. This was where Shen Wei, the Yi migrant I'd met in Sichuan, had worked assembling mobile phones.

The train trip to Dongguan took three hours from Guangzhou. My first sight of the city depressed me immediately: a mass of grey concrete absorbing cheap labour from afar. The drabness of the matchbox factory buildings seemed of a piece with the grey sky. As I walked the oppressive, dust-laden streets, I found it hard to breathe.

Dongguan has a migrant population of more than eight million; its local population is just over one million. It's fair to say that the entire city has been built by migrant labour. Yet the majority of its migrant workers have no proper status in the city, giving Dongguan the reputation of a world factory constructed and maintained by ghosts.

During the recession, of all Guangdong's cities, Dongguan suffered most – or more accurately, Dongguan's migrant workers suffered most. The deterioration began in 2007, when 909 foreign-owned firms in Dongguan went bust. By the end of the year, the first wave of workers, tens of thousands, had left. Layoffs increased in 2008. Many of the migrant workers who lost their jobs had been in Dongguan for more than a decade, devoting the prime of their working life to the city. They'd arrived at a time when the government was proclaiming 'Labour is a virtue': at the height of Deng's reform era.

I talked to a woman in her twenties named Shan who said she worked in a furniture factory a few miles away. She hesitated to discuss her own workplace, but when I asked about layoffs in Dongguan, she told me that there had been a large number of dismissals at a company called Dongguan Guo Xin Shoes Ltd, where a friend of hers, Lin, was still working. She couldn't tell me more. I asked to be introduced to her. Lin was reluctant to meet, and so I suggested to Shan that I call her for a chat.

Even on the phone, Lin wasn't willing to tell me much – probably as one of the few at the plant who hadn't yet been dismissed. But she described how on 23 April 2008, Dongguan Guo Xin Shoes Ltd had announced the dismissal of 400 workers on the factory floor. Lai Caiyun, who had worked there for more than ten years, fainted at the news. Most of the workers at the shoe factory were like her – they'd devoted years of their life to the company. The thirty-six-year-old Ms Xi from Sichuan had been making slippers at Guo Xin Shoes for nine years. When she was dismissed, her ten-year-old child was still going to school in Sichuan and waiting for her to send money home. Ms Xi found it hard to get work elsewhere because aside from manufacturing slippers she had no experience or skills. Worse still, she was now over what many companies in the area called the ideal working age. She was told when she looked for a new job, 'We prefer to employ the under twenty-fives.'

I tried to persuade Lin to put me in touch with one of these laid-off women workers. Finally, she gave me the phone number of twenty-nine-year-old Ms Peng. Over the phone, Ms Peng said that she'd come to Dongguan at the age of seventeen and had met her husband at the factory. She said that the workers produced two million pairs of shoes a month and that overtime work till 11 pm was considered an easy day. Their wages were low – 600–700 yuan (£55–64) a month, but went down to 200 a month during the off-peak season, when there were fewer orders to fill. As for minimum wage, the workers there never even knew what it was supposed to be. When I visited, in the summer of 2009, layoffs and bankruptcies were continuing in Dongguan, despite government reports that boasted of quick recovery. The first thing I heard on my bus trip into town was that a large Taiwanese-owned furniture company had just laid off about 300 people, at least a third of its workforce. All of them were migrants from Sichuan province and the Guangxi region. Some, who felt that they would not soon find new jobs in Dongguan, returned home to their villages. This was less difficult for those from Guangxi, which neighbours Guangdong province;

Sichuan is more than 1,000 kilometres away. Some tried to get new jobs elsewhere in Guangdong, and others were sent to make clothes and shoes in Zhejiang province, half a day's train trip from Dongguan. Zhejiang is a hub of light industries, such as shoe and textile manufacturing, and has pulled in many migrant workers in the past three decades.

I went to inspect Zhitong, the largest labour market in Dongguan. Zhitong charges ten yuan per person to register for potential work – a lot cheaper than the surrounding agencies – and an additional 100 yuan for 'intermediation' if workers want the labour market staff to put them in contact with prospective employers. Hundreds of ads were displayed on a billboard outside the building. One was from the Mei Wei Group, a Hong Kong firm:

> Our head is Tang Qing Nian, the brother of Tang Ying Nian, Hong Kong's current director of the Bureau of Political Affairs. We are urgently seeking seventeen-and-a-half-year-old to thirty-five-year-old males and seventeen-and-a-half-year-old to twenty-eight-year-old females. Must be hardworking, with no contagious diseases. Must be healthy and fit, able to work back-to-back shifts. Wages increase to 770–850 yuan (£70.7–78) a month, after probation, with food and lodging included.

'This ad is aimed at the new arrivals from the countryside,' a voice said from behind me. 'They think we're all stupid when we first get here.'

I turned around. The speaker was a man in his forties. His dark brown face distinguished him in the crowd. He had thick black hair and a small growth of beard, as if he hadn't shaved for several days.

'Are you looking for work?' I asked.

'For sure!' he said. He looked up at a line of job ads from foreign and joint-venture textile companies in Zhejiang. 'Employers from other provinces are all recruiting here. They know they are bound to find loads of rural migrants who've just lost their jobs!'

I looked down the ad board, and saw a large number of ads from joint ventures outside of Guangdong. I also saw that this job seeker had not taken notes on them. 'Aren't you interested in these jobs?' I asked.

'Yes. But I won't get them. They are all looking for younger and fitter migrants. I wouldn't stand a chance,' he said calmly, shrugging his shoulders.

His name was Mr Lu, and he was from Guangxi, in the southwest, formally known as the Guangxi Zhuang Autonomous Region, set up in 1958 as one of the five autonomous regions in China. His village, Yonghe, was a long way off. The difficult bus trip went along mountain lanes and crossed the Butou River. All he'd seen along the way was acre after acre of barren land. Over the Butou was Meihua Butou township, where he'd caught a minibus to Hezhou, another half day's journey, and he was still only 53 kilometres from Yonghe. From Hezhou, he'd travelled another 400 kilometres by bus to Dongguan.

'Those terrible bumpy mountain lanes,' he said, 'keep my village isolated from the outside world. But that secluded little place is not a haven free of troubles. It is a hell hole.' I was curious to find out what he meant.

The first thing that Lu wanted to tell me about himself was his ethnic identity. He came from the Zhuang group in Guangxi, the largest ethnic minority in China. There are 18 million Zhuang, and more than 90 percent of them live in Guangxi – the rest are in Yunnan, Guangdong, Guizhou and Hunan provinces. Most Zhuang have been assimilated into the dominant Han-Chinese culture, and the majority of them speak Mandarin and practice Han-Chinese customs. The post-1949 policies on ethnic minorities had actually followed the Chinese nationalist tradition formed since the beginning of the twentieth century. Assimilationism is at the centre of the concepts of nation and nationality, or *minzu*. The founder of the Chinese Nationalist Party, Sun Yat-sen, theorized the assimilationist policy toward ethnic minorities in his 'five-group coexistence' (*wu zu gonghe*), which encompasses the Han, Man (Manchurian), Meng (Mongolian), Hui, and Zang (Tibetan) groups. His policy of ethnic identification and recognition, which at the same time ruled out the possibility of self-determination for ethnic groups, was inherited and maintained, in theory and practice, by the Chinese Communist Party (CCP). The CCP developed it further, into the classification of fifty-six ethnic groups in China, and ensured the predominance of the Han majority by also adopting the Chinese Nationalist concept of an all-encompassing 'Chinese nation' (*Zhonghua minzu*). Under these policies, Lu told me, the Zhuang people gradually lost touch with their own language and culture. 'Although we keep our customs and costumes and our dance, they're really just tourist attractions,' he said. He could understand the Zhuang language but couldn't speak much of it, and he was married to a Han Chinese woman, not a problem in Yonghe, because cross-cultural relationships and marriages between Zhuang and Han Chinese were common, and there were a number of mixed families in the village.

Back in Yonghe, Lu had grown rice on two *mu* of land, but the crop was small, and the income not enough to feed three people. For the young, there was no employment and little farming to do. Life in the village for them seemed like a dead end. Since the early 1990s, young people had been leaving to search for work in Guangzhou, Dongguan, Shunde, and Shenzhen, all along the Pearl River Delta. At first, just a few hundred had gone. They had only primary or junior high school education and few skills, but they were determined to make a better living. Most were only able to find work in garment or shoe manufacturing or construction. A decade later, the number of migrant workers from Yonghe had doubled: The remittances the early migrants sent home had encouraged more people to leave the village. An increasing number of women were leaving, too. By the mid 2000s, more than half of the 5,000 village residents had gone away to work. Most of them were between sixteen and twenty-five years old. Middle-aged and older people stayed behind and raised the migrants' children.

Lu was an exception. In his early forties, he saw little hope for his family unless he left them to find a city job. While he was away, his wife not only carried on with farming but also began logging, like many of the other villagers. She sold the timber to traders in Hezhou town, who resold it elsewhere. Lu told me this was another impact of the reform era on the villages of Hezhou. The beautiful forest that he had grown up with was being gradually whittled away. Villagers who didn't have enough land to farm cut down the trees to survive. The local government let them do it, stood by while the village wasted its own resources. There were no regulations to limit the damage. Their mountain hills were barren now; what he had loved most about his home, the landscape, was gone. The ruthlessness of sheer poverty in the new era had destroyed it. Yonghe was an exhausted and ugly place now – as he called it, a hellhole. 'No good will come of it,' he said.

Lu decided to leave the village in order to fund his daughter's university tuition fees, which would cost him ten months of city-level wages. His daughter, now nineteen, was eager to succeed in her studies and to live in a city one day. She planned to study finance and hoped to raise her parents out of poverty. The education costs were high, but Lu believed in working for his family, and deplored the desperate parents in Baohe, the neighbouring village, who were rumoured to have sold their young daughters into service in households in Shanghai and other rich cities. One father sold his daughter for 2,000 yuan (£183.7) and was much condemned for it by the Baohe villagers, Lu told me.

Lu himself had grown up in an orphanage. He didn't know any adults apart from the two female staffers at the place – he remembers their faces were as cold as the concrete floor. He spent almost all of his time in the small library, which was filled with books about Mao and revolutionary China; by the time he was six he had taught himself to read. Perhaps as a way of seeking a role model, he joined the Chinese Communist Party (CCP). 'I wanted to feel I belonged and was protected. I believed that the Party would take care of me, like a parent.' Back then, Party membership meant patronage and social protection. Lu had been emotionally loyal to the Party all his life. Even in adversity – he described the time before the reform and opening up as 'living in deep water' – he had maintained his trust and his belief that the bad times were equally shared. In those days, he'd never seen the world outside of the village. When communal production, geared toward meeting big targets, couldn't feed the growing population, he blamed the incompetent cadres, not the Party itself. When peasants who couldn't bring up their kids began to give them away to better-off relatives, he blamed the irresponsible individuals, not the economic system of the community.

But then came the era of the reforms and opening up. At its very beginning, before the 1980s, he was growing 200–300 catties (about 12–18 kilos) of rice from each *mu* of his land, earning an average of 200–300 yuan (£18 – £27.5) per year, an income well below subsistence level. He was desperately poor and worked hard, hoping for a better future. A few years later, each *mu* of his land was growing 600 catties of rice, and as prices had gone up, his income improved. He thought that people were finally beginning to see the possibility of an end to starvation in their villages.

When he reached the age of twenty-five, Lu volunteered for a post as a propaganda cadre, dealing with all the publicity work for the village administration. He was well liked at the time, and his application was instantly accepted. He was much encouraged by this, seeing it as the Party's recognition of his loyalty. But during his time there, he couldn't close his eyes to the bribery and profiteering going on around him. For each project that required approval from the department, one or more of his colleagues would be taking a big 'red envelop' (*hongbao*, a bribe) in exchange for the official's cooperation. How could party cadres behave in this way? This was Lu's first experience of corruption, and he was very confused. He didn't want to be counted as one of the bribe-takers.

As Lu recalled the past, he had a bitterly disgusted look on his face.

'I wanted to break away from this circle,' he said. 'I even became frightened that, if I stayed any longer around this corruption, I would be dragged into it myself and would never be able to get out…'

He left his Party position and got himself a job working as a machine operator in an electricity supply plant. His pay was a pittance, but at least he had peace of mind. During this period, he thought about withdrawing from the Party altogether, but he didn't act. He had put so much faith in the Party, and was finding it difficult to disengage totally. A year later, however, news came to him from a cousin in Beijing that forced him to reconsider once more what being a Party member really meant. It was 1989, and the cousin's news was the carnage in Tiananmen Square. Lu hadn't heard about any deaths from the official media. He didn't know that the 'riot' referred to in the newspapers was in fact a massacre by the state. 'People are getting killed,' his cousin said on the phone. Lu became frightened – he felt unable to make sense of what was going on anymore. The Party to which he belonged was killing civilians in the streets of the capital. He finally decided to withdraw his membership.

These years in Dongguan had opened his eyes. 'As a migrant, I witnessed the huge income gap between the city and the country. I saw capital poured into the coastal provinces, into the Pearl River Delta, while interior provinces were utterly neglected. For me, this huge gap is the most distinctive characteristic of the era of the reform and opening up.'

When I met Lu in town again the next day, he told me he had not had much luck in his job search. He had just been to an interview for a dishwashing job in a restaurant, and had been turned down because he was too old. How young do you have to be to wash dishes? I said. He simply shook his head. He said his age was the formal reason they gave him when he showed up for the interview. He smiled bitterly, and said that actually this wasn't his worst experience in Dongguan – that had been his first job search this year. It was a rainy day. He called the number on a job ad and was offered an interview. He was so excited, he put on his best white shirt and rehearsed answers to all the questions he might possibly be asked. But as soon as he arrived, he was turned away: His electronic worker's card had expired. The card was required, and he hadn't known. Lu grudgingly made his way back to the labour market in the pouring rain. Cars sped past him, splashing him with dirty water, but he didn't care, since he'd failed the 'interview' anyway. Then two men had started following him along the pavement. From the way they sneaked behind him, and local talk he'd heard about pickpockets, he knew that they were thieves, waiting for the right opportunity to target him. He ducked into a shopping centre to hide, and found himself surrounded by things he could never afford.

Still Lu remained in Dongguan, even though, since early 2009, half of all Guangxi migrants who'd been laid off there had gone back to farming and timber trading in their home province. Now, outside the labour market, he looked depressed. 'No jobs today,' he murmured. His voice was lifeless. He told me he'd been to an interview at an electronics firm the day before – his second job interview this month. He'd been rejected again, this time because he hadn't taken his medical tests, a requirement for this particular company. Demoralized, he decided to try another labour market, called Houjie, situated in a more run-down part of town and open only on Saturdays. It was held outdoors and was only for rural migrants. That afternoon, many migrants who'd had no luck at Zhitong had gone there. Even though the wages offered at Houjie were the lowest around, companies seemed to have no problem recruiting workers – people there were very eager to get whatever jobs they could. Christmas was coming, the orders from the multinational companies would increase soon, and Lu would likely find a job. The question was, what kind?

Liu Min, from Sichuan, comes from the first generation of rural migrants, and describes himself as 'from the village'. But Liu Min has spent all his life migrating for work: He is no longer accustomed to village life. He eats a lot of Cantonese food, listens to Taiwanese pop music, watches Korean movies and reads world news online. He's not unique. In fact, he said, the majority of those under the age of forty in his home village, Suining, in eastern Sichuan, are out working in cities in their own or other provinces.

Liu Min began his life of migration when he was seventeen. He'd never had any education after primary school, but in Suining it was an unspoken rule that rural kids went out to work. His parents still farmed the land and they needed him to bring in an extra income. He found himself a brick-burning job in a kiln in Shanxi in 1990, earning 7.5 mao (a mao is worth one tenth of a yuan) per day – a normal rate for teenagers from the countryside – and was thrilled at receiving his first payment, to him a symbol of the beginning of his independence. He sent almost all of his wages home and stayed on the job for a year. Then he was lured into a more unusual line of work, one that paid better: gold mining. Two decades ago, gold was discovered in the mountains of Gansu province in the north-west. Many Sichuanese youth joined the army of gold diggers and went up to Gansu. Liu Min, like many others, was very excited at the prospect of fast money.

Forty youths were hired by a small private recruitment company and went up to Gansu together. It was a one-day bus trip through endless wasteland. The more barren the view out the window, the more worried they felt. But when they arrived at their destination, things brightened up. The snowy mountains thrilled them – this place was vastly different from the relatively warm climate and green rice fields of their native Sichuan. In Gansu, they drank clear, fresh water in the valleys and admired the natural beauty around them. They chopped down trees from the surrounding forest and made them into log beds to sleep on. Each day, they got up early to watch the sun rise. Liu Min loved watching the snow freeze on his shoes.

The work, though, involved high risks and was physically very demanding. Gold digging wasn't a rosy job when you got down to it. You had to dig up loads of heavy sand and stone and haul them on your shoulders all day long, before you could start breaking the stones into pieces in search of gold. You also had to keep an eye out for soft and shifting sand: instead of solid ground there might be water underneath. Liu Min said that some kids were not careful and had walked onto soft sand. It collapsed, and they drowned.

Those who survived spent every single day breaking up stones and digging up sand. Lin Min said it was the most primitive manual work he'd ever done. On some days, he found enough gold to put a smile on the team leader's face. On other days there was nothing at all. Although the air was fresh and clean up in the mountains, the weather was changeable. At times it rained heavily, and they had to find a shelter between the rocks and wait for the sky to clear. At other times, it became too windy and cold to work.

Liu Min said if it had not been for the harsh weather conditions and the risks involved, he'd have stayed. It was good money – on a good day, he could make 50 or even 60 yuan! That was more than twice what he could have earned in a day on a manual job in Chengdu in those days. But after forty days he'd had to quit – he simply couldn't keep up with the pace of work. He felt exhausted and wasn't able to produce enough.

Liu Min never thought he would come to work in Guangzhou. Other Sichuanese migrants had talked about it being an unfriendly place with a strange culture and an impossible dialect. The Guangzhou police were supposed to be tough, always looking out for migrants who hadn't applied for temporary residency permits, arresting and detaining those caught without permits and charging them a fine.

But Liu Min was a romantic: He had ended up in Guangzhou because of a woman. He'd met her in a Chengdu teahouse when she came to visit an aunt who had married a Sichuanese. She was drinking green tea with her aunt in a café when Liu Min sat down at the next table. He noticed her instantly. She was eighteen and looked a little pale. When he stared at her, she turned to him and said with a strong Cantonese accent, 'What's your favourite tea here?' He liked her 'sleepy, Japanese eyes' as he described them, and the pinkness of her cheeks, which she told him wasn't makeup. They spent the entire week meeting each other in Chengdu, chatting in teahouses about their lives and strolling around the ancient residence of the Tang poet Dufu in the centre of town. When she returned to Guangzhou a week later, she invited him to come and meet her parents. Liu Min was nearly nineteen, young and in love, and his fear of Guangzhou didn't matter anymore.

But he had nowhere to sleep the night he arrived in the city. He thought to himself: Wait till tomorrow morning and things will brighten up when she meets me. Liu Min found himself a corner under the bridge for the night. He was all alone. As he was bedding down for the night, a van driver got out of his vehicle and approached him. The man was carrying ten other migrants in the van. 'Do you want a lift somewhere?' he asked politely. Liu Min, shivering in the cold, thought it would be a good idea to find cheap lodgings in town. Once he got in the van, the driver turned and said to him: 'I'm charging you only five yuan each. Understand?'

Liu Min nodded, reassured because he wasn't alone, and handed five yuan to the driver. As the van steered through the city, Liu Min looked out carefully for a cheap place to stay. But the van drove farther and farther away from the city centre. No one had any idea where they were going.

Halfway across the city, the driver suddenly stopped the van and ordered, 'Get out! All of you! Now!' He had already taken their fares.

Liu Min grudgingly got off the van with the other migrants, who unloaded their bags onto the pavement. No one had expected this and no one knew how to respond. Liu Min didn't feel he could fight this treatment. They were all strangers in this city. He decided to follow the others, who were walking in a group, looking for a place to sleep for the night. They all looked exhausted; like him, they had all just arrived in this city. All of them were first-timers there. 'Welcome to Guangzhou,' he said to them, sarcastically. After an hour's trek back into the city centre, they found a flyover on a busy road, which was empty and clean – likely the work of migrant street cleaners. The migrants sat down, leaned against their bags, and tried to get some sleep.

The following morning, Liu Min woke up to bright sunlight shining on the flyover. It took him a few seconds to remember what had happened the night before. He reached into his pocket and found only ten yuan left. He had to see her. He got up and rushed to the train station and spent the last bit of his money on a rail ticket to Longgang, where the girl of his dreams lived. The eighteen-year-old was delighted to see him. He had really made it to Guangzhou. But now he must meet her parents, who were living with their daughter. She led him into their apartment. He politely introduced himself and said he'd come all the way from a village called Suining, in Sichuan. 'Where?' said the father. They weren't impressed. A kid from the countryside. 'What are you aiming to do in Guangzhou?' the father asked. Liu Min said he wanted to find work in a factory. Any work. By then, there was open contempt on the man's face. He said to Liu Min, 'My daughter will be marrying someone local when she reaches her twenties.' Liu Min hadn't even proposed marriage, but it was obvious that the girl's parents didn't approve of them furthering their relationship. Worse still, she did not fight for him.

Liu Min decided to leave Guangzhou, to spare himself of any more humiliation. He felt utterly defeated. Suddenly he remembered that he did not even have the cash to return home! The final humiliation was having to ask the girl to lend him some money. She did. She gave him twenty yuan and a bag of Cantonese steamed buns to eat on his journey home.

Liu Min could have stayed in Guangzhou and tried to find work. That would have been the practical thing to do. But he felt he couldn't face up to a lonely life there, without even a single acquaintance. He couldn't face up to further defeat. So he went back to Chengdu with a broken heart. Back home, he began to resent life in the village and, in fact, his origins. To be born into a peasant family, he said, was like having a brand on your body that you could never wash off. Whatever you did, wherever you went, it would always be there. His first quest for love had made him see that.

When he turned twenty, Liu Min felt he must go out to seek work again. This time, he went to Chengdu. There were many rural migrants of his age there, doing all types of manual work. Someone from his village suggested that he rent a motorbike and make money transporting people from train stations. He followed the advice. On his first day as a motorbike-taxi, he worked at North Station, and had ten customers and made thirty yuan. During lulls, he chatted with a number of young people from nearby villages. They all thought that the job wasn't worthwhile and were considering going south.

Two months later, Liu Min saw a young woman coming out of the station, looking for a cab. He approached her. She said she'd just come from Guangzhou, to visit a friend. There must be something about Guangzhou, Liu Min thought to himself. Her name was Zhen Zhen. She was in her mid twenties, wore a pair of black-framed glasses, and was smartly dressed in a silky black top and black miniskirt. He offered to show her around Chengdu, as he knew it well.

'I'm thinking of going to Guangzhou to look for work at some point,' Liu Min told her over a cup of tea in his favourite teahouse.

'You should,' Zhen Zhen said. 'That's where the jobs are. And now you know me.' Liu Min took this as a sign of her interest, and so he went, again, on a southbound train, three days after having met her.

Despite his impulsive decision, Liu Min was mentally better prepared this time, ready to make a serious effort to find work in Guangzhou. He didn't know quite how to start, but he'd had experience of operating a motorcycle taxi in a city. At the stations in Guangzhou, he saw many migrants doing that job. They were all newcomers, from Sichuan, Hubei and further away. The large number of them meant that there was a great demand. So he got himself a cheap second-hand motorbike and went to work.

It was really tough at first, because Liu Min didn't know Guangzhou at all. He was still learning the map when he started the job. 'This is a massive city,' he kept saying to his customers.

Some of them waited patiently for him to find their destinations on the map, and others simply left and looked for other motorcyclists. Also, since he couldn't speak a word of Cantonese, he couldn't understand much of what his customers were saying, and some of them took advantage of that and paid him less than they owed.

But this time in Guangzhou, love came his way. Zhen Zhen, the woman who had encouraged him to come to Guangzhou to work, started to see him regularly. She was fun loving, and showed him some delightful parts of the metropolis. Once, on her day off, she took him to a sunflower garden half an hour to the south of the city. He'd never seen such a magnificent garden in Sichuan or anywhere else. They strolled along in the middle of the sunflower field, breathing in the fresh air that they didn't usually have in Guangzhou. On the bus trip back, Liu Min asked if she minded having a boyfriend from the countryside. She told him that she actually came from the outskirts of Guangzhou and wasn't precisely urban herself. He laughed. He began to find her adorable: He loved her openness and her unconventional outlook on life. He looked forward to each meeting, always on her day off.

Zhen Zhen worked at a garment factory, and one day, she told Liu Min that she'd be able to introduce him to the job. 'I've got my first real job in Guangzhou!' he said excitedly. That evening, as they were dining out to celebrate his new career, Liu Min proposed marriage. He couldn't be more sure. She didn't hesitate to say yes.

For a traditional wedding, the woman has to return to the man's hometown for the ceremony. So Zhen Zhen went with Liu Min back to Sichuan, and they had a beautiful wedding in Suining, his home village. Firecrackers deafened everyone in the streets that day. Twenty tables dressed with red cloths were laid out in the middle of the village, and all those who knew the family were invited to join the feast. Liu Min's parents were so proud: Their son had gone out to work in the city and had even brought back a bride!

Back in Guangzhou, Liu Min, the newly married man, started his new job at the factory. The work was ironing clothes. It paid

870 yuan (£79) a month, which wasn't enough to live on, especially now that he was a family man and must take on the responsibility of supporting his wife's parents as well as his own back in Sichuan. He ended up working two jobs: the garment job in the daytime, and the motorcycling job at night. Unfortunately, in just his second month, his workload at the garment plant was decreased and his pay cut by more than half. He was told that this was normal in Guangzhou. Then the following month he was laid off, along with twenty other workers. He couldn't believe it. There was no explanation. No redundancy pay. Was this also the norm?

Liu Min was to realize in the following decade that random and unfair dismissals were indeed the norm. And bad luck had nothing to do with it. He got a warehouse job shelving goods at a company called Xiong Wei Ltd. He was paid a piece rate instead of by the hour, and by company policy, all workers were owed two months' wages and paid in the third month. Liu Min was told that this was always the rule. But it was very difficult to live without wages for two months. He had no choice but to continue with the motorcycling job in the evening in order to make ends meet.

At Xiong Wei Ltd, Liu Min and other migrants from Sichuan, Hunan and Yunnan worked fourteen to fifteen hours a day. They were given no days off for a month. Was that the norm, too? Liu Min wondered. What next?

After six months, the boss suddenly wanted to 'adjust' their wages, but this time Liu Min refused to accept the 'norm'. He had his pride and his dignity, and he said no. He was dismissed immediately, without pay. There was no one to turn to for help. Liu Min tore up the factory's rota book in front of his boss, to show his frustration. Then he stormed out.

But he had to carry on earning and supporting his family, so Liu Min was prepared to tolerate most things – even the police. Once, he and his coworkers were stopped and searched on the street and arrested because they didn't have their temporary residency permits with them. The warnings he'd had from fellow Sichuanese migrants many years back turned out to be true. 'It was as if we were foreigners,' he said. 'But real foreigners never need to show their documents on the street. I realized that without that piece of paper, you are a ghost.' That night, as a punishment for not carrying the permits with them, they were made to wash the floors and clean the toilets in the entire two-storey police building, working till late at night to finish. In fact, this was also the norm – the police often abused their power this way.

Liu Min dreamed of being his own boss and setting his own terms. He wanted to use the money he'd saved to set up a food shop or drugstore of his own back home. He did not want to remain a person without status in the southern metropolis. But his wife, Zhen Zhen, objected to the idea of returning to Sichuan – she wanted a life in Guangzhou.

Liu Min didn't want to leave Zhen Zhen behind, but he felt that to better himself he had to take risks. He did not want to spend the rest of his life toiling in a factory, never certain that his next paycheck would be delivered. He made a final decision to return to Sichuan with his savings and open his first food shop in the village – a place where you could find any everyday thing you needed, from a bottle of cooking oil to a bag of fresh spinach. To his delight, his parents were able to help out and took pleasure in looking after the shop. With his own hands, he had finally set up his little family business.

Zhen Zhen divorced him. She announced her decision over the phone. Just like that. She didn't give him a chance to change her mind. Her mind was made up. She felt let down by Liu Min; she couldn't understand how he could leave her behind for his new business. She saw that as selfishness and was unable to forgive him. 'It seems as though my life is just a series of high-risk adventures,' he said to me. 'Maybe deep down I knew that Zhen Zhen wasn't really suited to me. She just doesn't take big steps in life.'

But Liu Min had underestimated his closeness to Zhen Zhen. The divorce depressed him more than he expected. For months, he wasn't able to focus on running the shop. Eventually, he suffered losses and had to give up the business.

He returned to Guangzhou, secretly hoping that Zhen Zhen would return to him one day. She never did. Needing to send money home to his parents, he began working again in mid 2007. This time, his job was in a poorly ventilated garment factory in the eastern part of the city, where he sewed labels onto T-shirts for eleven hours a day. It was dull, but at least he no longer had to do motorcycle runs in the evening – and he no longer had to shoulder the burden of supporting his in-laws. At the same time, he felt that his life had become purposeless.

In the spring of 2009, he was laid off, in the middle of the recession, along with thirty others. All of the dismissed workers were owed two months' wages, which went unpaid.

Liu Min walked the streets of Guangzhou, wondering if love would come his way again. For a decade, his dreams had been dashed by the ruthlessness of life and the harsh changes in this southern city. These dreams, he knows, had been shared by his entire generation of migrant workers, who had given the city their sweat and blood.

In the Shadows of Olympians:
Unorganized Workers in Beijing

One summer evening, I was taking a walk in east Beijing, just seven metro stops away from Tiananmen Square. I wanted to avoid the underground rush hour and just walk for a while. Along a dusty main road packed with private cars and cabs, I happened to walk past a metal-built shack – so tiny it was barely noticeable – crammed in between two hotel buildings. I was curious and looked through the cracks in between the metal. I was amazed by what I saw: a middle-aged weary-looking couple sitting inside. I went round to the other side where a metal door stood open. The couple stood up immediately as I said hello.

'Do you live here?' I asked.

They nodded. The shack was actually more the size of a shed, the ceilings no higher than the couple's heads. How could anyone live in this cramped space, no more than three square metres, with no facilities at all? It was completely dark inside. No electricity. By the dim street light that shone through the cracks, I saw beds made of bricks at one end of the space. There was nothing to keep them warm in the winter apart from the metal skin of the shack and possibly the gas stove in the corner, which I later found out they used for cooking.

I asked where they'd come from. 'Guangyuan city, Sichuan province,' the woman replied, starting to chop up vegetables next to the wok on the stove. They introduced themselves as Mr and Mrs He. They worked for a construction company in Beijing on a different project each year. This time, they'd been here for six months, working on a building project in this area, along with fifty other Sichuanese recruited by a labour contractor from their home-town. The other workers were housed in a basement dormitory two blocks away. Mr and Mrs He's metal shack had been provided by the same contractor as a 'favour' because they were a couple and 'needed some privacy'. Typically, migrant construction workers are given poor-quality housing by employers, many of whom charge a fee for it. These accommodations are always overcrowded and often lack running water, just like Mr and Mrs He's shack.

'Come in, you can come in,' Mrs He said politely, smiling. I stepped indoors and stood there watching her carry on chopping vegetables, as there was no place to sit down. Mr He sat on his brick bed, resting. Mrs He said that none of the workers on the project had seen a contract. They knew nothing about their entitlements or rights under the Labour Contract Law. They were to be paid at only the end of the year – a common practice, despite the fact that it violates a legal requirement that construction employers pay workers each month in full.

'We are lucky enough. At least we think we'll get paid – because we were paid on our project in Beijing last year. Some people from our hometown weren't. In that situation, there was little they could do. You can't take your boss to court if you yourself don't have residency status in this city, which most of us folks don't. And if you can't provide contractual proof of your claims, you can't sue, can you?'

Besides, there are the heavy legal costs, impossible for migrant workers to deal with. Arbitration alone would cost a worker 420 yuan (£38), and average monthly wages for migrant workers in Beijing are no more than double that amount.

'The building project will last till the end of the year, and we will return home for the Chinese New Year. Next spring, we will be back in the capital and placed on another project – I think it will be just like this one, with similar conditions. I don't think it will be anything different, because this was what we got on our first job in Beijing, last year.'

Mrs He told me she was cooking for the team of builders. This was an extra job for her. When the food was ready, she had to take it to them in the other building. I saw that she was busy, and said good-bye to them.

Outside, I thought about Mr and Mrs He's fatalistic mindset. With no one to turn to and no resources to fall back on, they felt they must simply accept whatever was given to them. But I also knew about the sharp increase in the number of labour disputes in recent years (see previous chapter) – sharp even according to numbers from the Ministry of Public Security, which were probably conservative. The *China Labour Bulletin* wrote about workers' growing awareness of their collective power:

> Workers proactively sought better pay levels, better working conditions, shorter working hours, and payment of overtime. They were no longer prepared to suffer in silence or simply walk off the job as they had done in the past, but instead developed their own positive, innovative and usually effective solutions to their problems ... Workers have seen plenty of evidence from media reports, blog posts and word of mouth that strikes, protests, roadblocks and sit-ins are effective methods of achieving their goals, and they have greater confidence in their ability to defend their own interests by such means.[1]

The first modern unions in China were formed in major cities such as Beijing, Shanghai and Guangzhou in 1918, in a country carved up by imperialist powers and warlords. Prior to this, guilds, established by the old handicraft industries, were the main form of workers' associations, developed during the Qing dynasty. Guilds were based on trade loyalty and internal solidarity among workers and employers, and were an obstacle to the development of organisations such as unions that operated in the interest of workers as a class. Although guilds were still prevalent in 1918, the growth of large-scale industries had shaped a new landscape of working-class organization. The concentration of these industries brought a concentration of the working class. As youths from the countryside migrated in large numbers to work in major cities, the system of province-based guilds and other old forms of organization, such as secret societies, eroded. According to Jean Chesneaux, author of *Chinese Labour Movement 1919–1927*, China's proletariat in the late 1920s consisted of about 1,500,000 factory workers and 1,750,000 other industrial workers, and like the migrant workers today, they largely originated from the countryside, to which they were socially and economically tied. But widespread anti-imperialist sentiment quickly politicized many of these workers, despite their lack of experience in organizing. Since the May Fourth demonstrations in 1919, workers' movements had always been based on two fronts: anti-imperialist and anti-warlord. This focus was evident particularly in 1922 and 1923. When the May Fourth Movement began, workers were still the rearguard, rallying behind students and intellectuals for the 'development of national industries' and the 'promotion of national products'. During boycotts of foreign goods, factory workers were encouraged to increase Chinese production. Soon, these workers began to realize their own collective strength and started to organize spontaneous strikes across the country. A distinct characteristic of their growing militancy at this time was solidarity: strike actions often spread very quickly, from one industry to another, across regions. By April 1927, according to the CCP, 2.8 million workers had joined trade unions.

Since its founding, the CCP had actively worked to raise the consciousness of the nascent working class. A main focus of the party's work was to combine 'the propagation of socialism' with the organization of a labour movement. Each of the CCP's local branches was running a workers' publication, such as Shanghai's *Labour Field* (*Laodongjie*) and the *Voice of Labour* (*Laodongyin*) and *Workers Monthly* (*Gongren Yuekan*) in Beijing. Schools were also set up for workers, to raise their awareness of the need to form trade unions.

On May 1, 1925, the second national labour congress was held in Guangzhou, and proclaimed the founding of the All-China Federation of Trade Unions (ACFTU), the first national trade union organization in China.[2]

This was the heyday of Chinese labour activism, when workers were organizing their own boycotts and strikes against imperialism. By early 1927, more than half of the CCP's 58,000 members were workers, according to Arif Dirlik, a noted scholar of twentieth-century Chinese history. Their militancy and strength frightened Chiang Kai-shek, the leader at the centre of the Moscow-directed anti-imperialist United Front between the Kuomintang and the CCP. He tried to curb the power of the labour movement, using the ACFTU to impose restrictions on workers' self-organization. In 1927 he led a massacre of tens of thousands of workers and trade unionists. After that, workers no longer played a significant role in the CCP's rise to power.

The ACFTU today is open to anyone who wishes to join – a worker files an application, which is reviewed by his trade union group and then approved by the trade union committee. In theory, ACFTU membership guarantees the right to vote and be elected to union positions and the right to take part in the running of trade union affairs. However, in reality, ACFTU is largely a 'paper union', playing a bureaucratic role and colluding with employers. It depends on the support of the enterprises to meet its membership quotas. In most cases, the nomination of union representatives is based upon negotiations between the trade union bureaucracy and the employing businesses, which jointly vote for the committee, who then elect a chairperson. Workers are left out of the entire process. Today, the ACFTU, with a membership of 134 million people, is both the world's largest trade union and one of its least effective.

Because strikes are illegal in China, workers must take industrial action spontaneously, without the involvement of trade unions. As citizens, they are not permitted to form their own civil organizations. In fact, 80 percent of existing civil groups in China are illegal.[3] The other 20 percent, the legal civil groups, are mostly subdivisions of government departments (*guakao*), and 'exist in between cracks'. Other civil groups that enjoy legality and resources are fishing societies, poetry and calligraphy societies, and the like, formed by retired cadres. These are the only organizations that get registered easily and enjoy abundant funding.

In November 2011, when I was trying to find out about civil groups in Xinjiang, the Uighur Autonomous Region, I spoke on the phone to Dr Liu Kaiming, head of the Institute of Contemporary Observation (ICO), China's first NGO on behalf of migrant workers, founded in 2001 in Shenzhen. From the beginning, the organization was refused official NGO status; Dr Liu had to register it as a limited company. In 2003 and 2004, he applied again for an NGO registration and was again rejected, although the ICO had funding amounting to one million yuan (partly from UC Berkeley) as well as a venue. Dr Liu later attempted to register it with the Labour Bureau in Shenzhen, and was turned down. In 2005, he applied once more, this time emphasizing the ICO's cultural role, stating its intention to set up a library for migrant workers. Once again, his application was rejected.

Dr Liu has given up the fight for NGO registration, although he has encountered many difficulties running the ICO as a limited company, a status that limits its operations to research, training and counselling, rather than advocacy, and poses particular difficulties with support and funding. He and his colleagues have always run the ICO with a 'crisis consciousness', knowing it could be closed down at any moment.

Dr Liu said that there was a strong demand in China for the formation of civil groups, as the opening up of the market had created many social conflicts. 'But the government has not been willing to loosen up its grip,' he told me. 'It fears that civil society organizations will grow beyond the control of the state. It fears the power of the people.'

In Daxing district, in southern Beijing, I visited Yellow village, which has a population of a few thousand, mostly migrants. This is where SOS Children's Village, the British charity, has set up housing for abandoned children, many of them from migrant families. As Beijing's migrant communities continue to grow, so has the number of children abandoned by parents unable to rear them under difficult circumstances. The village looked quiet and peaceful. Curious, I walked through the gate to take a look at the buildings inside. A man came out of the security room and walked slowly toward me. He was a security guard, judging from his uniform, and still in his thirties, but his back was bent and he looked unusually thin and frail.

'How can I help?' he said.

'I'm just looking around,' I replied. 'You speak with a familiar accent. Where are you from?'

He said he was Shandongese, but from Heilongjiang province, and so had neither a Shandong nor Beijing *hukou*.[4] He laughed, showing white teeth. His *hukou* was still in Heilongjiang. His hometown was 200 kilometres from Yantai, in Shandong. The Shandongese are the largest group of migrants in Daxing, and most of them work in security, construction, or street gardening. However, Beijing isn't the top choice for Shandongese peasants, who more often seek work in Qingdao and Jinan, the largest cities of their own province.

The heat was oppressive, without the slightest breeze. Buses and rickshaws went past, stirring up more dust. A man who looked in his late fifties was hawking honey juice on the side of the road. His beehives sat right next to the cups of juice, on a stool.

We stood watching the scene, and my new friend mentioned that the honey drink hawker was definitely not from Beijing, either, because he was brown-skinned, as if he'd done farming all his life. After ten minutes, he looked at his watch and saw that it was time for his break. I invited him for a cup of tea, and he pointed to a café with an awning over the front door across the dusty street. As we walked over, he told me his name was Xuan. 'The ancient wisdom says that when you reach the age of thirty, you ought to know your way,' he said. 'But look at me, thirty-eight years of age, and good for nothing.'

Inside the café, people were eating hot pot, kept warm by small gas bottles sitting at their feet. Children were singing and shouting noisily around us. Xuan said he wasn't hungry. He just wanted to talk.

'This job of mine,' he said over a glass of Coke, 'is all I have.' He looked out the window and stared at the honey-drink seller passing a cup to a woman and her child. 'I was lucky to get it, from a Shandong recruiter back home. He works for the security company and gets paid 100 yuan for each worker he recruits. Not a bad deal for him. And the job enables me to stand on my own feet. I'd burdened my family for far too long.'

He said that his village was tiny, with only seventy to eighty households, 200 to 300 residents. He had come from a typical proletarian family in the true sense of Mao's words. Three of his uncles had fought for the Revolution. They were young, ambitious and patriotic. They believed that they could do something for their country. His father was a *ganbu*, a CCP member and cadre, too, a loyal one. During the difficult times of the 1950s, when all efforts were put into collectivist production to develop the country, Xuan said, people were meant to be selfless: petty crimes like stealing were considered a huge offense. Another village family was caught stealing wood. Just a few pieces. They were publicly criticized and punished for it. And because they had the same surname as Xuan's family, people believed they were related, and Xuan's father lost his position as a local cadre.

Reputation was everything then. There was no way that his father could make a good life for his family with that false accusation of theft hanging over him. He had to leave Yantai. His children understood that he was doing it for them. He went to Heilongjiang, where many Shandongese had gone in those bad times. In a way he was quite lucky, because he got away from the village before the Cultural Revolution started.

Xuan believed that the original intent of the Cultural Revolution was good. He said the problem was that no one – probably including Mao himself – really knew what socialism was or how to bring about socialist change. The result of ignorance was 'mad practice'.

Xuan didn't think that the Maoist rhetoric upon which this 'mad practice' was based had been abandoned with the advent of the economic reforms and opening up. He said Deng Xiaoping wouldn't be what he was without Mao. In fact, the People's Republic of China wouldn't be what it was without Mao. The ruling clique, he said, has kept Mao on his pedestal to legitimize developing China through the world market. His legacy was the only bit of socialism – or something that looked like socialism – they'd got left in their bag.

Xuan had felt hopeful in the first few years of the Deng era, believing that the reforms might bring real changes to their impoverished village, where life was so much dominated by the influence of the village cadres. He thought that at last, people like him would be able to go to college and not have to keep singing praises of the Party or be controlled by the cadres anymore.

When the household responsibility contracting system was initiated in autumn 1980, villagers all signed contracts with the local production team.[5] Under this decollectivization process, they could farm their own plot of land and increase their production. However, Xuan said, the demarcation and distribution of land had led to a lot of conflicts, as some peasants were assigned bigger plots than others. The amount of land you were given determined your income, and thus your future. Corruption made the situation worse. Ninety-five percent of the village land had been privately contracted, leaving just five percent for public use, and that had been gobbled up in bribes to village leaders – 'adjusted for private use'. The cadres continued to dominate and make life difficult for the villagers. They went wild on taxes, and peasants like Xuan spent all their labour earning the money to pay them. The worst and heaviest taxes were imposed during Deng Xiaoping's time, the so-called era of reforms. 'We were taxed out of our lives.' said Xuan, resentfully.

Villagers couldn't go on living on the land. They had to seek work elsewhere just to survive the tyranny of local leaders. When the tax system was finally abolished, in 2006, the government called it 'putting an end to 2,600 years of the imperial system'. Xuan wondered why that couldn't have been done earlier, why their leaders had retained the imperial tax system long after removing the landlords. But for sure, the government couldn't have done it any later – the peasants were boiling with anger and if the government hadn't lifted the heavy taxation, there'd have been a second revolution – a peasants' revolution.

Indeed, rural protests, like urban ones, have increased sharply in the past decade. In 2004, there were, as officially reported, a total of 74,000 rural protests involving more than three million people, most of them impoverished peasants overburdened by taxes.

Those dreadful years, Xuan said, drained his village's economy. In 1991, he'd stopped working on the farm. He and his seven siblings all had to leave Yantai and find new ways of making a living. They moved their *hukou* to Heilongjiang.

The four brothers, including Xuan, went first to Harbin, the capital and largest city in Heilongjiang; later, their four sisters joined them. Harbin then had a population of five million and was one of the northeast's rapidly developing economic centres. There was plenty of work. Xuan's second eldest brother found a job as a labourer on a building site, and urged the other brothers to join him. Xuan, who had a heart condition, felt he wasn't fit for hard labour, so he joined his elder sisters in the town's textile factory. They all lived under the same roof, shouldering housing costs together.

Once they'd made some money in Heilongjiang, they wanted to move their *hukou* back to their home village, but it was very complicated and difficult. Xuan's eldest brother returned to Yantai, but couldn't restore the family's *hukou* because the village administration asked for a registration fee of 3,000 yuan, an arbitrary amount. The village bureaucrats profited off the villagers in any way they could. Xuan's brothers and sisters couldn't meet their demand, so they remained nonexistent, unregistered 'black households' (*hei-hu*) in their own home village.

Xuan said, 'I was myself asked to pay a bribe to the police through the general secretary of the village production team. The secretary said to me that if I paid him 3,000 yuan, he would get it all sorted out for me. What he meant was that he would give my money directly to the head of the police station. In total, I would have had to pay 4,000 to 5,000 yuan. I didn't have it. So I, too, a 'ghost' in the village, like my siblings.' Only their mother, who never left Yantai, still has *hukou* in Shandong.

Xuan didn't think he could take the matter to higher-level cadres, because of the mutual protection among officials of all levels, a practice called *guan guan xiang hu*. 'Our village chiefs and officials do this kind of profiteering all the time. We all detest them, and we have quite an antagonistic relationship with them. But on the surface we have to remain polite in order to survive. Just like the US and China. China doesn't like the US, but has to maintain a 'good' relationship, at least superficially. There is no way I could report this village general secretary to the top. I'd have no connections to back me up if and when I ended by getting myself into trouble.'

I could see that Xuan was growing increasingly more despondent as he spoke. He sighed deeply, then said with a bitter sneer, 'Do you know what democracy means in China? It means good connections. It means knowing the right people in the right places. There is no consciousness of the need for democracy here. If you have good connections, you are a free person to do whatever you like. If you have good connections, you can buy your status. We cannot dream of such a concept as democracy if we don't even have a bloody *hukou* where we live, can we? If we are not even treated as residents, what rights do we have to speak of?'

What about a Beijing *hukou*? After six years in the capital, Xuan still hadn't got that either. 'I wish I could qualify,' he said. 'But it's impossible.'

The truth was, villagers like Xuan only qualified for temporary residency permits, which effectively make migrants second-class citizens. In 1982, the government enacted the vagrancy law that allowed police to arrest anyone who couldn't show proper household registration documents. As a result, rural migrants in the cities were subjected to endless abuse and violence at the hands of the police. Since 1997, migrants who hold a stable job or source of income, which must be in a secondary or tertiary industry, or in management or professional services, and have owned their place of residence for more than two years have been eligible to apply to transfer their rural *hukou* to one of 450 designated towns and cities. The rules are not only tough but also irregularly applied. For example, they do not specify a minimum property value for the residence a migrant must own, and local governments often set it very high. Such stringent qualifications are impossible for the majority of migrants to meet, and very few have managed to apply.

In 2001, in response to migrant workers' expressed anger, the central government announced a plan to abolish fees and simplify temporary residency permit application procedures. However, the plan, like most of central government's initiatives, lacked a coherent administrative policy, and had never been properly enforced on the local level. In 2003, Sun Zhigang, a migrant worker, was beaten to death while in police custody after being detained for not carrying a permit. This incident incited a great deal of anger among workers, and the *hukou* permit law was repealed. However, the China Labour Bulletin reports that even though some cities began to abolish their temporary residency systems the same year, enforcement in general was ineffectual. In 2005, some cities, such as Shenyang, reintroduced temporary permits. In 2008 and 2009, temporary residency permits for migrants were still required in every city I visited.

In any case, for Xuan, returning to his village to work on the land will never be an option. And except for his eldest brother, none of Xuan's siblings will ever return to farming, either. His eldest brother, Xuan told me, believed he had the duty to look after his mother and was the only one living with her. And he farmed because in the village there was no other work. Unfortunately, the family owned only three *mu* of peanut-growing land, producing an annual income of 1,500–1,800 yuan. One *mu* yielded 300 catties of peanuts, worth about 1,200 yuan (£109). Deducting the cost of chemical fertilizers, the profit per *mu* was 500–600 yuan. Other types of crops, such as fruit, would be much more profitable, but the family didn't have the money to invest in making such a change.

Xuan looked at his watch and said he had to go. It was now dark outside. I walked with him back to his workplace. He was going to have dinner in the canteen and then go on the night shift, from 6 pm to 8 am the next morning. And then he would sleep for four hours, before his next shift began.

'The security company I'm working for is getting everything out of me when I'm getting little out of them,' Xuan said. His company supplied all the guards to the SOS Children's Village, and like many security firms in Beijing recruited mainly from the countryside. Migrants worked without contracts here, and, in Xuan's words, were expected to keep quiet about it. They'd be told they had contracts, but never received or saw them. When Xuan once asked about it, on all of the guards' behalf, the director of the company said to him: 'Who's making trouble?' Xuan had to take that as a 'no'.

Xuan said he and his colleagues worked seven days a week for 900 yuan (£81–90) per month, that is, five yuan per hour. What he resented most wasn't the low pay, but the industry rule that their wages be paid a month in arrears. He didn't see the justification for it. He had imagined that workers at a global charity would be entitled to many rights, and was disappointed to find that it wasn't like that at all. There was no sick pay or holiday pay. The only right granted by the company was the right of workers to cover each other's shifts. An employee who wanted a day off could have it on those terms, but it was unpaid leave and considered a favour. The housing provided by the company, right inside the village gate, was crowded – four workers to one room. SOS Children's Village apparently never checked to make sure the security company that supplied their labour observed the labour laws. (At the time of going to press, the charity had not responded to the above.)

For Xuan, the overcrowded housing situation was not as hard to endure as the loneliness and isolation of living and working in Beijing. Working as a migrant in a provincial township, as he had in Heilongjiang, was quite different from doing it in the nation's capital. The rural-to-urban transition was tougher for him. He found it difficult to integrate himself into the local Beijing communities, where he felt the lack of a common experience and language. Beijingers, in his view, saw themselves as being at the centre of culture and migrants of rural origin at the margin. The feeling of alienation – of being a permanent outsider – was the most painful thing for him.

Xuan regretted not having the money to spend on travelling home. He missed his mother. He was the youngest among his siblings, he said, and his mother used to spoil him. In a way, he envied his eldest brother for being able to work at home and look after her, and thought he could do it better himself. Xuan used to wash his mother's clothes for her.

He was sending his wages back home regularly. But his monthly living expenses in Daxing, one of the poorest places in Beijing, came to around 400 yuan, almost half of his earnings, and he was also being sucked dry by debt.

'I still owe 36,000 yuan (£3,270) to my brothers,' he said. 'I borrowed it to pay for medical treatments for my heart condition in Shandong.' Years ago, Xuan had a girlfriend back home. She left him when she discovered that he was suffering from a heart disease that would always require expensive treatments. Xuan knew that he couldn't have afforded to marry her – getting married cost an average 100,000 yuan (£9,000), because as part of the proposal you had to buy a place to live, as well as pay for the wedding itself. As a poor man in poor health, Xuan knew he'd never be able to even think about a wife. He said he'd come to terms with it; getting married wasn't so important, really, he'd got used to being on his own. More important for him was that he had burdened his family for twenty long years with his illness. He wanted to pay back the debts as soon as possible.

He didn't see much hope of finding a better-paid job. He'd been thinking about ways to make good money – his cousin came up with the idea that he might set up a family service agency, sending

Shandong women to work as domestic helpers in Beijing. But Xuan wasn't the agency-boss type.

However, it was a fact that many migrant women from Shandong went into domestic service in the capital. Household workers in Beijing are primarily migrant women, mostly between thirty and fifty years of age. Their lot is no more enviable than Xuan's. According to the International Labour Organization (ILO), 35 percent of domestic helpers in Beijing work more than ten hours a day and are not paid for overtime. More than 60 percent of them have not joined any insurance scheme. There are no legal provisions in China covering working conditions for domestic jobs. These migrant women are seen as temporary workers doing casual labour, and have no protections at all.

Xuan knew that the migrants' lack of organization was preventing them from winning fair pay – and that the Chinese state and companies knew this, too. 'We are like scattered sand,' he said. 'There are millions of us, but without power as the largest army of workers.'

I asked if he thought that an independent trade union was what people wanted.

'Very few of us would even understand what a trade union is, let alone want to form one! And anyway, it's not allowed,' he said. 'I don't know what socialism is. I can't read Marx. But I know what socialism is not. It's not what we have here in this country.'

Xuan and I stayed in touch. We met again in Beijing a few months later, as the city was celebrating the 'birthday of the Motherland' – the sixtieth anniversary of the People's Republic. Xuan had never visited Tiananmen Square, despite having lived in Beijing for six years, so we went together. He wanted to know what it looked like off the TV screen. We entered on the south end of the square, at the front gate, which the People's Liberation Army had occupied following their Civil War victory in 1949. Here was where Mao declared the formation of the People's Republic: 'The Chinese people have finally stood up!'

Thirty-four floats and tanks were still on display, surrounded by crowds. Xuan watched them and sighed. 'How much those in power care about face!' he cried. 'Their face is much more important and expensive than our bare bottoms.'

I tried to imagine what it was like for him – a former peasant selling his labour cheaply to pay off money he'd borrowed for medical care – to watch this parade of advanced weaponry, these tanks and missiles, this most elaborate display of national strength. This was where the People's Liberation Army – who have been given credit for the peasant revolution of 1949 – just as famously crushed the student and worker demonstration of 1989, and where rural petitioners, who continue to arrive daily in efforts to have their grievances addressed, were officially banned during the celebrations.

Later that evening, I waited with Xuan for the bus that would take him back to his night shift. 'You know, I'm not without ambitions,' he said. 'When I've paid off all my debt, I will be able to start thinking of my future.' As I watched him push himself onto the over-crowded bus, I thought of how frail he looked.

When I checked in with him by phone in February 2012, Xuan had still not managed to clear the debt he owed to his brothers, because his wages were so low. He had left his job at SOS Village. Working and living in that tiny space by the front gate had got to be too much: He'd had little interaction with anyone apart from taciturn colleagues who were just as demoralized as he, and he'd felt totally cut off from any other community. His younger cousin, still in his late thirties and more streetwise in Beijing after years of working there, had suggested that he change jobs and had found him a full-time position as a greeter in a department store in the busy central Chaoyang district – the trendiest area in the capital that Xuan had ever seen. The greeter job pays 1,200 yuan a month, slightly below the capital's minimum monthly wage (which was raised to 1,260 yuan on 1 January 2012). When I asked what his work duties were, he answered with bitter humour: 'Standing stiff and bowing low.'

8

Go West! The Migration
Industry in Rural Fujian

As I rode the train into Fujian province, just east of Guangdong, the radio broadcast news about celebrations for the sixtieth National Day of the Motherland. None of the passengers around me seemed to care – since radio broadcasts on the train are compulsory, they had probably become deaf to them.

The Day of the Motherland commemorates the peasant revolution that overthrew the old powers: imperialism and the landowning classes. But strangely, the newscaster mentioned neither the peasants nor the Revolution, but instead spoke of 'peaceful reunification', a message aimed at the people across the Taiwan Strait: 'In the near future, we will complete the historical mission of uniting the Chinese nation.' Clearly, the real purpose of the broadcast was to celebrate national sovereignty and national consciousness. '*Laobaixing* will fight for the glory of the Motherland.'

That term *laobaixing* kept coming up: '*Laobaixing* wholeheartedly celebrate the birth of the nation.' Meaning 'ordinary folk', *laobaixing* is the only word the Chinese media use to refer to China's citizens. The word for citizen is never heard.

I asked some migrant workers who were standing in the aisle by my seat what they thought about this. A middle-aged man from Anhui province had a theory. '*Laobaixing* is a feudal concept, actually, meaning the ordinary masses ruled by the few,' he said. 'The concept implies that we are not supposed to make demands or talk back, let alone revolt.'

He might have been an admirer of Lu Xun, one of China's greatest writers. The concept of *laobaixing* has a centuries-old history and it continued to be used, with political implications, by republicans and revolutionaries alike, in the twentieth century and beyond, as it could mean either the law-abiding populace or the leader-worshipping masses. Lu Xun – also a socialist – challenged the idea of *laobaixing* implicitly in his works in the 1910s and 1920s, when he created caricatures of the passive masses who habitually take life as it is, concerned about their immediate circumstances but uninterested in doing something to change them. His comic character Ah Q dreads bad luck and moans about being mistreated but sneers at the concept of equality. The notions of 'citizen' and 'citizenship' imply entitlements and responsibility; *laobaixing* are expected (by those who use the term) to be the passive recipients of rights granted as an act of benevolence by the rulers. That is the fundamental difference: 'citizens' are active, while *laobaixing* are not.

I arrived at Fuqing city in central Fujian, a province that over three decades has seen tens of thousands of its people leave villages and townships to seek better opportunities abroad – mainly in Japan, the US and Europe. Fuqing, with a population of 1.2 million, is a growing city with a seafood industry and a developing export-led trade. Although its concrete landscape isn't appealing, the outskirts are surrounded by mountains and fields. It is in central Fujian that, typically, a variety of paths of migration converge: migration from the rural interior to the coast as well as the migration overseas departing from the coast itself. The outflow of Fujianese, primarily from the area around the capital, Fuzhou – mainly as a result of decades of low agricultural income and problems of land grab – and the counties of Lianjiang (particularly Dingjiang and Guangtou townships), Changle, Fuqing and Putian, began increasing after 1985, when most restrictions on emigration were lifted by the Chinese government. Before the Deng era, local authorities considered external migration similar to defection; since then, however, they have encouraged investment from Fujianese who have become established overseas, acclaiming this older generation of migrants as models for their home communities, and also encouraged a new generation to travel abroad for work. According to Professor Frank Pieke, who has taught modern Chinese studies at Leiden and Oxford, the local government plays an important role in enabling migratory flows, mostly indirectly in the Fuzhou area, but much more openly in Mingxi county in the interior of Fujian, where the export of labour is a top priority for the county authorities.[1] Since the reform and opening up, the government has actively facilitated international migration. Construction companies have been set up by the state to contract labour abroad, particularly in the Middle East and Africa. Chinese Overseas Subcontracting Projects Association, a national organization founded in 1988 and guided by the government, was established for this purpose. According to its 2009 figures, the association has 300 member enterprises and covers more than 100 destination countries. Li Minghuan, professor of Xiamen University, noted, 'In late 1980s, the number of workers contracted by large-scale state enterprises to work abroad was between 20,000 and 30,000. It increased to over 100,000 workers in the 1990s, and rose to more than 500,000 people in the 21st century. By the end of 2008, the number of workers had reached over four million.'

Throughout the 1980s and 1990s, central Fujian became one of the main sources of Chinese migration abroad. In the past two decades, migrants from here have formed the majority of undocumented migrant labour in Japan, the US and Europe, including the UK. According to Peter Kwong, a professor in the Asian American Studies programme at Hunter College and professor of sociology at the Graduate Centre of the City University of New York, some 200,000 undocumented immigrants have come from Fujian to the US in the past fifteen years.[2] Compared with Xiamen, Fuqing and the surrounding areas have not pulled in much investment and, as the local people say, 'there are few real jobs around here'. Young people who haven't had a university education – the situation of most villagers – can find only low-paid work in the manufacturing industries, such as the shoe and garment trades, and service industries. Clerical jobs are available only to university graduates, so most villagers are faced with gruelling assembly lines or long hours spent working in dead-end jobs in restaurants and hotels. And the older generation, those above forty years of age, have even fewer opportunities, and are at the very bottom of the ladder – especially the women. They can find work only in domestic service – all of the housecleaners and nannies I observed in Putian and Fuqing were middle-aged or older women from surrounding villages.

I visited the village of Juwei, in Yinxi district of Fuqing town. It has a population of under a thousand and looks like an old housing estate tacked to the edge of town, but I saw new houses being built and a playground being dug up, with bulldozers around. Juwei is the home village of a Chinese migrant worker I knew from the UK, Xiao Lin. Xiao Lin, now forty-five, is one of the politest men I've ever met. He has a studious look, spectacles, and soft-spoken manner, and the nickname Bookworm. We met in 2006 in London's Chinatown, where he was working as a casual labourer unloading food products from factory vans for the supermarkets. I approached him to ask him about his work. He was open and articulate. After that, Xiao Lin and I would meet occasionally – sometimes at my home and others at his – and he'd share his thoughts and talk about his experiences working in London. In the entire time I'd known him, I had never heard him complain – not when he was dismissed for no reason from a bean curd factory in north London after two years of employment, nor when he was owed a week's wages by a British Asian restaurant on Whitechapel Road in east London. (He eventually got paid, after I visited the manager and warned him I'd have him up before a tribunal.) Xiao Lin seemed always to take life as it is. Was he an example of *laobaixing*?

Xiao Lin had told me a lot about his past and how he'd migrated. But it wasn't until I visited his home village that I understood the force that drove him. His wife, Ah Fen, met me on the main road by their village and took me to their apartment. She was the same age as Xiao Lin, and looked worn out. Deep lines of hard work were written in her brown face. She was warm and hospitable, holding my hand as she walked me through the village and led me to a first-floor apartment, newly built, made possible by the money Xiao Lin sent. They'd just moved in, from their old residence on the other side of the village. The first thing she did when I sat down was prepare a plate of *guangbing*, a flat sesame bread filled with seaweed and minced pork, a local specialty.

Guangbing are named after Ji Guangqi, the general who drove the Japanese invaders out of Fujian in 1562. It was invented because the general didn't want to slow down their marching speed for meals– the breads were shaped into rings so his soldiers could wear a string of them around their necks. Following the general's victory, the recipe for this bread became popular – minus the hole in the middle. They tasted delicious and are good as an appetizer before your first Fujianese meal.

Ah Fen had been selling *guangbing* for a living when her husband attempted to migrate to the West for the first time. She'd picked up the food business again during Xiao Lin's stay in England. She had been running her own street food stall until a month ago. She said age was catching up with her, and as the family's economic situation had improved with the money Xiao Lin was sending, she felt that she could afford not to work for a while. 'I'm on a break,' she said, with a tired smile.

Xiao Lin went abroad for the first time in 1995. Before that, he and his wife had owned a piece of land, on which they grew rice and sweet potatoes. But their farming income was too small to support their aging parents. One day, the local authorities announced that they were taking over the land of the village for commercial use – the village committee had decided to sell it to a developer to build private properties and department stores, without consulting the villagers. No compensation was promised. The villagers were outraged. They got together and went to protest to the committee. They demanded proper compensation for the 200 households in the village. Fearing that the protest might escalate, the village committee said that the villagers would be given a one-off compensation of 7,000–8,000 yuan per *mu*. Most villagers had only two or three *mu*. This one-off compensation was much too cheap, Xiao Lin said. Villagers would be left without means to survive.

They had no choice but to carry on their fight against this land grab. Xiao Lin helped to lead a protest that lasted three years. Every day, the protesters held village meetings and organized demonstrations in front of the village committee building. There was no further response from the authorities. The villagers' land was taken from them by force. To continue the fight, the villagers elected three representatives, one of them Xiao Lin, to go to the land bureau in Beijing to hand in their petition against the land grab. The six-hour train trip from Fuzhou to Beijing was paid for out of money put together by all the villagers for their action. When they arrived at the land bureau, they presented their petition, but the officials told them that they needed to visit the central discipline committee instead. So they did, but officials there ignored their demands and wouldn't even look at their petition. 'Go back to talk to your Fuqing municipal government,' they were told.

Predictably, the Fuqing city government ignored the petition, too. In response, Xiao Lin and others organized a protest attended by 300 people, who marched together to the city government building. 'Return our land!' 'Save our livelihood!' the protesters shouted out their demands. For an answer, the city government sent the police. Two protesters were arrested and detained for six months.

The villagers realized that they were powerless in the face of the authorities. They returned home, dejected. Although some still fought on, others accepted the offer of a small piece of land (just under ten *mu* were allocated for the entire village), without proper compensation in money. Then many disillusioned villagers began to borrow money from relatives and moneylenders in nearby villages, in order to leave the country and seek other means of livelihood. Xiao Lin, then twenty-nine years old, decided he must leave, too. He felt that he had run out of choices. The majority of the villagers had opted for going abroad, because then they'd be able to earn ten times more than they could in local cities like Xiamen. The investment was seen as well worth it. Xiao Lin, following advice from other villagers and decided to try his luck in the US, like so many others.

He borrowed $20,000 from his relatives in and around the village. It seems an unthinkable amount of money for people with so little, but migration was such a tradition in Fujian that people would always help family members to go abroad, trusting that the migrants' achievement would benefit the entire family. He used it pay a well-known Changle 'snakehead', or man-smuggler, to arrange his journey. Different snakeheads charged different prices for passage to the US. Migrants were willing to pay whatever it took to leave China. Those from Changle were charged more than those from Fuqing, since there were stronger social networks of Changle migrants in the west coast cities, such as San Francisco and Los Angeles, giving new migrants from the same city a greater chance for success there. Fujian's smuggling trade was also dominated by Changle snakeheads, because they were the first group of smugglers in the province. In those days, Changle migrants went to the US, using the UK only as a transfer point, because they had few social networks established there. (For similar reasons, most Fuqing migrants went to Japan.) The average price for US passage then ranged from $20,000 to $30,000; today it's $30,000 to $40,000. It usually took a migrant three to four years to pay back the loan, borrowed from relatives or moneylenders (or, quite often, both). Normally, the migrant paid the smuggler a third or half the fee before setting off. On reaching the agreed-upon destination, he or she called the family in Fujian and ask themed to pay off the rest.

The day before his departure, Xiao Lin spent half a day packing his clothes. His wife Ah Fen insisted that he take his winter jacket – and packets of instant noodles and shredded dried beef. And, of course, a bag of her *guangbing* to sustain him over the next couple of days. There was no embrace and neither of them shed a tear. Xiao Lin felt anxious about going on a small boat across the

Pacific, but he didn't share his worries with Ah Fen. He felt that she had already a lot on her shoulders: a two-year-old daughter to raise on her own. Xiao Lin wasn't sure when he would return home, but thought he'd come back after a few years if he made enough money. The snakehead had given him no instructions except in which cities he should change buses, how to get to the port, and which hotels he should book into in various places along the way. Xiao Lin had no idea what the journey would be like, not even which US city he was bound for.

He set out alone from Fuqing, boarding a bus to Guangzhou. It was the first time he'd ever seen that city. Following the snakehead's instructions, he waited in a hotel room near the train station, paid for by the snakehead. He began to feel more anxious about the trip, and spent most of his next two days smoking alone in the cheap, tiny room. The hotel staff hadn't even prepared clean bedding here. In the evening, Xiao Lin ate two of the *guangbing* his wife had prepared for him. Each one was large and stuffed with much meat, and would keep him going. Two days later, still following instructions, he came down to the train station to meet his pickup man, who was thirtyish and had a Fuqing accent but wasn't interested in conversing with Xiao Lin. They went to the bus station, where the man picked up three other migrants from Fuqing. He then put the four of them on a bus heading to Taishan, a small town by the sea, 140 kilometres west of Hong Kong. Xiao Lin liked the look of Taishan – the streets were clean and there was green space aplenty. He knew that the town was famous for being the 'home of the overseas Chinese' – he had heard about Taishan being the birthplace of the overseas Chinese game volleyball. Taishan has always had a tradition of migration: the overseas Taishanese population has reached 1.3 million, and up to 500,000 Chinese Americans claim Taishanese origins. Xiao Lin walked around town with his three Fuqing co-travellers all day. It was Chinese New Year's Eve and people were at home with their families – and most shops were closed. The four men all telephoned their own families. Xiao Lin told Ah Fen that he would be on the ship quite soon, and that everything would be fine. Then he and the others strolled up and down the port a few times. What's on the other side of the ocean? One of them said that he was feeling excited about the trip. The other two chatted merrily about what they'd like to do once they'd reached the US. But Xiao Lin kept quiet. He only hoped that they would actually get there. His companions had come from another village and had paid a different snakehead. The pickup man who had led them here met up with them at 10 pm that evening, just before putting all four of them on a small fishing boat.

Within two hours, the fishing boat had ferried them to a huge cargo ship, about ten metres long, parked in the middle of the ocean. Xiao Lin could almost hear his heart beating. He and the other three migrants had no idea where they were – they had heard from the pickup man that the cargo ship wouldn't be too far from the Philippines, but no one could really tell them.

A long rope ladder hung down the side of the cargo ship. A man on board told the four migrants to climb up. 'Hurry,' he said to them. Xiao Lin could hear people talking – it sounded as if some migrants were already on board. The four from Fuqing climbed up the long rope ladder, slowly, one by one. It took three minutes for the first man to reach the top and get on board. It didn't look easy; he was waving and shaking as he climbed. When it was his turn, Xiao Lin had to throw his small bag of food away – the packets of noodles and other snacks that Ah Fen had prepared, so as to hold tight to the ladder and not fall into the deep, dark sea below him. He'd never been so frightened in his life.

When they were finally all aboard, they found they'd been only the second group of migrants to arrive. There were many more fishing boats to come with people from Fuqing and Changle. They had to wait for five to six days before the ship was full. When there were over 400 people on board, they started to move.

The ship was from Panama, bound for Los Angeles. The eleven crewmembers – Xiao Lin had no idea what nationality they were, but thought they were most likely from Panama –had been paid to smuggle them through.

Their living area was three huge storage containers at the bottom of the ship, each of which could accommodate up to 200 people. There was no other cargo on board. Most of the migrants were from Fujian – and as usual, the Changle natives dominated. Only twenty to thirty were women, and most of them were married, with children they had left behind. Xiao Lin was herded into one of the containers, along with 200 other people, and settled down. Some of them laid out their clothing on the floor and tried to take a rest. No one had proper bedding because they'd been told not to bring any, as it would overload the ship and take up too much space.

The snakeheads in Fujian had assigned the task of managing the trip to twenty migrants from Changle, most of whom had made a similar trip before. These migrants had been chosen when they approached the snakeheads to arrange for their trip, because they were experienced and knew what to expect during the crossing. Their compensation for managing the others had been a discount on the fees for their own crossing. These 'leaders' were asked to communicate by phone with the snakeheads in Fujian every day and to report on situations. No one on board thought much about these men's roles but simply followed whatever instructions they gave. They were also responsible for feeding the 400 travellers. They found some used round oil containers, cut off the tops and then built cooking fires in them using scrap lumber. They had been given meal plans and ingredients for the entire trip. Still, the food supply was so limited and distributed among so many people that each traveller got only two bowls of watery congee (rice porridge) with pickled vegetables each day. The water supply ran out after fifteen days, and they were forced to drink seawater.

It was cold – February, just after the Chinese New Year – but especially with no bedding. Xiao Lin had only a small bag of clothing with him – and some biscuits he'd put into his pockets before leaving home. They had been told not to bring much. His three pieces of clothing were not enough to sleep on. The cold kept him awake. So he'd sit up and work on a chart he'd drawn up of how many days they have been at sea and what happened on each day.

Then he'd try to sleep again in the cold. He said that he was always gazing up at the high ceiling of the container, like the vault of a warehouse 'I felt the ship drifting in the ocean,' he later recalled, 'and I felt I was just drifting permanently.'

Often, he lay there talking to Ah Wen, a man from Changle who sat next to him. Each traveller had a tiny space, and kept to it, because the container was so crowded. Ah Wen had tried to go to the US three times already, by the same route and the same snakehead. The first time he was caught on the fishing boat before he could board the cargo ship. During the second and third trips, his ship was caught carrying Chinese migrants when they reached the US. Ah Wen wouldn't give up. For him, there was no hope of bettering his life back on the farm. Like many from his home village, Ah Wen was still in debt from his previous trips – he owed 200,000 yuan that his relatives and moneylenders loaned him for the first crossing; the snakehead does not charge an extra fee if the migrant fails to reach the destination country and would like to try a second trip. Ah Wen believed it would be worthwhile. Xiao Lin was worried that they might get caught halfway there and sent back. But Ah Wen reassured him that the crossing was easier these days, judging from other people's experience, and that it should take about one month, if all went well.

Two weeks had passed. The next ten days became even harder to bear, as the food supply dwindled and the migrant leaders were constantly checking the supply and calculating the number of days the food would last. Rationing became tight. All Xiao Lin could think about was how to survive the journey. Anyway, he had nothing else to do.

Then, a few days later, the ship suddenly stopped moving. They were in the middle of the Pacific Ocean. Real panic broke out inside the containers. *What's going on?* Everyone got up from their sitting space and was asking anxiously for an explanation. Before long, someone brought the news that the ship had broken down, and that they were between the Marshall Islands and Hawaii. The crew had been asked by the Chinese leaders to repair the problem. But after half a day, the crew hadn't been able to fix anything, and one of the Chinese leaders came downstairs with the rumour that the crew-members were beginning to despair. Still, no one expected what happened next: All eleven crew members jumped into the sea in an attempt to escape the situation – possibly because they didn't know what the Chinese leaders would do and they feared punishment. Five of the crew swam back to the ship almost immediately, real-izing the stupidity of their plan and gasping for air, and the Chinese leaders threw the rope ladder to them and pulled them back up as they climbed. The other crewmen never came back to the ship, and everyone assumed they had drowned in this bottomless ocean. Another rumour began to circulate: The crewmembers had been disputing with the snakeheads over payment and had decided to down tools and damage the machinery in protest.

All they could do now was wait to be rescued. Xiao Lin looked at his own chart and saw that it had been exactly a month since he'd left home. A long month without windows. And now his destina-tion seemed unreachable.

Four days later, a few US helicopters appeared above the ship – the noise of their blades could be heard within the containers. Xiao Lin felt a coldness through his spine. He couldn't speak. Ah Wen went quiet, too. Everyone looked, but obviously they couldn't see anything from where they were. Then they all sat down and waited. When the news that troops were boarding the ship trickled down into the warehouses, the migrants began hoping that they might be sent to the US, instead of back home. The US border officers kept that hope alive, taking them to a military camp on the Marshall Islands, telling everyone they would be sent to the US. The migrants lived with this hope throughout their one-month detainment on the islands.

Finally, on the last day, the US officers herded them from their cells after providing them with one last meal, shackled them and loaded them into buses filled with other migrants and brought them to an airfield. They were finally leaving. This was the first time Xiao Lin had ever flown. It was the same for most of the others.

Xiao Lin thought that this was the day he would be arriving in the US, but his hopes were dashed in an instant when the first hundred of them boarded the plane. There, unsmiling Chinese immigration officers were standing in a row, on a passenger plane, to 'welcome' the migrants back home.

On their arrival in Xiamen, the second 'welcome' the failed migrants received was the border officers' request for a heavy penalty of 20,000 yuan (£1,810) from each of them. The thought of bringing this further burden on his family devastated Xiao Lin. He felt he was going to collapse. But he held back his tears like everyone else. He was kept at a poorly maintained detention centre in Xiamen until he could pay up. At least half of the migrants couldn't pay up and had to wait at the centre. Few households had telephones at the time, so Xiao Lin asked the chief officer to send a messenger to his village to bring the news to Ah Fen, so that she could come to get him out with the required fee. He had to wait for five days for Ah Fen to borrow the fee from a moneylender in Fuqing and then travel by bus all the way to Xiamen. On seeing him, Ah Fen burst into tears, for the first time. They were now in huge debt, poorer than ever before. They didn't speak a word on the three-hour bus ride home.

The village protest over the land grab was still continuing when Xiao Lin came home, as if nothing had changed. A fellow voyager from his village, after being sent back home, asked the same snakehead to send him on a second trip and left the very next day to go on the same sea route to the US. Much later on, they heard news that he had arrived after a month, found himself a job in a Chinese restaurant and settled in Los Angeles. He'd put up with low wages in the catering trade for a year before moving into building work, which earned him relatively good money. Over the years, he managed to build a three-storey house back in Juwei village.

Disheartened by his own experience, Xiao Lin decided not to attempt the passage again, and to try to make a living at home. His failed migration had left both him and Ah Fen bitter about their lives. Ah Fen thought that perhaps he was not meant to go to work

in the US. Was this destiny? Meanwhile, there were no real employment opportunities in the areas surrounding their village. Villagers
had either left to go abroad or had gone to work in another city
or province. Those who remained were older people or children.
Xiao Lin knew he wouldn't be able to stay long. Six months later,
he was introduced by a friend into the seafood wholesale trade
in the northeast, transporting seafood products from Fuqing to
Heilongjiang. But the competition became fierce and the small
margin of profit wasn't worth the struggle. Then, in early 2000, a
friend told him about Europe. He said there was plenty of work to
be had in Britain and Italy – and money was especially easy to earn
in London.

Following his friend's advice, Xiao Lin found a snakehead in
Fuqing. (People find a local snakehead or facilitator in their own
part of Fujian, and en route to their destination country, they will
be picked up by local snakeheads along the way.) One popular
route to Britain in those days was overland through Germany. To
get to Germany, Chinese migrants usually travelled to Moldova
first, with a proper passport, on a business-visitor visa, which was
quite easy to obtain for Moldova. The snakehead arranged all
of these documents for Xiao Lin. All Xiao Lin had to do was to
bring his passport with him to the airport. Again he had to borrow
heavily from moneylenders – the China-to-Germany trip cost
85,000 yuan. The Germany-to-Britain leg he was told to arrange
when he arrived in Germany. So Xiao Lin flew to Moldova, where
he was supposed to destroy his passport. From then on, he would
travel 'undocumented'. In Moldova, he met with a local Chinese
snakehead and was instructed to join a group of fifteen smuggled
Chinese migrants, with whom he would travel through Ukraine
and Slovakia to Germany. The snakehead took them in a van that
night, driving all the way to Ukraine.

In the Ukrainian mountains, Xiao Lin and the others were led
by two pokerfaced, Ukrainian snakeheads with shaved skulls. They
were soldiers and were familiar with the geography. Suddenly the
two soldiers waved their hands and ordered the Chinese migrants

to run, as fast as possible, to avoid the border officers who might come up behind them at any moment. One of the soldiers said loudly that they had to run fast, so to be there in time for the pickup. Those who couldn't keep up would be lost in the huge, deep forests and would not be able to find their way out. Alone in the mountains they would certainly die. That could happen even in good weather conditions, never mind now, in the dead of winter. One teenage boy was travelling alone without any adult. After an hour, he was so out of breath that he couldn't run anymore. Xiao Lin tried to physically push him forward, urging him to move on. 'Come on, we have to go fast.' But he was too tired to continue and after ten more minutes, he stopped walking. The other migrants didn't even look at him, just kept moving forward. This was a matter of survival. No one would wait. But Xiao Lin continued to urge the boy on, saying that his family would be looking for him and wondering where he was if he became lost in the mountains. When the teenager gave up walking, Xiao Lin hoisted the boy onto his back and carried him the rest of the way, ten more miles along the mountain path.

When the group started to walk downhill, Xiao Lin felt that they might be near the end of the harsh trek. In a distance, he could see dots, little houses. Where was this? He had no idea, but felt a little more hopeful. They kept on, behind the two Ukrainian soldiers.

Half an hour later, they finally walked out of the forest and up to a wire fence near the mountain's foot. This was the border to Slovakia, and the soldiers took knives from their pockets and cut the wire. Then they let the migrants through.

Still following the two soldiers, the migrants reached the hilly outskirts of a village and were told by the soldiers to stop and wait in front of a tree. The pickup would come. But the local snakehead for the next part of the journey didn't appear. Just as everyone began to be worried, the two soldiers suddenly made a hand gesture indicating their departure, then simply left, without a word of instruction.

Xiao Lin and the other migrants stood there, not knowing what to do. They waited, hoping that their contact would show up eventually. He didn't. The border officers did. Apparently, some local villagers had told them about the strange group of foreigners. They were taken to a nearby detention centre, where officers tried to talk to them, without success. They had no way of understanding one another, and the border control office wasn't about to hire a Chinese interpreter. Not knowing what else to do, the officers decided to detain them. Xiao Lin counted the days on a scrap of paper in his pocket as he waited for freedom. Ten days. Twenty. Twenty-eight. The officers began to wonder how far they could stretch their limited resources to keep these migrants. Finally, a month later, an officer opened the cell and let everyone out. He drove them to a nearby railway station. Then he wrote down the address and phone number of the Chinese embassy in Slovakia, and passed the piece of paper to the Chinese migrants. Xiao Lin said nothing, but thought, Who in our situation would be stupid enough to get in touch with the Chinese embassy?

Xiao Lin used his mobile phone to call the snakehead in China for help in rearranging the rest of the trip. Two hours later, another snakehead, a young Slovak, was sent to pick them up. He spoke no Chinese and only a few words of English, but showed them into his van. Then he drove them to a Slovakian town a few hours away. Xiao Lin had no idea where they were. But there, the group of migrants was divided into four separate vans, and three hours later, they crossed the border to the Czech Republic.

When the migrants finally reached Germany, they were picked up in a small town – they never learned its name – by a local Chinese snakehead, Ah Qiang. Ah Qiang was in his thirties, came from Yuqi township, Fuqing, in Fujian, and stood out from the crowd with his shoulder-length hair. Xiao Lin said that he appeared confident but never looked you in the eye when he spoke. He was a peasant, like them, and had only been to primary school. Ten years before, back in Fujian, he'd worked as a local 'connector'—someone who links snakeheads with potential clients. But he was ambitious and wanted to make more money. He wanted especially to get to Europe. He applied for a tourist visa to Moscow. From Moscow, he hired a Chinese snakehead to arrange his trip into Ukraine. Seeing all the other incoming Chinese migrants, he realized what profits he could be making himself from the human-smuggling trade. In Kiev, he began to work part-time as a local snakehead, receiving migrants en route and sending them on to their next pickup point. As his business grew, he was able to settle in Germany, where he began to work full-time as a human-smuggler. Now he was rumoured to be the focal pickup man in Europe, the one to whom snakeheads in China sent group after group of migrants.

When they arrived in Germany, Ah Qiang would direct them to different destinations in Italy, Spain, France, or the UK. The migrants had arranged their journeys through different snakeheads and a loose network of connectors in China, and all had different fees to pay. Those on the China-to-Germany route were charged 85,000 yuan (£7,720) each, half in advance, as was common practice. Once in Germany, they were to call their families in China, who would pay the remainder. To Xiao Lin's surprise, Ah Qiang asked him for an additional 5,000 yuan (£454), for 'extra costs on the trip'. He was in no position to argue, so he called his wife and asked her to seek a loan for him from a moneylender.

Ah Qiang had become one of the best-known Chinese snake-heads in Europe. Someone by the name of Ah Zhong was known as the number one after 2000, when the monopoly of the notorious Mr J., who since 1997 had smuggled up to 20,000 people from China to Britain, was brought to an end by the tragic deaths of some of his migrant cargo, who suffocated in the back of a lorry in Dover. (He went unpunished for lack of evidence, but lost his stranglehold on the trade.) Ah Zhong filled the gap he left, making enemies across Europe, where many Chinese smugglers competed to expand their trade in the early 2000s, and was eventually shot dead by his rivals in Moldova. Since then, Ah Qiang's star had been rising; he began to enjoy a new monopoly, bringing thousands of Chinese migrants into Europe.

Once the families of Xiao Lin and the others had paid off the snakeheads back in China, Ah Qiang put them on trains to go wherever they wished. Xiao Lin was advised to choose a certain town where he might be able to claim political asylum. Ah Qiang got him the ticket and sent him to the station. Xiao Lin never knew what the town was called, simply followed his instructions. When he arrived, he was detained in a camp. His movements were confined to the town and he wasn't permitted to work, defeating his real purpose in coming to Europe. He desperately wanted to move on, and just at this time, friends of his in Italy told him that there was going to be an amnesty there, an opportunity to earn legal status and a living. Xiao Lin decided to give it a try.

First he had to reach Italy, and without papers that wouldn't be easy. On the train from Cologne to Paris, he was constantly looking out for train conductors, frightened at the prospect of being caught without a visa or even a passport. Between Paris and Florence he developed a tactic to avoid surveillance on the train: He went from carriage to carriage, constantly changing seats. He felt self-conscious; he seemed to be the only Chinese person on the train.

But he reached Italy, and began working at a garment factory while he waited for a reply to his amnesty application. After four months without one, he decided to move on to the UK in search of better-paid work. So far, he had not managed to clear off any of the Fujian loans, and on the phone, Ah Fen spoke very worriedly about their load of debt.

The problem was getting to the UK. He called a well-known snakehead in France who arranged hundreds of journeys per year and was known to be very reliable. He told Xiao Lin that a trip from Italy to England cost 40,000 to 50,000 yuan (£3,636–£4,545, the price since then has nearly doubled). Where was Xiao Lin going to find this amount of money? He called Ah Fen, and promised her that this would be the last loan they'd take from a moneylender. Ah Fen was already depressed about the debts they'd built up over the years. She felt they were trapped. But what could she do? They'd gone so far, there seemed no turning back.

Eventually, the snakehead promised to put Xiao Lin 'first on the list'. When he arrived in Paris he was housed for three days in what is known as a duck house (*yazilou*), an overcrowded apartment shared with forty other migrants, all of them awaiting passage to the UK. During his stay, Xiao Lin left the apartment a few times, trying to get some fresh air. He was fascinated by a bakery at the street corner: He'd never seen these delicious-looking pastries before. He longed to try some but had no cash to spare. He just stood at the window gazing at them.

Throughout his time in Paris, Xiao Lin was never given any information or even a vague idea of when he might be on his way to Britain. Wait, was all anyone said, until one night he was told he was leaving immediately, with three other migrants. They were driven in a car to the outskirts of town and asked to get on a lorry parked on the side of the road. They were told to hide in the sleeping compartment above the driver's seat on a lorry heading toward Dover.

The overnight ride felt like eternity. There was no water to drink, and barely enough air to breathe. Most of all, there was the fear: This was the very last part of his long, harsh journey, and he dreaded getting caught. He did not want to fail.

But this time, Xiao Lin reached his destination country. It was 6 am, and they were in Dover! The four migrants couldn't contain their relief. The lorry driver pulled into a quiet car park a few miles away from the port and let them out. Xiao Lin took a deep breath, stretching his arms and legs. He was finally standing on the soil of his final destination – a country with plenty of work. He wanted to call Ah Fen right away and tell her the good news.

Xiao Lin considered himself fortunate when it came to finding work. The undocumented Fujianese are the largest Chinese migrant community in Britain, numbering up to 80,000, and they have relatively well-established social networks in major cities all over the country. It took Xiao Lin two days to locate his first job: his hometown contact introduced him to a Liverpool pub owner and restaurateur, Mr P., who ran a cockle-picking business in Barrow-in-Furness, in Cumbria. This English businessman employed a chef from Fujian in his restaurant and had become acquainted with the Chinese community – and with a pool of Chinese workers eager to do all kinds of work that the British wouldn't do (or would do only for a high price). Mr P wanted them for his cockle-picking business, and asked his chef to bring them into the trade.

Since the early 2000s, cheap Chinese migrant labour had been much sought after by local cockling businesses. Cockle production in Britain is mainly for export to Spain, with some domestic consumption. Local cockle pickers had already been in the business for years, working for a wage two to three times that paid to the Chinese. When Xiao Lin arrived in Liverpool, his contact took him to a three-bedroom house in a run-down part of town where twenty other Chinese migrants were living. There were already two Chinese cockle-picking teams, each comprising forty people, all employed directly by Mr P, who owned three houses in Liverpool for their accommodation. His son drove them to work on the sands every day.

A cockle-picker's life is very disciplined. Working hours must follow the tides. On mornings when work started at six, Xiao Lin and other migrants would get up before five. After breakfast, their employer's son would pick them up and drive them to a town called Barrow-in-Furness (Chinese migrants simply called it Barrow), 46 miles (74 kilometres) from Liverpool. Xiao Lin had never had to travel so far to get to work. He watched the coastline along the way in amazement. Barrow is a small Cumbrian town, with a population of around 47,000, set at the north end of Morecambe Bay and surrounded by mountains. When Mr P sent his new team onto the sands, it was the first time Barrow's town folks had seen large groups of Chinese people in the flesh. The coast here is wide and long, as if to accommodate a large number of workers. When they were working, Xiao Lin would put on his Wellington boots and raincoat and walked onto the sand beach. As the sea receded, he could see miles and miles of sand stretching out toward the horizon.

Chinese workers, in groups, kneeled down on the sand to rake out the shiny cockles. Xiao Lin found the work strenuous – a long day of bending down gave him a backache.

When they finished the shift, the workers would come back to shore and their bags of cockles would be counted up by Mr P's assistants. Workers were paid according to the number of bags of cockles they'd raked and collected. One 25 kilo bag was worth £5. Later, other teams would be paid £6 or £7 ($9.6–11) per bag. Xiao Lin began by making £35 a day, but soon became more skilful and quicker, and made slightly more.

The number of pickers on the sands of Barrow gradually increased. Teams employed by different people sometimes worked the same beach. Production demands were high and competition was fierce. During the summer when days were longer, some employers asked their workers to do double shifts: They would start picking at 7 pm when the tide receded and work for three hours before the tide came up. During the night, they would sleep on the grass right above the beach, and go down again early next morning and pick till 11 am or noon. By the tidal charts, there would be ten days in a month that you could work double shifts.

By early 2004, there were about ten teams each with forty to fifty Chinese cocklers working along Morecambe Bay. They were run by local cockling 'gangmasters', as labour providers in Britain's shellfish-gathering, agriculture and food-processing industries are generally called. Some local gangmasters using a Chinese labour force worked with Chinese recruiters, who become their translators, accountants, tidal timekeepers and managers. The cockles were processed locally and then distributed to supermarkets all over Britain as well as to multinational companies like Dani Foods, based in Spain.

Xiao Lin had been working his hardest ever since he arrived in Liverpool. But the cockling wasn't paying enough. His frequent phone calls with Ah Fen only increased his anxiety. He had to earn more – and faster. Then one night, on a street corner, he became involved in a conversation with a friendly man from Fuqing who

introduced himself as Tian Long, Heavenly Dragon. He was tall
and longhaired and outgoing and said he'd only just arrived in
Liverpool, and made his living selling roses in a pub. He was doing
well, earning £50 a day. 'That's more than I earn doing cockle
picking,' Xiao Lin said. He felt tempted to follow Tian Long into
the trade. Then, a week later, he heard Tian Long had fought with
a number of Chinese newcomers who were also selling roses. He'd
wanted to protect his territory. Soon, all over Liverpool's Chinese
migrant community, Tian Long became known as 'the rose dealer'.
Xiao Lin was always telling people about him – he admired Tian
Long for his daring, adventurous character. The Heavenly Dragon
became Xiao Lin's first friend in England.

Two months later, however, Tian Long told Xiao Lin that
he was giving up selling roses. More and more young Chinese
people were coming into the area and starting the same business.
'I can't keep having fights with people, can I?' he said to Xiao Lin.
'Especially not when they're younger and fitter than me.' One day,
while strolling around Liverpool's Chinatown, Tian Long bumped
into a Fuqing townsman, Lin Liang Ren, called Ah Ren, who was
recruiting Chinese workers for a cockling team run by 'John', a
well-known gangmaster in the cockling trade. 'Why don't you
come and join us?' Ah Ren said. Without any other work options,
Tian Long took up the offer immediately.

Like other gangmasters, John preferred the Chinese because
they were productive – under great pressure to earn, to pay off
their debts and to support their families – and two to three times
cheaper than locals. John depended on his recruiter Ah Ren to
bring Chinese workers into the trade. Ah Ren, then twenty-nine,
was relatively new to cockling – in 2003 he'd been in Liverpool
studying English and his cockle-picking brother persuaded him
into joining the trade – and more diligent in meeting production
targets than in watching the tide charts. Checking tidal times the
day before setting out to work is essential in cockling. The tide
recedes and rises every eight hours, and there are only four really
safe working hours for each shift. All of the local cocklers had a

tidal timetable with them and strictly followed the rules, and in winter, when days are shorter, they tended to work fewer hours. But the Chinese labour force run by the gangmasters was sent out to work in the dark, in dangerous tidal conditions, to maximize company profits.

Knowledge of geographical and current weather conditions is also essential: where the quicksands and shifting gullies are; how fast the tide is coming in. Safety equipment is a must: a cockle-picker needs a suitable communication device, either a VHF marine band radio or mobile phone, and a location device, ideally a GPS (Global Positioning Unit), or at least a compass, to return to shore in adverse conditions. Highly visible clothing is also necessary, a torch for night work, and whistles and flares in case of fog or mist. None of these basics had been explained to the Chinese workers – not by the local gangmasters, nor by their direct recruiters. Certainly John had never informed his workers about health and safety requirements for working at sea, or given them any training. As for the tidal timekeeping, he'd passed that on to Ah Ren, who had passed it on to his own assistants, who knew nothing about tidal charts and gauged the times by their own 'common sense'.

On the night of 5 February 2004, Xiao Lin was taking a break, talking with his coworkers in the apartment in Liverpool. He called his friend Tian Long, who was picking cockles in John's team, fifteen miles away. That night, as the timetables had shown, the tide was moving fast and extremely unsuitable for working. The gangmasters of the other Chinese teams had asked the workers to stay home and rest. Xiao Lin's team had been off work for two days. But at three that afternoon, after local cocklers had finished their work and headed home, Ah Ren pressured his workers to go picking in Morecambe Bay. On the way to the Bay, one of the team's two vans broke down. Workers got out and discussed whether they should return to Liverpool or wait for a second transport to the Bay. Some said they'd heard other teams were taking a break, and they should, too. 'Let's go back,' they pleaded. Nineteen-year-old Zhifang, from Putian city in Fujian, said, 'No way! We have to work. There are many orders. We can't stop work!' In the end, half of them decided to return to Liverpool – Ah Ren still owed some of them wages, they didn't see the point of working so hard for him. The others, however, afraid of offending Ah Ren, stayed waiting for the second van bound for the bay.

Xiao Lin had called Tian Long to wish his friend a happy Lantern Day. Every Chinese person celebrates this colourful festival, which falls on the fifteenth day of the Chinese New Year, as a day of love and joy – some call it a Chinese Valentine's Day.

'The tide's coming up,' Tian Long said anxiously on the phone. It was around 8:30 pm and he was caught in the water. It sounded as if he was trying to get back to shore. 'I have no time to talk now. I've got to go,' he said.

Xiao Lin never saw his friend again. The following morning, he heard that at least twenty-three Chinese cockle pickers had drowned in Morecambe Bay.

More than forty of them had been out there, the only team working that night. Ah Ren was an ambitious recruiter and manager, and wanted to take over John's team for himself. At the time, John was paying him £15 ($24) per bag of cockles and Ah Ren paid the workers £12 ($19), making small profits as a small middleman. He wanted to be a real gangmaster, cut out the middle buyers and work directly with the clients. He wanted to increase production to meet the high demands from the multinationals. The cockles that the Chinese workers picked the night of 5 February were to be transported to Spain the next morning. When Ah Ren sent the workers onto the sands, there'd been one hour left before the tide would start coming in. He knew that he was breaking the rules. He should have told the workers to come back to shore before 7 pm at the very latest.

One of the workers had a stomachache that night and decided to knock off early. It took him an hour to walk back to shore. When he turned back to look at the others, he saw the tide coming in fast. It was 8 pm. Ah Ren wasn't around. Where was he? He was playing majiong with a few friends in a Chinese restaurant in Morecambe town centre. He had given the tide watch to two assistants – Tian Long was one of them – who were also working out on the sands. At 8:30 pm, the workers realized the tide had come up faster than they could escape. They were stranded in between the gullies – they hadn't known the gullies were so deep. When they filled with water, it was impossible to swim across, and most of the workers couldn't swim, anyway. They tried calling emergency services, but none of them could say more than 'Help us!' 'Sink in water!' 'Help!' Tian Long called Ah Ren. 'Think of a way to save us!' he pleaded. Ah Ren rushed back to the shore and saw the tide roaring in. He dialled 999, but when they picked up the phone, he panicked and lost his English. Partly because of this, the rescue arrived late. Only one of the stranded workers was saved.

Twenty-one bodies, men and women aged eighteen to forty-five, were recovered from the bay in the days that followed. The twenty-second wasn't found until autumn 2010. One was never found. Fifteen cockle pickers survived. The workers were all undocumented. Twenty-two of the dead were from Fujian province. One was from Shandong – no one even knows her name.

The initial response from the British media was disappointing. There was an attempt to minimize the significance of the disaster by calling it a 'Chinese tragedy'. Most tabloids and broadsheets were fixated on the criminal nature of the organizers of Chinese cockle-picking work. Much of the discussion focused on the Chinese snakeheads and their possible influence on the trade. Justice was formally satisfied when after a seven-month-long trial that ended in March 2006, Lin Liang Ren, a man at the bottom of the industry, was given a fourteen-year prison sentence for twenty-one counts of manslaughter. No one above him in the cockling business was affected.

But British society had learned something from the tragedy: A group of foreign workers had died working in one of their industries, on their soil. They could no longer say that this was not their business (as they had after the Dover tragedy in 2000, when 58 smuggled Chinese died of suffocation in the back of a lorry). They reacted with shock and shame, as they learned about the working conditions of the many migrant workers who made such a huge contribution to their country. Thanks to this new awareness, the Gangmasters Licensing Act that had been passed in June 2004 was enforced in October 2006 by the formation of the Gangmasters Licensing Authorities. Unfortunately, the act covers only labour providers in the fresh food produce and packing industry, shellfish gathering, agriculture, and horticulture. And the GLA, under-funded and understaffed, is not as effective as it could be.

From the beginning, I'd wanted to understand what lay behind the events that night – what had made it possible for Chinese migrants to be subjected to such exploitation, exploitation that had cost their precious lives. I'd gone undercover at various British workplaces to get a glimpse into the background of the Morecambe Bay tragedy, and established contact with the families of the drowned workers – to raise money for them so they could pay off the depressingly heavy debts that were preventing them from moving forward with their lives.

While in Fujian, I wanted to visit some of these families, whom I had kept in touch with over the years. The first person on my list was Liying. Her younger brother, Xu Yu Hua, and her sister-in-law, Liu Qin Ying, were both drowned at Morecambe Bay, and Liying was raising their orphaned son, Xu Bin, now twenty. Liying, an office assistant, makes 800 yuan a month. Her father is retired, and she's the sole breadwinner. She devotes most of her time to taking care of Xu Bin; her own fourteen-year-old daughter lives with her father in Fuzhou, a two-hour bus trip away from Putian county, in central Fujian, where she lives.

I travelled down to Putian, two hours from Juwei, to see her. At the bus station, a woman in simple white shirt and blue jeans came up to me joyfully. It was Liying. She embraced me warmly. She held my hands and said to me, 'There are so many things ... so many things I have to tell you.' We had never met before, but I felt I'd known her a long time; we had been writing and talking to each other on the phone for years. Liying looked much frailer than her pictures, and worn. Still in her early forties, she had dark shadows under her tired eyes; her cheeks were pale and thin.

We took a rickshaw to her home in Putian's Jiangkou township, where we walked through dusty lanes of glaring sunshine. Jiangkou had just a few streets, and there was little trade besides a few fruit stalls. Liying showed me into an old two-storey house of plain concrete, where she lived with her father, her younger sister and Xu Bin. Inside, the floor was concrete, too. The windows were small, and there wasn't enough light coming through. The ground floor had been let to builders from Yunnan, who were working on project sites in Jiangkou.

As her father was still in the local temple, where he went once a week to pray for peace for the family, Liying took me up to the second floor to meet her sister. Liying's sister had a tragic past. At a young age, she was abducted by a local man and for days was imprisoned and repeatedly raped. When she was eventually found, she was so traumatized that she had lost her ability to make sense of the world. Since then, she had never spoken or exchanged thoughts with anyone, including her older sister. Now in her early thirties, she was still locked in her tormented inner world.

She lived alone in her large, completely unfurnished room – there wasn't even a bed, because she never slept on one. I was struck by the bareness of the concrete floor and walls. And then I saw her, kneeling in a corner, eating rice and bits of meat from a metal bowl with her hands. The local government was giving the family fifteen yuan (£1.3) a month to support her sister, Liying told me. This was clearly insufficient. Liying said that applying for disability benefits was extremely complicated. When you put in an application, someone from the civil affairs department would come to visit and assess the needs of the applicant. Liying had a full-time paid job, and her family had been unable to convince the authorities that more support was needed. 'We look after her as well as we can,' said Liying. 'Xu Bin is very good to her. He always prepares food and brings it up to her.'

Liying led me back to the first floor, where everyone else lived. It also had a concrete floor, without much furniture – it did have a dining table and a few chairs. There was a tiny kitchen at the top end of the room. Xu Bin had just returned from school. He looked thin and studious, and wore glasses. He nodded at me, smiling, when I walked in. 'Nice to see you, Ms Pai,' he said politely. Then he pulled out a chair and asked me to have a seat.

I congratulated him on passing the national college-entrance exam, for which he had spent the entire year preparing. Passing this exam meant future opportunities for the youth here – for most people, climbing the educational ladder is the only way they can possibly lift themselves out of rural poverty. Xu Bin was one of the few in the neighbourhood who had managed to do well in the exam.

Xu Bin smiled modestly and said he could have done a lot better – he actually wanted to retake the exam the following year, so he could go to a better university.

He stood up and pointed to some pictures on the bare wall: photos of his parents. I went up to have a closer look. They were both smiling – these were pictures of happy occasions, family gatherings, taken just before they left home to go to work in England, when he was fourteen. His father had been a van driver, earning no more than 600 yuan a month, and his mother had farmed the tiny piece of land just behind their house. They'd begun to feel the strain of making a living when Xu Bin was five or six. They'd wanted to decorate the house and make it a nicer place for the family to live, but that wasn't possible on their income. They'd wanted to provide better for every family member. Xu Bin's father hadn't thought it possible to find any decent employment at home. He'd heard from other Putian residents about working in England. One of them said his relative had gone there, and that many employers were recruiting Chinese people to work in restaurants and other trades.

Xu Bin's father was much encouraged. He left first, and his wife followed after two months. 'I was opposed to her plan to go to work in England,' said Xu Bin, sorrowfully. He hadn't wanted his dad to leave, and now he was losing his mother. He was too young to understand his parents' desperation. He was close to them both and didn't want to be without them. 'She insisted,' he said now. 'She thought they'd earn faster if they were both working in England.'

'We heard little about their life once they arrived, even though we talked every other day on the phone. All we heard was that they changed jobs a lot, for reasons I didn't know. They hadn't managed to send much money home, maybe because they changed jobs ... They didn't tend to talk much about themselves, but were always asking how we were – how I was doing at school.' They never made enough to pay off their debts, which were transferred to Xu Bin.

Liying was making tea for us in the kitchen while we sat talking. Xu Bin paused, looking out the window. Then he moved the chair slightly, away from the bright sunlight that was shining on his face.

'You don't need to talk about all this if you don't want to,' I said.

'No, I'm fine,' he replied firmly. 'I want to talk about it.'

I let him continue.

'That tragic night was the night of the Lantern Festival,' he said. 'We were calling my parents, just to ask how they were, but it was difficult to get hold of them. I called and called. I got worried. They would normally answer my call, whatever they were doing. But there was no news from them throughout the night.' The last time Xu Bin tried them it was 7 am in China. No answer. His parents had already drowned.

'We were told about the drowning by the police in England – their Chinese interpreter informed us by phone. I didn't want to believe it. For a long time, I wanted to believe that they were still alive.'

I was silent. I thought about those letters Liying had written me, telling me how quiet Xu Bin had become – how he had withdrawn from the world around him.

'I gradually accepted the fact that they were gone. Gone, forever. I've come to terms with the reality that I am alone.'

Xu Bin looked through the opened door at his aunt Liying, who was still preparing tea in the kitchen. 'I am so lucky to have such a kind-hearted aunt. She has been looking after me, at the expense of her own family,' he said.

During the year after we met, Xu Bin worked extremely hard to prepare to retake the national exam – and this time, he was satisfied with the results. Now, in 2012, he's studying at Xiamen University. In the summer, he comes home to Putian to do part-time work locally, to supplement the family's income. He says that getting a good education and making a good living in future is the only way he can thank his parents for the sacrifice they'd made for him.

Later on, Liying took me to meet the parents of Lin Zhifang, at nineteen the youngest of those who drowned at Morecambe Bay. They'd come down from their home in the mountains to sell dragon eyes, a fruit similar to lychees, and sugarcane in the local market. They were standing in front of their stall when we approached, and greeted us warmly. They offered me a large bag of dragon eyes.

'This is tough work,' I said, 'Selling fruit in this heat.' It was over thirty degrees centigrade and they'd been standing in the sun all day. They were wiping sweat off their foreheads.

'Oh, we're used to it,' Mr Lin said. He explained that they had worked on the land all their lives until a few years ago, when they decided to stop farming. 'We are too old and the farming income was just not enough to live on,' he said. 'Now we depend on selling these fruits for a living.'

Liying brought us some Fujianese seafood noodles from a nearby café, and we all went to her office to sit down for lunch. Zhifang's father told me that every time they met Liying, it would remind them of their son, because it was Liying's brother who, with the best of intentions, had introduced their son to cockling in Lancashire. Although the memories were painful, Zhifang's father had made peace with them, and there was no feeling of blame. Between the two families, there was only deep empathy for each other's losses.

As we ate, Mr Lin told me about how Zhifang had worked in a

factory for two years before leaving for the UK. He was the eldest son, and what he wanted most was to build a house for the family. At the time, they were living in a cramped, one-story rented apartment up in the mountains. There were only two rooms; Mr and Mrs Lin had slept in the sitting room while Zhifang and his brother and sisters shared the bedroom. He'd wanted to make their lives better, and never could have done it in Putian. So he'd followed the footsteps of other people in their community and gone to work in England.

'Who knew he'd be gone forever?' said Mr Lin. He lowered his head, as if to hide his deep sadness.

At the time of his death, Zhifang left his parents with a debt of 200,000 yuan (£18,300, $31,744), owed to a moneylender for his passage. The burden meant that Zhifang's younger brother, who had passed his exam, couldn't afford to attend university. Instead he got a job in the factory where Zhifang's two sisters were already working. In February 2010, their debts were finally cleared by the donations from the UK, but Mr and Mrs Lin carry on their fruit sales and their two daughters are still in the factory, because there are no other work options for them. Their son, however, is once again considering attending university.

Lin Zhifang's mother let her husband do the talking – she did not speak much Mandarin, the official language taught at school. But she looked at him intensely, and every now and then reminded him in Fujianese of things she'd like to say, particularly about the heavy burden they'd inherited: Their lives were buried under a mountain of debt. Every few minutes, she peeled a few dragon eyes for me and urged me to eat them. A few times when her husband spoke of Zhifang, she too looked down, remembering the loss of her son, and wept. Too proud to show her tears, she wiped them away before they began to roll down her face. As she did this, I realized that Zhifang had looked exactly like her. I'd seen him among the photos of Morecambe Bay victims published in newspapers all over Britain. He'd had his mother's round, innocent eyes, the same full lips, and the same kindness etched in his smile.

Two days later, I visited Yan Chun, widow of Dong Xin Wu, now in her early forties. Dong was thirty-nine when he drowned at Morecambe Bay. He'd been a cobbler in Fuzhou and decided to migrate to the UK to improve his income. I'd never met Yan Chun before, but she had got in contact with me through Liying. She'd called me many times to ask me to help her raise money through the newly set up Morecambe Victims Fund. Dong's family owed 200,000 yuan (£18,300, $31,744). Later, they would pay it off with donations from the UK, but when I visited in 2009, they were still deeply in debt. When Yan Chun opened the front door of their family farmhouse in a village on the outskirts of Fuzhou, her eyes looked swollen, as if she'd been crying. There was someone else sobbing inside the house. Then I saw a woman in her eighties – Dong's mother-in-law. On seeing me, she fell to her knees. The sight of such grief overwhelmed me.

'Please, please help us!' she begged. She wouldn't stop crying. I didn't know what to do, or what to say. She wanted me to help her raise money for the family to pay off the debts.

I knelt down and tried to raise her from the floor. I promised her that I would report their desperate situation to the public in Britain, and do my best to raise the money.

Yan Chun pulled her mother up and took her into the main room. I followed them in. While Yan Chun laid her mother down on a long bench, I observed another older woman sitting on the other side of the room, staring into space. Yan Chun told me that she was Dong's mother. I went up to greet her. She gazed at me with vacant eyes. A middle-aged woman sitting next to her explained that she suffered from dementia. The subsidy the family received for her was only 150 yuan per month, and the newly introduced medical insurance for villagers was a joke – patients could only claim insurance if they were hospitalized, and then only 20 percent of the costs.

We introduced ourselves. She was Fang, Yan Chun's neighbour, a retired clerk in the local propaganda department who often helped look after Dong's mother. Now Yan Chun came to sit down by the large table in the middle of the room, and talked about her situation. She worked as a cleaner in an insurance company, earning 800–900 yuan (£73–82.5) per month. She'd been depressed, at times suicidal. She sobbed as she told me that she couldn't bear to go on living like this, yet despite the hardship, she had to live – not for herself, but for her son.

'My son was only fifteen when his father died,' she said. 'He was so traumatized that he didn't want to go to school anymore. He wanted to work, to help the family. He wanted to serve the army in Tibet because they'd pay him 100,000 yuan and that would help clear off our debts … But we would never let him go. I certainly wouldn't. I have already lost my husband.'

Then there was the pressure from the moneylenders – phone calls and visits. She dreaded them, not because the creditors might harm her physically but because they continually shamed her. She had no dignity left. The indebtedness had exhausted her.

Fang tried to turn the conversation, to take our minds off the debts. Even within the brief twenty minutes of my arrival, I'd realized that her presence created some positive atmosphere in the house. She went out and soon came back with a large bowl of fish ball soup for everyone to share, for lunch. Yan Chun dished out soup for her mother and mother-in-law, but neither woman moved her spoon. Fang began talking humorously about her old job, telling me about the 'ugly face of the Chinese Communist Party', I could see that she brought at least some laughter into this unfortunate household.

'I had to organize all the displays and put up all the posters in town,' she said with an impish smile.

'Did you put up all the posters of "socialism with Chinese characteristics"?' I asked, jokingly. In Fuzhou, there were distinctive slogan banners on the street walls: 'Socialism with Chinese characteristics enriches the countryside'; 'Socialism with Chinese characteristics builds harmonious society.'

'Of course, that was all my work,' she replied. 'As an expert, I can tell you this – When you see the word 'characteristics', you should know it means 'fake'. 'Socialism with Chinese characteristics' therefore means fake socialism. This is all part of CCP performance art.'

Despite tragedies like Morecambe Bay, Britain continues to be one of the major destination countries for migrants. Chinese migration to the UK dates back to the early nineteenth century, when Chinese sailors began arriving in British ports – Liverpool, London, Cardiff. China's defeat in the Opium Wars of 1839–1842 had forced open China's own ports to British commercial interests and led to increased trade between Britain and China. In East London, a Chinese seamen's community was formed in Limehouse, which was known as Chinatown for the next seventy years.[3] There, low-paid seamen from Guangdong, Zhejiang and Fujian were recruited by British shipping firms such as the East India Company. But the largest wave of Chinese migration to the UK, during the 1950s and 1960s, consisted predominantly of male migrants from Hong Kong, including the rural villages of New Territories, who mainly found employment or set up businesses in the catering trade.

Only during the era of the reform and opening up – which coincided with the toughening of Britain's immigration policies – did undocumented migration from China really begin. The recent immigration cap on non-EU migrants and the strengthening of border controls in Europe has frustrated the demand for overland smuggling and made it much more expensive. Given the desperate circumstances, many Fujianese parents are thinking and planning for their children to travel to the UK in a completely different way: as students or asylum-seeking orphans.

Local agents (*zhongjie*), nicknamed licensed snakeheads or 'modern-day snakeheads' by many Fujianese, are making huge profits from the growing demand for student visas to the UK. These registered connectors (*laxian-ren*) work in Fujian's local communities, relying on social networks to reach their clientele. And like the 'unlicensed' human-smugglers who operate covertly, these 'aboveboard' agencies take no responsibility for anything except getting the students to their destination.

At a dinner in Fuqing I met a woman, Ms Shen, who runs a well-known agency in town. She arrived late to the event, and stood out as she walked into the room. She looked businesslike in her tight, knee-length black skirt and shiny gold belt. Everyone seemed to know her and be eager to befriend her. And as she herself told me, she was a prominent member of her local church, the source of most of her clients.

'That's handy – you have both your spiritual and financial sides covered,' I joked.

She smiled. 'Well, yes, we do business with a conscience.'

Her company charges 100,000 RMB (£9,170, $15,872) to arrange for young Fujianese – from seventeen-year-old students to young workers in their early twenties – to study in Britain. Her clients are placed in language schools all over the UK.

Ms Shen said that this was a fair price and included the first year's tuition fees as well as visa arrangements. Later, however, one of her clients told me that the agency fees alone are £8,000, nearly 90 percent of the total cost.

At dinner, Ms Shen only picked at her food. It was obvious that she took no interest in that aspect of the evening. She was too busy answering questions about the services her company provides.

'I've been there myself,' Ms Shen always tells her potential clients with an empathetic smile. 'I used to work in Australia … without papers. It was really tough and I know what it's like.'

'Business is good, particularly since spring 2009,' she said to me. 'There are about 500 language schools in the UK to which you can apply. Representatives from fifteen schools came to Fuzhou to talk about their packages and recruit students. It is easier to apply if you are already in high school or university.'

'How many people have you got student visas for this year?' I asked.

'Oh, many,' she said, clearly unwilling to give specifics. 'Maybe a few hundred.'

Many of Ms Shen's clients are in the Jiangjing township, one of the biggest sources of migration from Fujian. Jiangjing, situated to the southeast of Fuqing, has a population of 92,000, and is administratively divided into twenty-six villages. It is largely agricultural and has attracted few industries, and the local government talks about developing Jiangjing's 'characteristic industries': furniture manufacture and food processing (vegetables and fruit). As these have not been sufficient to provide employment for the township's youth, most young job seekers have migrated. A large number of Britain's undocumented Chinese migrants – some 10,000 – come from Jiangjing. Many of the fifty-eight migrants who died in the Dover tragedy came from there, as did the smuggling kingpin responsible for their deaths, Mr J, who until that scandal was a well-known Chinese community leader in London. At the height of his business, he was smuggling seventy to eighty migrants a day. More than 100 'connectors' worked for him; he paid his *laxian-ren* a few thousand yuan for each client recruited. For the China-UK journey, he charged the client 180,000 yuan (£16,800).

Other smugglers in Jiangjing send clients to the US to work. However, since 9/11 US border controls have been much more stringent and the sea route to the US has become extremely difficult and unpopular. The number of smuggled migrant workers bound for the US has decreased. The new informal migration there is via student and tourist visas.

Despite the hardships involved, the success of this continuing migration trend is the first thing you see when entering Jiangjing: endless rows of massive, European-style houses. It was an odd change of scene from all the poor villages I'd been visiting nearby. Viewed from a distance, the township, with its flashy high-rise buildings, looked almost as unreal as a piece of Fujianese landscape. As I drew nearer, I saw the large balconies and the grand gates of the new houses, which I was told had cost at least a million yuan (£90,900, $145,766) to build. But when I walked past them, I realized that most of them were still empty; they stood silent, like memorial monuments to the migrant labour that had made them possible.

In Jiangjing, I visited one of Ms Shen's clients, Fang, who was getting ready to leave for Britain with a friend. I arrived at one of the European-style houses, three storeys high and with a well-landscaped front garden filled with beautiful pots of flowers and plants. Fang and her mother welcomed me in, sat me down in their marble-floored sitting room, and peeled apples and oranges for me. I couldn't help noticing the high ceilings, and the stylish winding wooden stairs leading up to the second and third floors. Eighteen-year-old Fang hadn't completed high school yet, but she couldn't wait to leave. Anyway, there you didn't need to provide exam results or any other qualification to apply for a student visa – all that the language schools in England wanted was cash. Fang was an outgoing girl, talking and laughing a lot. She seemed excited at the prospect of going to study in England, in the company of her good friend Yan. They sat next to each other, chatting about the trip they were about to take.

Fang's mother was in her late forties. She wore a short, sleeveless navy blue dress and looked younger than her age – almost like Fang's older sister instead. She said she would be on her own when her daughter left. Her husband and her brother were both working in the US, and their migration had truly transformed her life. 'This house is my brother's,' she told me. 'His success is envied in our neighbourhood. I wouldn't have been able to live in such a house if it hadn't been for him. He's been in the US for more than ten years and made a fortune working on construction projects.' Her brother's wife lived upstairs with the couple's young son and hoped to join her husband in the US at some point. Their wealth was seen as an example of what migration could accomplish. Fang's mother said she hoped to build a new house of her own one day. Maybe not like this one, but a house half its size would be good, and would cost only between 400,000 and 500,000 yuan (£40,000–50,000, $64,124–80,155). She didn't seem to want to talk about her husband, but instead described her latest migration plan for the family, sending her young daughter to England. No doubt this was part of the home-building scheme: Fang would try to study and work at the same time. Once in the UK she could get a job through hometown contacts there, most likely in a Chinese restaurant or takeaway. She'd be expected to earn around £180 ($288.5) a week and send a large part of it home.

I knew that a migrant living in the UK would have to earn this rate for at least six to seven years steadily, without significant periods of unemployment, to be able to build a house that cost 500,000 yuan. Fang's mother seemed at ease with family members working in different parts of the world, separated for a very long time.

'When will your family come together again?' I wondered out loud.

She smiled knowingly at my question. 'When we can.' She paused, then added, 'We Fujianese are different, you see. Our migrating ancestors left us with this legacy: You mustn't sit and take what is thrown at you in life. You must always endeavour to improve your living standards. You must do better. It's a traditional Chinese idea that "fallen leaves must return to their roots" (*luo ye gui gen*). But it is the Fujianese thinking that fallen leaves must find roots where they fall.'

Fang told me that Ms Shen's agency had promised Fang accommodation in England as part of the package – which also included visa procedures and an offer from a language school – costing 100,000 RMB (£9,170) in all, before the family put in the application. The price was standard and no one usually bargained. But once the deal was done, Ms Shen mentioned to Fang in a casual phone conversation that Fang would have to find her own place to live in London. 'It's easy to find a room over there,' Ms Shen said to her. But Fang would be new to the city and hadn't the slightest idea how to find a place – nor did she speak enough English to do so. She would have to rely on hometown contacts. This did not seem to worry her – problems with the agency are seen as part of the migration process, and problems with accommodation were not unusual. Why make a fuss about it? 'Everyone else can do it. Why can't we?' was the common attitude.

In Jiangjing, as in many other towns in Fujian, new houses are always built on ancestral land. It is an expression of pride, not only for family members individually, but also for the name and tradition of the family itself. Even for migrants who settle permanently overseas, it is still important that the houses they build in their native towns, with years and years of earnings sent home, be on land the family has always owned. That explained the empty mansions I'd wondered about when entering Jiangjing. I learned that at least a third of all this new construction had been supervised by relatives of migrants living abroad, and even when these family members didn't move into the houses themselves, they took pride in looking after them. These untenanted houses, I realized, were seen as emblems of how hard-working migrants were enriching their families and their homeland.

'Have you got to my home yet?' asked Mr Cai anxiously. He'd called me from London an hour before I reached his home village of Jiatou, Xincuo township, in Fuqing. I'd met Mr Cai when walking past a building site in east London and had since invited him for tea at my place many times. He'd found our meetings a nice little break from his stressful and isolated working life in London.

Xincuo, a seaside town, is about an hour by bus from Fuqing. Jiatou is a tiny fishing village within the township of Xincuo, and has only a few thousand households. However, it is dotted with symbols of successful migration: a few new houses already stand handsomely in the neighbourhood, and more are in the process of being built. More than half of the families here, though, are without migrant members, and their homes look run-down and old, some needing repair work, making a sharp visual contrast to the prosperity of others in the village. Mr Cai's new house, three storeys high, towered over the old farmhouses around it. Each floor, supported by grand imitation-Greek pillars, had a pretty balcony large enough to hold a summer barbecue.

Cai's wife, Xiuyu, answered the door. She seemed to be in her early forties, had short black hair and was casually dressed in a pink T-shirt and black tracksuit trousers. She greeted me warmly and led me inside. I couldn't contain my amazement at the beautifully decorated interior. From the marble-floored lounge, a wide winding staircase led to the two upper floors. To the left of the lounge was a large kitchen, furnished with modern appliances and pine cupboards.

'It's magnificent!' I gushed. Xiuyu seemed very pleased.

'This is all from my husband's nine long years in England!' she said. The house had cost 600,000 RMB (£55,018) to build. It had been completed three months ago, and she'd moved right in.

'Have you sent pictures of it to him?' I was referring to her husband, who had not come home once in the entire nine years.

'Of course!' she said merrily. 'He's very happy with the style and structure.'

Xiuyu introduced me to her neighbours, who were gathering in her sitting room to play cards. Six or seven of them, all middle-aged women from the next-door farmhouses, were chatting happily. Cai's younger brother, in his thirties, was also there, joining in the game. He was shirtless, on a short lunch break from his own building site. They all looked up and greeted me. One of the women said: 'Isn't this house wonderful? I wish my husband could build me a house like this!' She looked genuinely envious, and everyone else laughed. Cai's brother said proudly that without Cai, the house wouldn't have been possible. Now its spacious lounge was a communal social venue for the village women, many of whom were alone because their husbands were working abroad in the US and UK. Their husbands might not have been there long enough to be able to afford houses like Cai's.

Mr Cai, now forty-eight years old, began as a fisherman. He'd never got beyond primary school. He grew up learning about the fishing trade from his father, who owned a good boat. They had worked together, and when sales were good, in the early 1980s, Cai and his dad used to jointly earn 10,000 yuan (£916, $1,587) a year. But that was far from sufficient for their extended family: his parents, grandparents, him and his brother, both single at the time all lived under one roof.

Cai made his first labour migration abroad to Taiwan at the age of twenty-seven. He'd heard that you could earn five or six times more working in construction or manufacturing there. Back then, before the cross-strait travel ban was lifted in 1987, migration from China was strictly controlled, limited to a tiny number of exceptionally allowed family visits. As there was no formal migration channel for the Chinese, Cai, like many other Fujianese, had to be smuggled in.

In Keelung, the port of Taiwan at which he arrived, Cai called up a Fujianese man whose phone number he'd got from a friend in Fuqing. This man was well connected and knew contractors who employed Chinese workers on construction projects in Taipei. Cai ended up in a town called Xinzhuang on the outskirts of Taipei and started working as a labourer, loading concrete and helping out on a building site. He was earning the equivalent of 1,000 yuan a month, higher than what he earned at home, but hardly sufficient for him to pay back his loan, let alone send money to his family for anything else. He lived with a number of other Fujianese workers a few blocks from the site. Unfortunately, this residence was situated quite close to a police station, and at the time, there was a perceived increase in the number of Chinese being smuggled from Fujian to Taiwan, and a growing police focus on 'catching the illegals'. Within a month of arriving in Taiwan, Cai was arrested in a police raid on his workplace and was immediately deported back to China.

Young and undiscouraged, Cai next went for the popular option of Japan. A smuggler in Fuqing arranged the journey: Cai followed his instructions, travelling alone by bus to Kunming in the southwestern province of Yunnan. The trip took nearly two days. Once in Kunming, he met with his pickup man, joining other migrants who were already there. Before dusk, they arrived at a border town, where they waited till late night to be led across into Burma. In Burma, the migrants were picked up again by a local man and taken to a cheap hotel room, where they rested for a day. In the evening, they set off again – this time in a van, all the way to the border of Thailand. Cai had no idea where he was; he had lost all sense of direction. All he could remember was being taken into Thailand. From there, he was put on a plane to Singapore. After a few days' wait, he was instructed to board another plane, from Singapore to Japan. He began to feel hopeful, thinking that now he'd reach his destination soon enough.

He never boarded that plane – he and the other migrants were all arrested at the airport. They were taken to the police station and two days later were given Singapore's punishment for breaking the law: They were whipped by an officer. Immediately afterward, they were deported.

At least being deported again to Fujian was no disgrace there. Back home, deportation was seen as simply part of a migration scheme gone wrong: No one would blame him for the doings of governments.

In the following two years, Cai tried to find work in and around his village, to no avail. There was no way he could return to fishing now. He had big loans to pay off, totalling 150,000 yuan, from his failed attempts to go abroad. He knew that no job he could get in Fujian would pay well enough to clear off that debt. In this situation, he was easily persuaded into another migration. This time, some villagers told him that he should go to the US. There were relatively strong Fujianese networks there.

Chinese presence in the US dates back to the 1800s, when Chinese migrants, most of them from Guangdong province, were sent to build the Transcontinental Railroad. The predominantly male workforce tolerated poor working conditions, formed their own communities and eventually settled, despite much anti-Chinese prejudice and discrimination. In 1882, the first piece of anti-Chinese legislation, the Chinese Exclusion Act, formally shut the US borders to Chinese workers. From then onward, the Chinese communities became enclosed and self-reliant.

The Chinese Exclusion Act was repealed in 1943 when China joined the Allied Powers during the Second World War. In theory, this repeal also lifted the ban on granting US citizenship to Chinese residents.

But in fact, it was only after 1964, when the Civil Rights Act was enacted, and 1968, when the Amendments to the Immigration and Nationality Act came into effect and race-based immigration quotas were eliminated, that the nearly eighty-year-old barrier to Chinese immigration was finally completely removed.

Since the era of reforms opened China's doors in the 1980s, a growing inflow of Fujianese migrants has transformed American Chinese communities. Migrants from Lianjiang took the lead, quickly finding their own space in US cities. They were followed by wave after wave of peasants and fishermen from Changle and their descendents, who through the 1980s and 1990s risked their lives entering the US by sea, lured by stories of the long-term settlement enjoyed by earlier migrants. Then came the people from Fuqing. And news of these migrants' successes in western cities, such as Los Angeles, encouraged further waves of migration from the Fujian.

The number of Chinese migrants in the US grew from 27,000 in the 1960s to 124,000 in the 1980s and 420,000 in the 1990s.[4] Between 1980 and 2002, 911,000 Chinese settled in the US.[5] In 2002, more than 700,000 temporary migrants, mostly students and skilled workers, were admitted as well.

The Immigration Act of 1990 was intended to limit the influx of low-skilled migrants in particular, and since it came into effect visa quotas for skilled migrant labour have been ten times higher than quotas for low-skilled or unskilled workers. When the latter group was denied access to legitimate migration channels, temporary and irregular Chinese migration increased. The number of Fujianese migrants who chose to be smuggled into the US grew fast. Tens of thousands of them paid smugglers high fees and braved the perilous sea crossing only to end up in the lowest-paid jobs in the garment and service industries. As US border controls tightened, the sea route became even more dangerous. Hearing stories of failed attempts, eventually Cai abandoned his

US plans. A friend who was already working in London had told him that there was a great deal of work to do in British construction and the industry seemed to have a liking for Chinese labour. As Cai was still indebted and couldn't find decent work locally, he decided Britain was his only chance, and in the summer of 2001, he went.

Again he had to borrow heavily from the moneylenders. The snakehead who arranged his trip charged him 180,000 yuan (£16,500, $28,579). He was given a Korean passport and instructed to fly to Hong Kong and from there to Japan. In Japan, he was met by a local snakehead who helped him board a plane direct to London. He was now deeper in debt than ever, and determined to succeed. When he arrived in London, Cai's friend introduced him to a number of Fujianese labour contractors who were recruiting workers from their home province – preferred because they spoke the same language – for building sites, all over London. These Fujianese recruiters usually worked for a layer of British Asian middlemen who took on building projects – both houses and hotels – from private landlords and companies. The hiring was always arranged in an informal manner and payment was not guaranteed. A Fujianese recruiter would sometimes be approached by one of these middlemen on the street and asked to provide a team of workers. Frequently, Cai heard, when the job was done the middleman simply disappeared without paying the recruiter, and so the workers were not paid, either. Still, construction remained a popular trade for male Chinese migrants, as jobs were relatively easy to get. Cai and his co-workers estimated that there were at least 30,000 Chinese builders working in London.

Cai has been lucky enough to stay employed most of the time. He told me he thinks the main reason is that he stuck with one recruiter all these years, despite a few short bad periods when there wasn't much work. Usually, construction workers go from one employer to another, seeking available jobs. Cai remained loyal to his recruiter from Fuqing, and built up a good working relationship with him. Even when there was an immigration raid on a nearby site and the other workers on his team scattered, Cai didn't leave the job. As a result, his employer trusted him, and his 'rice bowl' was secured. Cai gave his utmost and never asked for a day off. Sometimes he worked nonstop for a month. Within two years, he managed to pay off the money he'd borrowed to enter Britain. He wasn't alone in this achievement. Paying off 180,000 yuan was possible if a migrant could keep working, without long intervals between jobs.

Cai doesn't understand the concept behind 'workaholic'. His sole purpose for being in Britain is to earn as much as possible. On average, he makes £1,500 per month, and sends £1,000 home. But without papers, he cannot return himself. 'When my father passed away, I couldn't go home to attend his funeral. When my mother passed away last November, my family called me and I told them I couldn't leave England. What else could I have done? I have no passport. I just can't go back.'

In their newly built house, Xiuyu led me up the wide marble staircase to the second floor, where her air-conditioned bedroom is. The bed was also new, with pink sheets and bright red pillows. The walls looked freshly painted. 'That's your room,' she said, smiling and pointing to another large, well-decorated bedroom on the other side of the staircase. She generously pressed me to stay overnight, but Liying had already booked a hotel room for me in Fuqing town centre, which I couldn't refuse. Then she took me to the third floor, where two more large furnished bedrooms stood empty.

'Our daughter and son no longer live at home,' Xiuyu said quietly. 'Now I am totally alone.'

Her twenty-seven-year-old son, Aiguo, was working in Italy, one of tens of thousands Fujianese who were smuggled through Europe aiming for Britain but became stranded in other countries. Some of them waited for months in Italian cities with no promised date for departure; eventually they decided to stay and work. Aiguo was one of them –his snakehead never told him why he hadn't been able to get him out of Italy. But like other relatively new arrivals,

Aiguo had found employment in a handbag factory run and owned by earlier migrants from the rural outskirts of Wenzhou, a prefecture city in Zhejiang province. Wenzhou's lack of cultivated land (farmland accounts for only 10 percent of the prefecture's total area), coupled with a poor transportation system, made it difficult to survive there, and since the 1980s, international migration has been rapidly increasing, alongside internal migration among the Wenzhounese, according to Dr Wu Bin of the University of Nottingham, who has done extensive research on Wenzhou migration to Europe. By 2003, around 2.1 million Wenzhounese were living outside of Wenzhou, and by 2004 425,000 were living in ninty-three countries worldwide. The majority of them, 98.7 percent, are concentrated in France, Italy and the Netherlands. Dr Wu calls them Europe's Chinese Jews.

The rural Wenzhou Zhejianese are seen as adventurers and natural traders. They have travelled far and brought their skills and knowledge of the traditional textile industry with them wherever they settled. They form the majority of the Chinese migrant population in Italy, having pioneered Chinese migration to Europe long before the Fujianese began coming in the later 1980s. The Fujianese men and women, therefore, tend to follow the choices and patterns of employment already set out by the Zhejiang migrants, many of whom are now garment traders and factory owners. The Zhejianese and Fujianese speak completely different dialects and cannot communicate without using Mandarin, China's national language. They have formed two different classes in the Chinese communities in Italy – bosses and workers – and quite often are antagonistic toward each other.

Aiguo, like other Fujianese, had endured very low wages and long working hours under Zhejiangnese bosses, much like the Fujianese migrants working for Cantonese speakers in Britain. He and other male workers operated the machines that cut and shaped the handbags, while their female colleagues did the sewing, for a minimum of sixteen hours a day, seven days a week, for 500 euros per month.

Some worked like this for years. Others tried to save money to set up their own small businesses, following the Zhejianese model, but without experience, they often failed in their ventures. Still others attempted once more to reach the UK.

Aiguo spoke with his mother once a week on the phone. He told her that he'd recently fallen for a woman. A divorcée, his mother said, and frowned. Her name was Qin, and she'd been smuggled into Europe from Fuqing a few years before by the famous Ah Zhong, before he was shot dead. Her destination country was the UK, but while waiting in Milan, she became acquainted with a few Fujianese migrants and was introduced to a handbag factory job. At first, she simply wanted to bring in some income during the wait. But six months passed and she still didn't know when the next transport would be. So she stayed on in the low-paid factory job, earning about one third of the money she'd have been paid in Britain for the same work, to support her son back home.

'And I know about your twenty-two-year-old daughter,' I said to Xiuyu. Cai had told me about his girl one day when he was feeling depressed and worried about her. Her name was Yun, and she'd been smuggled into Britain when she was nineteen, in 2006. Xiuyu took out an album to show me pictures of Yun when she was fifteen, family pictures, with Cai and Xiuyu holding their daughter between them.

'Isn't she pretty?' Xiuyu said. 'Why don't you take this picture with you, to find her a man?'

'In England?' I asked, wondering what she'd think about having an English son-in-law.

'Yes, in England!' she replied with assurance. 'It doesn't matter if he's English or Chinese, just as long as he can give her a good life.'

On arrival at Heathrow Airport in Britain, Yun, following instructions from the man who had arranged her journey, told immigration that she was sixteen and an orphan. As expected, she was immediately detained and then put in a home run by Hillingdon social services near the airport.

According to Cai, the Fujianese were told by snakeheads that the best and easiest way for their children to enter and stay in the UK was to claim to be orphans. 'And in fact, looking at the stricter immigration rules now, this seems the only way,' Cai said.

'We chose to send her this way because we wanted her to leave Fujian,' he continued. 'There is no future in China for people of our background. What would you do if they were your children? Wouldn't you want a good future for them? We want our daughter to start a new life in England, and find opportunity.'

The current exodus of Chinese youth is predominantly from the villages and townships of Fujian, where there are few industries or employment opportunities to keep them. A large number of these new migrants are young women, leaving home for the first time. Some of them, like Yun, come to join their parents already working undocumented in Britain, although she wouldn't live with her father and could not tell the authorities that he was also in Britain. Yun's ideal plan is to live and settle down in Britain. Her parents hope she will take advantage of the educational opportunities as well as find employment to support herself, and, in the longer term, their own parents and extended families.

The smugglers usually arrange for these youngsters to arrive in their destination country with an adult. But the adult disappears on arrival, and the young migrants have been coached to say that they don't know the adult in any circumstances. They appear as unaccompanied minors and claim asylum as orphans, and are put under social care, since they are officially underage. Hundreds of them may be granted refugee status later on. Others leave social care and disappear into the informal economy with the help of relatives or hometown contacts.

Yun entered the Hillingdon home in 2006. Seventy-seven Chinese youths have been reported missing from this care facility since March 2006, but Yun was not one of them: She left Hillingdon in 2009 and began to live independently when she reached her official (false) age of eighteen. She is now studying in a local school (arranged by her care manager and free of charge) and working part-time in a restaurant. As she had claimed to be an unaccompanied minor when she entered Britain, in theory she could not return to China, and she therefore began an application for asylum in the UK. Compared with other youth in the same situation, she is fortunate, because unknown to the authorities her father was already working in Britain, and she was able to see him during the stressful period of her asylum application.

Since 2009, the British media have reported a growing number of children missing from care homes: between September 2008 and September 2009 145 children and youths disappeared. Of those, 90 percent had been officially categorized as unaccompanied asylum-seeking children. After I returned from China, I visited forty Chinese youths in a college in the Hounslow area of west London, where they were studying English, mathematics, health, and social work free of charge. They had all apparently arrived as unaccompanied minors, and Hillingdon had transferred them to Hounslow social services, where their education and care could be arranged. Their welfare officer at the college, who was looking after their learning needs, met me there. She said that she had found it difficult to communicate with these young people, as they had been very withdrawn and she had no idea about the possible trouble they were in.

Ten of the youths showed up that day to meet us. We were led by their welfare officer to an empty classroom to talk. It was obvious that they wouldn't open up in front of the group, so I tried questioning them individually.

Most of them spoke with a Fujianese accent, although some claimed they came from other provinces. They all told the same story. They were orphans; their journeys were arranged by family members or close associates; the adults accompanying them during the trip disappeared on their arrival in Britain; they are applying for asylum and are waiting for a decision; none of them want to return to China and in fact would have difficulty returning because they don't have any documents; they are all living on £52 per week from the social services, which will continue to support them until they reach the official age of consent; they're all working part-time outside of school hours.

Inside the classroom, the youth sat together quietly with the welfare officer while I talked with them one by one. A timid-looking seventeen-year-old girl with long hair told me that she was from Shaanxi, but she spoke Mandarin with hardly any accent, so it was hard to tell which province she really came from. When I asked if she was all right living here, she nodded gently but struggled to hold back the tears in her eyes. I asked her how long she had been here, and she said eight to nine months. Then she confided in me. 'I am very worried,' she said quietly in Chinese, so the welfare officer couldn't understand her. 'I am worried about my asylum application being rejected.'

'What if it is? What are you going to do then?' I asked.

She shook her head sorrowfully. 'I really wouldn't know what to do if that happened,' she said. 'I wouldn't know. But I don't want to return to China. I really can't. I am still in debt.'

Another teenage girl, who held her hands clasped together, looking anxious, told me in a Fujianese accent that she was seventeen and that she had lived in an orphanage in Henan for a month after her parents died in an accident. Her journey to England had been arranged by her priest at the orphanage. She hadn't had to pay a penny for it.

'Are you the only one who was sent here to England from that orphanage?' I asked.

'There are other children here from that place,' she said. She seemed completely sure. 'The priest arranged for his contact to take me into England. I called him uncle.'

I asked her what he was like.

'I can't really describe him,' she said. 'He looks white and speaks some Chinese.'

'You mean he's a Westerner?' I asked.

'I'm not sure,' she said, looking anxious again. How could she not be sure? My guess is that the story that she was telling me was fabricated – not a story that she was forced to tell, but one that perhaps she had been encouraged to tell. And my feeling was that these were not trafficked youths – their welfare officer's theory – but youths whose parents had paid for them to leave China and come to Britain to seek their fortune.

The girl continued: 'At that time, I didn't know I was coming to England. Uncle told me that he was taking me to a good place where "human rights are respected". We travelled together by plane, but when we arrived in England, he told me at the airport that he had "something to sort out" and would be back soon. But he never returned. I was left alone at the customs, and so I was detained immediately.' These were the same stories that Cai's daughter Yun had been telling the authorities.

Most of Britain's Chinese migrant youth were not trafficked into the UK, contrary to popular assumptions. Almost all of them arrived with the consent of their parents; in fact, most of their parents even encouraged or made the decision on their behalf and arranged for them to come to Britain as 'orphans' seeking a way to get around the increasingly more stringent British immigration enforcement. The profits international snakeheads reap are not the cause of the migration.

In fact, coercion usually happens only after young people arrive in the UK, explained Christine Beddoe, director of ECPAT (End Child Prostitution, Child Pornography and the Trafficking of Children for Sexual Purposes). The process of 'trafficking' does not need to involve and does not only occur upon crossing national borders. 'Although the majority of them may have been sent into Britain at their own will, they can become incapable of managing their own life direction and making decisions for themselves once in Britain, mainly due to their lack of language skills and experience of living abroad,' she said. 'The lack of social and institutional protection makes it worse – it makes it easier for them to become "trafficked" within the UK.'

Two young female Chinese migrants I met in the UK were from Meihua village, along the northeastern coast of Fujian, which I had visited when I was in China. 'Meihua' means plum blossoms, but what had caught my eye as I entered the silent town were the old-fashioned cobblestone streets. The housing blocks of apartments were run down, and there was little evidence of human life. Some of the shops looked semi-closed, with their metal doors half down, and there was no one around to tell me why. Where had all the young men and women gone? A twenty-minute walk down the road brought me to the coast, a tranquil sand beach that no one seemed to visit. A few fishing boats were in the distance. I could only see a small group of fishermen selling seafood on shore. Thirty years earlier, Meihua village had been dependent on fishing, a trade handed down for generations. But an increasing number of new people entering the trade had created a situation of 'superfluous labour'. Competition became too fierce; many fishermen had taken losses, and eventually left the sea.

Shuzhen grew up here. Her father was a fisherman all his life, a hardworking family man. 'We can see Matsu island from our seashore,' Shuzhen once told me. Matsu lies between Fujian and Taiwan; it's 100 miles northwest of Taiwan, in fact, despite being Taiwanese territory, but I couldn't see it from the beach where I was standing. Shuzhen's father and the other fishermen of Meihua spent all their time working at sea, and often went out as far as Matsu, which took an hour and a half in one of their boats. The majority of Matsu's families originally came from Changle in Fujian, a migration that began during the Yuan dynasty in the thirteenth century.

After the fishing trade declined, there was little left for them in Meihua. Some began seeking other employment, such as food processing, in the nearby towns. It became obvious Meihua was a dead end. Beginning in the 1990s, following the footsteps of migrants from surrounding villages, they began to venture abroad, to the US, Canada, Spain, and eventually the UK. As typical all over Fujian, out of the 30,000 residents in Meihua around half have left home to find work outside of the country. Today, only older people and children remain.

Shuzhen herself left at the age of twenty-three, in 2007. She had completed her finance studies in a vocational college, which her parents had paid for, but she didn't have the connections to get a good job, so she had been working as a saleswoman in Changle, earning 1,000 yuan (£91.7) a month. This was not enough to support her parents, who had retired. She thought about setting up her own shop, but she had no capital.

It was during this time that she met a young man from Meihua village, whom she grew to trust. He had been working as an accountant for the fishing business for years, but as the trade declined, he had begun to look out for opportunities elsewhere. Relatives working in England encouraged him to join them, promising him abundance of work and decent wages. After months of consideration, he decided to go to England to try his luck. Shuzhen thought that would be the end of their relationship. She had become fond of him, but he hadn't asked her to come with him.

Her parents, however, encouraged her to join her boyfriend. Many girls of seventeen or eighteen had left the village to go to Britain. Shuzhen hesitated – she had no family there; she'd be alone in a strange country. Her parents did not give up. Her father said he had a few friends working there who would be kind enough to help her from time to time; it would be fine.

Despite her reluctance, Shuzhen knew she had to leave home. She was the eldest daughter and needed to set a good example for her two younger siblings. She should be the first to leave the village to earn a living for the family. 'My father is so scared of being poor,' she said. 'Terrified. So he desperately wanted me to leave home – to go out there and change my destiny. "You are not destined to be poor," he always said to me.'

Shuzhen understood her parents' decision. 'If you had a future in China, you wouldn't send your children abroad in this way. You have no way out, that's why you choose to do so,' she said. She left home believing that her parents had put all their hope in her.

The couple borrowed a total of 270,000 yuan (£24,758, $42,868) from relatives and moneylenders to arrange her journey. Shuzhen travelled with another young Fujianese woman from Changle. Even at the airport, Shuzhen felt anxious and thought about returning home. But the woman from Changle reassured her: Things will be all right in England; there are many Fujianese migrants there. So they flew together to Malaysia, where they were picked up by a local Chinese man who spoke Mandarin with a heavy accent. The man put them on a plane to Japan. Shuzhen didn't like flying. She began to feel unwell, sweating throughout the journey, till they landed in Tokyo. There was no time to rest or wait around in Japan. The two women, without a guide, following the snake-head's instructions on the phone, soon boarded another plane, this one for Britain. For Shuzhen, this was all too unreal. On the plane, the Changle woman told her that she must destroy her documents before arrival, which she did.

Shuzhen arrived in Britain and passed the days that followed in a trance. She had no idea where she was and she didn't understand a word that was said to her by all those around her – not the immigration officers or the police. She was sent to a place that resembled a 'women's prison' – she did not know how else to describe it. She wanted to go home, but she knew she couldn't. The aspirations of the entire family were now on her shoulders. Time passed and she no longer felt anything, numb even to her incarceration, until one day, a month later, she was transferred to a detention centre. There, all day long, she had nothing to do but sit in the English classes that the centre had organized for the detainees. She wondered why they would teach her their language if they weren't going to allow her into their society. But she tried her best to learn some basics: how to greet people, how to order food, how to book tickets. Then one day, a fellow detainee advised her to claim asylum, and told her she might be able to get legal advice. She gave Shuzhen the phone number of an immigration lawyer based in Chinatown. Once she'd made the application, all she had to do was wait for their decision. Within a few weeks, she was able to leave the centre. Her boyfriend came to pick her up on her release.

They went back to east London, where he lived and worked as

a Chinese restaurant cook, a place called Leytonstone, quite far out from the town centre. It was a multiethnic community where locals and migrants of all backgrounds – Eastern European, Russian, Latin American – lived and worked side by side. Shuzhen also saw a number of Chinese migrants selling merchandise on the streets, which puzzled her at first. Was this the only kind of work they could find? Soon after, she and her boyfriend got married. They held the wedding dinner at his workplace, and although there were just three tables of guests, it was attended by all his Fujianese friends and her relatives in London. It was the happiest day she'd spent in England. Her new husband seemed the one person she could truly rely on in a hostile country.

They became inseparable. Shuzhen knew she would follow him wherever he chose to go. She followed him to Manchester when he decided to take up a better offer of work as an assistant chef in a Chinese restaurant there. The enthusiastic relative who introduced him to the new job also got her a job as a waitress in the same restaurant. Wages were low for a 'dumb waitress' (one unable to speak English), just £150 a week, but as the employer knew her husband's relative, she was raised to £170 a week after six months. But soon after that, she became pregnant and had to quit. That was two years ago.

During all this time, Shuzhen had been talking with her parents on the phone at least once a week. She missed her home village. She'd tried to learn English at Wai Yin, a Chinese women's community association in Manchester, but as she didn't interact with local people, her English was still limited to 'menu English'.

Now she was pregnant with her second child, and her husband was working to help her pay off the debt of £24,758. 'I wanted to go home, but I've lost the connection with life back in Fujian,' she told me. She no longer knew Meihua village – she was out of touch with friends and everything that had been happening there in the past three years.

I asked if she was planning to stay in England.

'Should I?' she frowned, kissing her two-year-old son's forehead as he sat in the pram. 'We are not part of society here. We are looked down upon all the time. At the hospitals, the rude white staff frown at our Chinese names ... At the nursery, my son is always bullied by white kids ... I wanted him to be educated here, but I don't want him to suffer from discrimination.'

Fortunately, Shuzhen has made the acquaintance of dozens of other Fujianese young women from villages around Changle and Fuqing who came to Britain in exactly the same way and are living here under the same circumstances. Some of them are younger than she is. Like her, many are waiting for the authorities' decisions to grant them refugee status – the only chance for them to be given regular status here. I asked her what she would do if her asylum application were turned down? How would she plan her future then? She said she would send her son back home, with the help of a friend with regular status, if and when the worst came. She would then go underground and concentrate on working and paying off the debts. 'I know that I should be setting a good example for my younger brother and sister at home,' she said, 'But I told them never to come to England. There's no need to come here and be second-class.'

Ah Chun also comes from a fishing family in Meihua village. Unlike Shuzhen, she's a born adventurer. At the age of thirteen, she left the village and went to study in a high school in Hubei province (which didn't cost her parents anything) with three other girls of her age. It was hundreds of miles away from home, but she feared nothing. She dreamed of becoming independent, and being away made her feel as if the whole world had opened up to her.

The four girls shared a dream: as they saw no opportunities at home, they would go abroad to start a new life. They imagined finding decent work and sending fortunes to their parents. They imagined space and personal freedom. One day they made a bet, on which one of them would make it to their destination country first. Ah Chun wanted to go to England. She'd heard stories about villagers working in England making enough money to change lives back home. The other three girls chose Japan and Ireland. Despite the higher risk of arrest there, Japan has been a popular destination country for Fujianese migrants because of its wages, higher than South Korea's. The parents of one of Ah Chun's friends borrowed from every relative they had as well as moneylenders to make a down payment of $1,000 to the local smuggler who arranged her journey, and they agreed that on her safe arrival in Japan on a cargo ship, the parents would pay the smuggler another $10,000.

The four girls left home around the same time, all with their parents' approval. Ah Chun left without completing her junior high school studies. She was fifteen. Her parents borrowed 200,000 yuan (£18,339, $31,754) from the moneylenders to pay for the snakehead's service. Ah Chun began her journey, in 2004.

She flew to Moscow on someone else's passport, provided by the snakehead, and from Moscow travelled with adults all the way. She was driven along with other migrants to Ukraine in a car. There were thirty of them at the beginning of the journey, but they gradually divided into smaller teams of four along the route, through Ukraine, Slovakia and the Czech Republic. Ah Chun really had no idea which countries she'd travelled through, except France, where she stayed the longest, for three months, waiting for transport to get them through the final leg of the journey. In Paris, she and two other female migrants had sneaked out of the apartment and to look at the city many times. She'd imagined it to be a romantic and pretty place, but she was surprised to find the streets filthy and grim, with indifferent pedestrians walking past in haste.

Finally, Ah Chun and three other migrants were sent on a lorry headed for Britain. The trip was difficult, as there was no food or water – and little ventilation in their crammed hideout in the sleeping alcove above the driver's seat. By the time the lorry reached Dover, Ah Chun had passed out. She was driven to a hospital in London – and that was where she woke up. She had no idea who'd sent her there (probably the lorry driver) or exactly where she was. She was totally alone. But she had reached her destination country! It was 2005, and she was now sixteen. Later, she learned that she was the only one of the four girls who made it to her planned destination. The other three were caught on arrival as they travelled on borrowed passports. They were immediately deported back to Fujian.

Ah Chun never hesitates to say that her bet changed her life. In Britain, she was put under social care as an unaccompanied minor and was given free support and education. While studying at a local school, Ah Chun also worked in a Chinatown restaurant for a time. The job paid less than £200 per week for eleven hours a day, six days a week.

I met Ah Chun for the first time in west London. She told me little about herself, but left her phone number with me. I called to ask to meet again. It wasn't until I visited her in her social housing (a ground-floor one-bedroom bedsit provided to her after she left the care home, as she was no longer a minor) in southwest London that I knew that she was the mother of two young children. She'd met a man from Fujian in London and had her first son with him when she was seventeen. Last year, she'd given birth to her second son. She was receiving £100 per week from social services, most of which she spent on her two young children. She also worked: Although her parents had paid off the snakehead back home, they still owed the sum to the moneylenders and relatives from whom they'd borrowed the money. She had to carry on at the Chinese restaurant to keep sending money home. But as she also had to attend school and look after her children, she was finding it difficult to cope. She didn't know how long it would take her to pay back all the debts.

'I feel really isolated here,' Ah Chun told me. She was giving her second son his bottle while he sat in the cot. 'Sometimes I think about my friends back in Fujian, the girls with whom I made the bet to go abroad. The village feels like a memory, so far away. Now I don't have friends around, and I don't even have time to go out. I have to look after the kids. And anyway I feel out of place with Chinese youth here – I'm too old to hang out with them.'

I asked her if she would send her children out of China, as her parents had sent her, if she were still living there. Would she leave her beloved children in the hands of an uncertain destiny in a country they knew nothing about and where they didn't speak the language?

'Yes, I would. I definitely would,' she said with total certainty in her voice. 'As a mother, I must find ways to ensure that my children are given opportunities to build their future. There would be risks, of course, but when they left China, their destiny would be in their hands. They would have the chance to change their life.'

Epilogue

Trouble on the New Frontier –
Ethnic Tensions in Xinjiang

During my time in China, I had met a number of job seekers who were migrating to Xinjiang, officially known as Xinjiang Uighur Autonomous Region, in the northwest. I had also visited a workplace in Shaoguan, Guangdong, where many Uighur migrants worked. These encounters made me want to return to Xinjiang, a region I'd travelled through briefly more than a decade ago. Now, in early September 2011, I decided to go and live there for four months.

Going to Xinjiang – or New Frontier, the meaning of the Chinese name of this most westerly region – has always invited much curious questioning and warning in China, and more often than not a stream of racially charged commentary about the region and its people. Talking about Xinjiang is like opening the lid on a long story of secrets and lies. This region, which takes up one sixth of the country and has a population of 20 million, remains hidden behind the media image of a restless, 'troubled' region. Rich in natural resources – its oil reserves account for a third of China's oil production and it is a major pipeline route into Central Asia – and significant in its strategic position, bordering Russia, Mongolia, Kazakhstan, Kyrgyzstan, Tajikistan, Afghanistan, Pakistan and India, Xinjiang is nevertheless seen as both culturally and geographically remote. It may be most widely known in the West today by the riots that broke out in 2009.

It all started in Shaoguan, a prefecture-level city in Guangdong province, when the labour authorities of Shufu County (known as

Kona Sheher in Uighur) in Xinjiang sent 818 Uighur men there to work in a toy factory owned by the Hong Kong firm Xuri Electronics, in May 2009. On 26 June, one month after the workers arrived in Shaoguan, two of them were killed and 118 people, most of them also Uighur migrants, were injured in a horrific outbreak of racial violence involving hundreds of people. The violence was started by vicious, racially motivated rumours that two Han Chinese women had been raped by a group of Uighur men.

On 5 July, about 1,000 Uighur people in Urumqi, the capital of Xinjiang, came out to protest against this racial murder of two Uighur workers. Heavy-handed intervention by the police to suppress the protestors triggered their long-repressed anger at the injustices they'd experienced. The conflict soon escalated into a series of riots in Urumqi, which resulted in the death of at least 197 people. A full-scale crackdown was launched immediately following the riots, and more than 1,500 Uighur people were arrested, some detained and others executed without trial. The two Han Chinese men who started the racist rumour and took part in the murder in Shaoguan were tried and executed while in Urumqi, and ten Uighur men who took part in the July riot were also executed.

The first thing I noticed as I stepped out of the chaotic Urumqi train station was the intimidating presence of fully armed police. The officers were carrying rifles and hustling the crowds out of the station gate. It was as if we were all escaping from a war zone. When I finally got free of the station area and into a cab, I found that the entire city was locked in traffic, caused by the tightened security controls. A two-month anti-terrorism crackdown had been launched all over Xinjiang, including the deployment of the 'Snow Leopard' Unit under the People's Armed Police, which had been stationed in Aksu, the capital city of Aksu prefecture, since early August. In Urumqi, surveillance was everywhere: CCTV was installed even in taxis; armed police were patrolling even job fairs in town.

Over the following months in Urumqi, I would be constantly asked by officers and the authorities to produce my documents.

Photocopies of my passport. Photocopies of my residency permit. Photocopies of my tenancy agreement. Even the well-guarded estate where I lived asked to have details of my identity. I came to learn that organizing your daily life in Urumqi isn't an easy task.

Urumqi, capital of Xinjiang, with a population of nearly three million, has developed beyond recognition in the past decade. Xinjiang used to be known for its natural beauty: the unspoilt Heavenly Mountain area and pine forest valleys at the border region; the tranquil desert towns; even Urumqi, where a community spirit was alive and in some southern neighbourhoods you could hear Rai music being played in the streets. Today, high-rise buildings cluster in the centre of the city. Construction projects are everywhere and developers are profiting like mad. The most striking sign of this 'development' is the thick grey smog that envelops the town year round: Urumqi has notoriously become one of China's most polluted cities. 'It gets worse in the winter,' people kept telling me. That's because the smog is caused not only by factories but also by energy use, from coal burning. In 2009, the city emitted 128,000 tonnes of sulphur dioxide and 61,000 tonnes of soot.

Over the past decade, the state has further promoted and encouraged mass migration into Xinjiang, both to exploit its resources and to 'Han-ize' the population in order to better control it. Muslim Uighurs are Xinjiang's ethnic majority, making up 45 percent of the region's total population, but they account for only 12.79 percent of Urumqi's population, due to massive Han-Chinese migration into the capital. Peasants have been recruited from all over China, in particular from neighbouring provinces, to work in the coal mines and oil fields, which are estimated to be twice as large as those in Saudi Arabia, with proven reserves of two billion tons of oil and 160 billion cubic metres of natural gas. But Xinjiang's oil industry is completely run by Han Chinese: the China National Petroleum Company recruited most of its workers from outside the province, bypassed the Xinjiang Petroleum Bureau in carrying out its exploration, and brought in Han Chinese migrant workers to construct a $14 billion pipeline that links the region's natural gas fields to Shanghai. As a result, the profits from the development of the region's rich resources have primarily benefited China's coastal East.

And Uighur workers passed over in Urumqi have few choices outside. Because of prevalent Han discrimination against ethnic minority groups, particularly Uighur Muslims, Uighur workers seeking employment or better pay would normally not consider migration to other parts of China a viable option.

I met Adel in Urumqi through a friend. Adel, a graduate in international trade studies, had taught Mandarin to Uighur students at the Science & Information College in Urumqi until the riot in July 2009. He spoke Mandarin more fluently than many Han Chinese people and was one of the most culturally 'integrated' Muslims I'd met in China. He recited ancient Chinese poems, socialized with Han Chinese, and even attended Chinese karaokes. Nevertheless, he told me, he'd been denied a job interview after the employer asked his ethnic origin and he'd replied that he was Uighur. He said that happened to many Uighur job seekers: 'Without connections, Uighur graduates find it virtually impossible to get into jobs in the state sector. You'd have to bribe your way in, which would cost you something like 100,000 yuan.'

He described the turmoil in the city on Sunday, 5 July 2009. Confrontation between the Han Chinese and Uighur people had escalated into violence. Adel was asked to go inside the college to protect the Uighur students, who had been told to stay there during the riots. Outside, people were getting hurt. Some had been stabbed to death. No matter what your personal views were or which side you took, if you were on the streets, you ran a high risk of losing your life. Things were completely out of control. Adel's students had never seen a riot like this and they were frightened. Only those whose families came to pick them up in a car were allowed to leave the campus. Adel stayed with his students inside the school for an entire week, during which they talked nonstop about the events taking place on the streets of their city. They also discussed what had happened in Shaoguan.

During the first three days of the riot, more than three hundred Chinese were out on the street searching for Uighurs to punish for the casualties during the first day of the riot. Dead bodies lay out on the open streets, and the living went into hiding. Adel's friends had all stopped work. By the fourth day, the food supply in the college had started to run out. Teachers like Adel risked their lives to go out and buy more. Meanwhile, Adel's wife was at home, worrying about him, and couldn't leave the house to come see him.

Adel did his best to protect his students. Despite his efforts, two of them, who had nothing to do with the riots but happened to be out on the street, were arrested. One of the students, a boy from Kashgar, was detained for a month without explanation. Shortly after his release, he was arrested again, for not carrying his ID – which the police had confiscated and which they never returned. Adel said that such senseless arrests and detentions were common, but the college administrators blamed him for his students' misfortune, and scapegoated and criticized him until, unable to bear further ill-treatment, he quit his job.

'And discrimination against ethnic minorities has continued to get worse since the 2009 riot,' Adel said. 'Now jobs are even harder for us to find.'

Thus a vicious circle is preserved, for the riot grew partially out of Uighur anger at institutional and personal discrimination, which is visible in the high level of unemployment amongst Uighur youth. In 2011, 80 percent of the 60,000 jobless graduates in Xinjiang were Uighur.

Kashgar and Khotan are among the least developed cities in the region – the net income per capita for peasants there is 76 percent of the national average, and according to figures from 2004, the incidence of poverty is 18 percent, almost twice as high as the national average of 10 percent. In the deep, snowy winter I spent in Urumqi, each labour market in town was still filled with hundreds of minority – mainly Uighur – job seekers from these southern cities, particularly from Khotan, situated in the deep south of Xinjiang, where prospects of development remain vague. Khotan lacks infrastructure and is hard to reach by public transportation – the choice is a thirty-six-hour train journey, or a twenty-eight-hour bus trip across the Taklamakan Desert. In Khotan, the most striking thing I saw, apart from the statue of Mao shaking hands with a Uighur peasant, was the grinding poverty, visible on every street corner.

At one Urumqi labour market, I stopped to speak to a tall, thin man in his mid twenties, dressed in a large leather jacket but still shivering in the cold. He nodded at me politely and told me he was a member of the Kyrgyz, an ethnic group that makes up only 0.9 percent of the population in Xinjiang. There are roughly 141,000 Kyrgyz living in China, most of them concentrated in Kizilsu Kyrgyz Autonomous Region in southwestern Xinjiang. He didn't want to tell me his Chinese name – he said it sounded too much like a car brand. To protect his identity, I will call him by the Kyrgyz name of Kylych. He had come to Urumqi from the town of Atushi, near the area bordering Kyrgyzstan, to study business management at Xinjiang University. He'd been born and grown up in Xinjiang, but did not want to stay there.

To fund his studies, Kylych had found himself a job as a labour contractor for Uighurs from southern Xinjiang seeking work in Urumqi's labour markets, sending them to building sites in and outside the city. But he wrestled with the problem of unpaid wages – once, he'd got a team of Uighur workers from Khotan to build a KTV building near People's Square in central Urumqi, and afterward the employer had simply vanished, without paying him the agreed 4,700 yuan, meaning that the Uighur workers didn't get paid, either. 'That happens a lot around here,' he said.

Then there is the institutional racism against ethnic minority migrant workers. This was the real reason why Kylych didn't want to stay in Xinjiang, or in China. 'There's no equality here,' he said. He was applying for a passport and was planning to go study and work in South Korea, where his relatives were. They told him that work was easy to find over there. He'd been waiting for a passport for a year. Often, it can take longer. He said that once he had his visa, he would not return to this country.

On one occasion, I invited him to dinner in my flat, and prepared him two popular Uighur dishes, *paulaw*, rice with diced carrots and lamb (originally from Uzbekistan), and *dapanji*, stewed chicken with potatoes. I asked him whether he had been visiting the mosque during his time in Urumqi, though he didn't seem particularly religious – like many other Uighur Muslims I've met, he sometimes drank alcohol in moderation. That evening, we shared a few glasses of Yili red wine.

'Not often,' he said. He looked slightly embarrassed.

He paused, and thought about it for a moment. Then he explained, 'The reason why I don't go to pray often is because there are rules that forbid us to practice religion. People are not permitted to visit the mosque if they happen to work in state institutions and state-run companies or if they are students at any level, from high school to university.'[1]

'I've heard of people getting arrested for it,' he said. His sister, currently a student at Xinjiang University, had also stopped praying at the mosque or in public.

Kylych seemed angry and solemn at the same time, struggling to find words to express his frustration. 'Despite these rules, people tend to carry on practicing their religion, quietly and secretly, in their private life, outside of college and work,' he said. 'In southern Xinjiang, particularly, people defy the rules and practice Islam.' Then he added, 'Most of the Muslims you'll find regularly in the mosques are jobless. They're the only ones with nothing to lose ...' He smiled bitterly. This was 'Islam with Chinese characteristics,' he joked.

During the 2009 riots in Urumqi, two of Kylych's friends from Kashgar and Khotan had been shot dead without trial on the street of Urumqi. They were Xinjiang University students and were protesting because they were angry at the state-imposed Han Chinese migration to poverty-stricken southern Xinjiang. On that day, 7 July, hundreds (some say thousands) of Han Chinese had held armed demonstrations in Urumqi and there were serious confrontations and violent clashes between Han Chinese and Uighur people in the streets. Kylych's two friends went out and joined many other Uighur protesters, shouting out their anger against Han Chinese domination. Kylych said that they'd wanted nothing more than what most Uighur youth would want: opportunities to develop themselves and their homeland. They knew that not everyone back home in Kashgar and Khotan was as fortunate as they were, able to attend a university. Most youth back home had no such hope of bettering their lives. Kylych's two friends cared about their communities and that was why they were out protesting.

As the confrontation continued in the streets, the police were reported to have used only teargas and roadblocks to disperse the crowds. But Kylych said that they had opened fire at the Uighur crowds and there had been fatalities. None of this was reported in the national press at the time.

That day, Kylych tried to get in contact with his two friends, but their mobile phones were switched off. He kept calling and there was no answer. He started to worry about their safety, because he knew there were casualties on the streets. It was only ten days later that Kylych realized they had been killed. Not only was he very upset about their death, but he also became very frightened for his own safety.

'I had a rail ticket to return home on 7 July, but I couldn't get on the train – all transportation was halted. I was very worried about my family in Atushi, and I couldn't get in touch with them; there was no connection on the phone line. And I couldn't send any emails, because internet access had been blocked. All I could do was wait in my dormitory in the university. It was like wartime. I was cut off from the outside world, and from my family.'

Only a month later, when Kylych finally got home, did his family tell him that during those days of the Urumqi riot, fear had permeated the air in Atushi. Although far away from Urumqi, their town had felt the impact of the riot – in fact, the entire Xinjiang region had felt it. Armed police were everywhere. Villagers in Atushi were given one bag of flour per household and then all shops were closed. No one was allowed to go out. No one dared.

Like Tibet, Xinjiang is considered an 'autonomous region', meaning that it has its own local government and greater legislative rights than the provinces. But in practice, it has only what Binh G. Phan, a Chinese academic, has called 'paper autonomy': While Chinese migration has been actively encouraged and planned by the state, ethnic minority groups in Xinjiang have been segregated to minimize their opportunities to govern. The Xinjiang Production and Construction Corps (also known as the *bingtuan*, or military corps), with two million members, has been stationed in Xinjiang since 1954, the year before it was established as an autonomous region. Nominally responsible for cultivating the region and defending the frontier, the *bingtuan* have built military agricultural settlements, introduced waves of migrants from China's interior, and served as an arm of the PLA in putting down civil unrest. For the Uighur people, the *bingtuan* are nothing less than a colonial institution.

'The real meaning of autonomy,' Kylych said, his voice dripping with sarcasm, 'is that in this multiethnic region, only one group dominates and makes decisions.'

He paused and looked around. 'Back in Atushi, my relatives and friends always said "the walls have ears". They would avoid talking about their political views, even at home.'

Under China's anti-terrorism initiatives, ethnic minorities who migrate to another country are considered potentially connected with international terrorists. Journalist Andy Worthington uncovered through Wikileaks that twenty-two Muslim Uighur men, mostly in their twenties, had been captured and jailed at Guantanamo from 2002–2006. Eighteen of them had left China at various periods of time during May and October 2001, and reached the Tora Bora Mountains in Afghanistan, where they found refuge in a small Uighur community that was later called a camp by the

US. There, they spent their time studying the Koran and planning to find a way to travel to Turkey or the US in search of work opportunities. But in October 2001, the community where they were staying was hit in a US bombing raid. One man died. According to the injured Yusef Abbas (ISN 275, still detained at Guantanamo), the others were 'covered in half a bucket of his flesh.' The group of men ran for their lives and crossed the Pakistan border, where they took refuge in a village that betrayed them, and ended up in a Pakistani prison. Eventually, these men were handed over to the US forces and were sent to Guantanamo in June 2002.

The US maintained that these Uighur men were probable members of the ETIM (East Turkistan Islamic Movement), described by China as a dangerous organization founded to achieve separatism through armed insurrection and terrorism, and that the ETIM was affiliated and supported by Al-Qaeda and other terrorist groups. They have no evidence to back any of this up. In fact, the Uighur men had not even heard about the 9/11 attack, as they had no access to media. As Andy Worthington reported, though they were captured in Pakistan 'along with Al-Qaeda members', the Uighur men had only wound up in their company because they were lost.

I often saw Chinese government warnings against the ETIM written on the inside walls of mosques in Xinjiang. The warnings always encouraged people to report on the organization. But no one in the region ever seemed able to tell me what exactly the ETIM was, nor has the Chinese or the US government ever defined it clearly. 'ETIM is probably defunct by now,' said Nicholas Bequelin of Human Rights Watch.[2] Others have doubted that the organization ever existed.

Little has changed for Xinjiang since the 2009 riot. The old secretary of the CCP's Xinjiang Committee, Wang Lequan, was replaced by a new secretary, Zhang Chunxian, in April 2010, but this represented no more than a new name and a new personal style. 'Make a watchful security stance the norm rather than the exception,' he

292 *Scattered Sand*

has reportedly instructed regional officials. 'Officials at all levels must harden their stance on opposing splittism and stepping up their crackdown on extremist religious forces and their activities.'

Meanwhile, the winter is lasting for migrants searching for jobs in the labour markets of Urumqi. As across all of China, the biggest 'security risk' for them is their inability to earn quickly and send money home to their families.

Acknowledgements

My thanks to the men and women who shared their stories with me during this journey, even though, for their own security, I cannot thank them by name. I'd also like to thank Professor Colin Sparks of Journalism, Hong Kong University, for his kind support and advice; Chang Yiru for her advice on conducting research in China; Mr Chen and his relations in Shenyang for their hospitality; Xiao Zheng and Qi for their great help in northern Shandong; Xiao Dong for his company in Henan; and Liying for her time in Fujian.

Millions of thanks go to Audrea Lim, my editor at Verso, for her deep sympathy with the issues, detailed feedback and advice, generous support throughout the writing, and restructuring of the book, which made a huge difference, and to my publisher, Tom Penn, whose commitment has allowed these socially marginalized voices in modern China to be heard. This book would not have been possible without them.

I'm very grateful to Professor Gregor Benton, Betsy Tobin, and Jeremy Riggall for their brilliant advice on my first draft. I cannot thank Gregor enough for his wonderful editing and unflagging support, or for his foreword. Big thanks to Jeremy for encouraging me from the beginning of the project, and to Betsy for her excellent critique and evaluation.

I'd like to thank John Davies, my very patient ex-partner, for generously and kindly being there for me throughout. He has always been a great source of strength; I will always remember what he has done for me.

Finally, I thank Leslie Hearson, Denis Wong, Bob Hughes, Lin Dong and Lisa Mok, for their kind and unwearied encouragement and support.

Further Reading

Benton, Gregor, and Pieke, Frank (eds.), *The Chinese in Europe*, Basingstoke: Macmillan, 1998.

Chang, Leslie T., *Factory Girls: Voices from the Heart of Modern China*, Picador, 2010.

Chen, Guidi, and Wu, Chuntao, *Will the Boat Sink the Water? The Life of China's Peasants*, PublicAffairs, 2006.

China Labour Bulletin, 'Going It Alone: The Workers' Movement in China (2007–2008)', July 2009, available at clb.org.hk/en/.

China Labour Bulletin, 'Swimming Against the Tide: A Short History of Labour Conflict in China and the Government's Attempt to Control It', October 2010, available at clb.org.hk/en/.

Fan, C. Cindy, *China on the Move: Migration, the State and the Household*, London: Routledge, 2007.

Gaetano, A. M., *On the Move: Women and Rural-to-Urban Migration in Contemporary China*, Columbia University Press, 2004.

Gittings, John, *The Changing Face of China: From Mao to Market*, Oxford University Press, 2006.

Human Rights Watch, *One Year of My Blood*, March 2008.

Nielsen, Ingrid, and Russell Smyth, *Migration and Social Perception in China*, World Scientific Publishing, November 2008.

Jacka, Tamara, *Rural Women in Urban China: Gender, Migration and Social Change*, M. E. Sharpe, Inc., 2006.

Kyle, David, and Koslowski, Rey (eds.), *Global Human Smuggling: Comparative Perspectives*, Johns Hopkins University Press, 2001.

Lee, Ching (ed.), *Working in China: Ethnographies of Labour and Workplace Transformation*, London: Routledge, 2007.

Lee, Grace O.M., and Warner, Malcolm (ed.), *Unemployment in China* (Routledge Contemporary China Series), London: Routledge, 2006.

Leung, Wing-yue, *Smashing the Iron Rice Pot: Workers and Unions in China's Market Socialism*, Hong Kong: Asia Monitor Resource Centre, 1988.

Luyn, Van, and Floris-Jan, *Floating City of Peasants: The Great Migration in Contemporary China*, The New Press, 2008.

Mallee, Hein, and Pieke, Frank N., *Internal and International Migration: Chinese Perspectives* (Chinese Worlds), London: Routledge, 1999.

Meisner, Maurice, *Mao's China and After: A History of the People's Republic*, The Free Press, 1999.

Meisner, Maurice, *Marxism, Maoism and Utopianism: Eight Essays*, University of Wisconsin Press, 1982.

Minakir, Pavel A. (ed.), Freeze, Gregory L. (ed. & trans.), *Russian Far East: An Economic Handbook*, M. E. Sharpe, Inc., 1994.

Murphy, Rachel, and the International Organization for Migration, *Domestic Migrant Remittances in China: Distributions, Channels and Livelihoods*, International Organization for Migration, November 2006.

Murphy, Rachel, *How Migrant Labour is Changing Rural China* (Cambridge Modern China Series), Cambridge University Press, 2002.

Murphy, Rachel (ed.), *Labour Migration and Social Development in Contemporary China*, Routlege, 2008.

Nyiri, Pal, *New Chinese Migrants in Europe: The Case of the Chinese Community in Hungary*, Ashgate, 1999.

Nyiri, Pal, and Saveliev, Igor R. (eds.), *Globalising Chinese Migration: Trends in Europe and Asia* (Research in Migration and Ethnic Relations Series), Ashgate, 2003.

O'Brien, Kevin J., and Li, Lianjiang, *Rightful Resistance in Rural China*, Cambridge University Press, 2006.

Pieke, Frank N., and Mallee, Hein, *Internal and International Migration: Chinese Perspectives* (Chinese Worlds), London: Routledge, 1999.

Pieke, Frank N. and Nyiri, Pal, *Transnational Chinese: Fujianese Migrants in Europe*, Stanford University Press, 2004.

Pun, Ngai, *Made in China: Women Factory Workers in a Global Workplace*, Duke University Press, 2005.

Seibert, Andreas, *From Somewhere to Nowhere: China's Internal Migrants*, Lars Muller Publishers, 2008.

Shelly, Toby, *Exploited: Migrant Labour in the New Global Economy*, Zed Books Ltd., 2007.

Solinger, D. J., *Contesting Citizenship in Urban China: Peasant Migrants, the State and the Logic of the Market*, University of California Press, 1999.

State Council China, 'China Migrant Workers Investigation and Research Report', 2006.

Wang, Fei-Ling, *Organizing Through Division and Exclusion: China's Hukou System*, Stanford University Press, 2005.

Wu, Bin, and Zanin, Valter, 'Working Conditions in Chinese Ethnic Workshops:

An Empirical Study in Textiles, Garment and Leather Sectors in Veneto, Italy', School of Contemporary Chinese Studies, University of Nottingham, March 2008.

Xu, Feng, *Women Migrant Workers in China's Economic Reform*, Palgrave MacMillan, 2000.

Yan, Hairong, *New Masters, New Servants: Development, Migration and Women Workers in China*, Duke University Press, 2009.

Yun, Gao (ed.), *Concealed Chains: Labour Exploitation and Chinese Migrants in Europe*, International Labour Organization, 2010.

Zhang, Linxiu, 'China's Rural Labour Market Development and Its Gender Implications', *China Economic Review*, Vol. 15, 2, 2004.

Zhang, Mei, *China's Poor Regions: Rural-Urban Migration, Poverty, Economic Reform and Urbanisation*, London: Routledge, 2003.

Notes

Preface

1 Aaron Back and Liyan Qi, 'China to Speed Up Reform of "Hukou" System', *Wall Street Journal*, 18 Dec 2012.

Introduction

1 In some cases, grain production figures were inflated up to ten times the actual production amount. This led to the state pressuring local units to submit more grain than they could spare.

2 A *mu* is equivalent to 666.66 square metres, or 0.1647 acres.

3 See paper by Fu Chen, Dr Liming Wang, and John Davis, 'Land reform in rural China since the mid 1980s', in Land Reform 1998/2, published by FAO (Food and Agriculture Organization of the UN), September 1999.

4 Maurice Meisner, *Mao's China and After: A History of the People's Republic*, Free Press, 1999, 468.

5 See 'Internal Migration and Stability in China', *Migration News*, No.10, Volume 3, October 1996, 1.

6 See Pavel A. Minakir, 'Chinese Immigration in the Russian Far East: Regional, National, and International Dimensions', in *Cooperation and Conflict in the Former Soviet Union: Implications for Migration*, Jeremy R. Azrael and Emil A. Payin (eds.), Santa Monica: Rand, 1996, 85–86.

7 See 'China's tide of migrant labour turns', *Asia Times*, February 5, 2009, 1.

8 See National Bureau of Statistics (NBS) at stats.gov.cn/english/.

Chapter 1. Exodus

1 Yuanli Liu, 'Development of the rural health insurance system in China', Oxford University Press, 2004, 159–65.

2 Even today, a person of mixed (Chinese and Russian) parentage, when recognized, will often be given derogatory names, such as *ermaozi* (meaning 'half hairy').

3 *Liaoning Daily*, 29 October 2010, 1.

4 *Liaoning Daily*, 21 February 2011, 1.

5 Ibid.

6 Ibid.

7 Garnaut, R., Song, L. and Yao, Y., 'Impact and Significance of state-owned enterprise restructuring,' *China Journal*, 2006, 35–65.

8 Hu Angang, *Crossing National Border: Human Migration Issues in Northeast Asia*, United Nations University, 2005, 72.

9 'No Way Out: Worker Activism in China's State-Owned Enterprise Reforms', *China Labour Bulletin*, September 2008, 5.

10 'No Way Out: Worker Activism in China's State-Owned Enterprise Reforms', *China Labour Bulletin*, September 2008, 12.

11 A study of the dynamics of rural society in China conducted by the Institute of Rural Development at Chinese Academy of Social Sciences (CASS) between August 2003 and June 2004 identified such land disputes as one of the major 'rural problems' since 2002. The study also suggested that the focus of peasant activism has generally shifted from issues of taxation to land disputes.

12 According to an estimate by the National Audit Office in June 2011, local government debts in China total 10.7 trillion yuan. See Tom Orlik, 'China Tallies Local Debt', *Wall Street Journal*, 28 June 2011.

13 According to the National Audit Office estimates.

14 Xinhua News Agency report, 25 June 2007.

15 The Labour Contract Law was met with resistance from multinational companies. Some companies reacted to the law by proactively dismissing workers who would have come under the new rules. In October 2008, Wal-Mart dismissed 100 employees at a sourcing centre in China. The company said the layoff was part of its global restructuring. LG and Olympus announced plans to lay off their employees. Carrefour China also asked over 40,000 of its Chinese workers to resign a two-year labour contract before December 28, 2007.

16 See report in the *China Daily*, 10 December 2009. Also see the *China Labour Bulletin* report for the same period.

17 See the Supreme Court's work report to the National People's Congress, published 11 March 2010 in *China News* (*Zhongguo Xinwenwang*), http://www.chinanews.com/gn/news/2010/03-11/2164257.shtml.

18 Ibid.

Chapter 2. Earthquakes in Bohemia

1 The Hundred Flowers Movement lasted for a few weeks in the summer of 1957. Its slogan was: 'Let a hundred flowers blossom and a hundred schools of thought contend!' Mao initiated the campaign of liberalization to encourage people to speak openly about their views about the national policies, but followed this up after a few weeks with a brutal crackdown, extracting forced confessions, punishing outspoken students with forced labour, and imprisoning many.

2 See Maurice Meisner's *Li Ta-Chao and the Origins of Chinese Marxism*, ACLS

Humanities E-Book, 2008, 52–70. Voluntarism was an important influence on the thought of Li Dazhao and Mao Zedong. For both of them, the forces of history are within the boundaries of psychological transformation and history itself is the record of psychological representations.

3 *Southern Weekend*, or *Nanfang Zhoumo*, is a weekly newspaper based in Guangzhou. It is owned by the Southern Daily Group, which also runs *Southern Daily* (*Nanfang Ribao*) and *Southern Metropolitan Daily* (*Nanfang Dushibao*). The publications in this group have conducted a great deal of excellent investigative reporting over the years – for which three of the editors at *Southern Metropolitan Daily* were arrested and many of their journalists detained and harassed. The group is recognized as the most daring, and the only investigative, media in China.

4 As reported by *Southern Weekend*. See above.

Chapter 3. Dust and Heat

1 'Bone and Blood: The Price of Coal in China', *China Labour Bulletin*, March 2008, 17.

2 Frank Pieke and Pal Nyiri, *Transnational Chinese: Fujianese Migrants in Europe*, Stanford University Press, 2004, 41–42.

3 The old disadvantage of Xiamen's adjacency to Taiwan now became a great advantage. Four business zones were established in the 1980s and 1990s to form clusters of investment from Taiwan, and the city has now pulled in more than $4.7 billion in direct Taiwanese investment. More than 2,700 Taiwanese investment projects in Xiamen are involved in industrial production; these are seen as the pillars of the city's economic development. As *China Daily* commented on 9 January 2009, 'Taiwan elements are now a crucial part of everyday life in Xiamen.'

4 The cases of people infected through blood transfusion continue to be heard. On 8 December 2009, a group of thirty-eight Henanese peasants, including four children, demonstrated in front of the health ministry in Beijing to petition the authorities for help. The protestors said that the clinics provided by the local authorities did not have appropriate medical supplies and that they had to travel to hospitals outside of their hometowns and pay the heavy medical costs themselves. Their disease had plunged them into debt. They demanded help and compensation. 'We have the right to live,' they said.

5 China has 560,000 to 920,000 people infected with the HIV virus and 97,000 to 112,000 full-blown AIDS patients, according to 2009 statistics from both China's ministry of health and the UN.

Chapter 4. The Dark Kilns

1 Chen Guidi and Wu Chuntao, *Will the Boat Sink the Water? The Life of China's Peasants*, New York: PublicAffairs, 2006, 172.

2 Similarly, research conducted by Li Shi, director of the Income Distribution and Poverty Research Centre at Beijing Normal University, shows that in 2002, 10 percent of the people in China acquired nearly 32 percent of the country's income.

Chapter 5. *'Bad Elements'*

1 Or compradors, a term dating back to the nineteenth century, referring to Chinese agents who took charge of Chinese employees and acted as business intermediaries on behalf of a foreign concern.

Chapter 6. *The Factory of the World*

1 Foxconn also established development centres in the US and Japan in 1994. In 1997, additional Foxconn plants started operations in the UK and the US. In 2007, the company and its subsidiaries owned plants in the Czech Republic, Hungary, Mexico, Brazil, India, and Vietnam. In February 2010, Foxconn workers in Ciudad Juarez, Mexico, rioted and set the plant on fire to protest against forced unpaid overtime.

2 'Mass incidents' is a term used to neutralize the implications of popular protests. In the face of rising labour militancy, the authorities have gradually adopted a more strategic position in dealing with workers' protests, attempting to 'remain aloof' in industrial disputes so as to avoid politicization. Editors of the state news agency, Xinhua, commented about 'mass incidents': 'We must avoid the politicization of mass incidents ... Party officials must pay close attention to mass incidents without making mountains out of molehills and seeing them as colossal "political incidents." Treating these incidents as antigovernment actions and subsequently suppressing them with strong force would be the precise method of exacerbating problems, and would have the direct result of aggravating the antagonism between officials and civilians.' Some 'mass incidents' in recent years have also expressed a rising anger against corruption and abuse of power by local authorities. In June 2008, for instance, more than 10,000 people rioted and set fire to a police station in Guizhou when the police covered up a murder perpetrated by relatives of local officials.

3 According to the Ministry of Public Security, 2006.

4 See *China Labour Bulletin*'s report, 'Going It Alone: The Workers Movement in China (2007–8)', July 2009, 49.

5 Ibid.

6 Ibid., 25.

7 The majority of workers at this plant are on a monthly base pay of 930 yuan, just above the local minimum wage.

8 The new rate plan was reported to be a three-tiered schedule built on a higher minimum wage of 1,550 yuan, which together with benefits could add up to an estimated total monthly earning of 2,800 yuan, according to the *China Post*, 22 February 2011, 1.

Chapter 7. In the Shadows of Olympians

1 See 'Going It Alone: The Workers Movement in China (2007–2008)', China Labour Bulletin, July 2009, 49.
2 Today, it is the only trade union in the country. Workers are not permitted to form independent unions.
3 He Sanwei, *Southern Weekend*, October 2011, 33.
4 The *hukou* is the household registration system, established in 1958, as mentioned in previous chapters.
5 The production team (*dadui*) is a basic administrative unit left over from the collectivist era.

Chapter 8. Go West!

1 Frank Pieke, 'Chinese Globalization and Migration to Europe', Centre for Comparative Immigration Studies, University of California, San Diego, March 2004, 5.
2 Peter Kwong, *Forbidden Workers: Illegal Chinese Immigrants and American Labor*, New York: The New Press, 1997, 9.
3 Local historian Leslie Hearson and I are documenting the story of Limehouse as a piece of oral history in an ongoing project titled 'East End Chinese'.
4 According to US Citizenship and Immigration Services (USCIS), http://www.uscis.gov/portal/site/uscis.
5 Ibid.

Epilogue

1 It is state policy in China to curb religious practice among ethnic minorities and to restrain the influence and growth of religions generally. Private companies may determine individually, on their own terms, whether to allow their Muslim employees to visit the mosque.
2 See 'Out of the closet: China's other Tibet', DissidentVoice.org, 5 January 2009.